"Slowing growth and rising inequality have become a toxic combination in western economies, notably including the US. This combination now threatens the survival of liberal democracy itself. Why has this happened? Some blame an excess of free-market capitalism. In this well-researched and clearly-written book, the authors demonstrate that the precise opposite is the case. What has emerged over the past forty years is not free-market capitalism, but a predatory form of monopoly capitalism. Capitalists will, alas, always prefer monopoly. Only the state can restore the competition we need, but it will do so only under the direction of an informed public. This, then, is a truly important book. Read, learn and act."

—**Martin Wolf**, Chief Economics
Commentator, *Financial Times*

"Tepper and Hearn make a compelling case that the United States economy is straying increasingly far from capitalism, a process that is having deleterious consequences for both productivity growth and inequality. The villain in their story is the growth of monopolies and oligopolies, abetted in many cases by government policies that either turned a blind eye to increasing concentration or actively encouraged it by creating rules to entrench incumbents. Their case is animated by passion but delivered in a detailed, analytical and factual manner that is still enjoyable to read. More importantly, it is not an excuse for despair but a specific set of policy recommendations for action."

—**Jason Furman**, Harvard Kennedy School, Chairman
of the Council of Economic Advisers (2013-17)

"Whatever happened to antitrust? In the US, it has for many years been effectively dormant as a tool to limit monopoly and monopsony power. Internet shopping isn't much help to a firm buying an input made by only one supplier, nor a consumer choosing between different brands all made by the same giant company, and workers can't easily switch to new locations and employers. The indisputable trend of rising concentration in American industry may be a major factor in the trend fall in labor's share of national income. This engagingly written book concludes with a powerful set of proposals to reverse the trend and make the capitalist market economy function as it should. Important – a must read."

—**Richard Portes CBE,** Professor of Economics, London Business School, Founder and Honorary President, Centre for Economic Policy Research

"In a compelling and deeply researched polemic, Tepper and Hearn describe a market that is broken. Increasingly, instead of delivering the benefits of competition to all, it is driving monopoly profits to the few. Regulatory and policy capitulation in the face of market concentration has put a dead weight on productivity and fostered inequality not just in the United States but globally. Their call to free markets from private monopolists and oligopolists should unite both left and right the world over."

—**Charles Kenny,** Senior Fellow, The Center for Global Development, Author of *Getting Better*

"This is an extremely important, timely and well researched book. Jonathan Tepper is himself a successful entrepreneur and he knows what "good" capitalism looks like. The current system, suborned by market abuse, corporatism, cronyism and regulatory capture and resulting in increasing inequality and anger amongst the wider population is badly in need of reform. If it is not reformed by people who believe in markets it will be reformed by people who don't and that would be bad news for everyone. Jonathan Tepper understands this well and I recommend his book to every member of the US Congress."

—**Sir Paul Marshall**, Chairman of Marshall Wace Hedge Fund Group

"Tepper and Hearn point out that, if current trends are left unchecked, the light at the end of the tunnel is a train driven by monopolists and oligopolists that a privileged few can afford a ticket on. This narrative of monopoly profits translating into lobbying and influence-peddling affects all of us in the price of drugs, airplane tickets, cable bills, banks, and even smartphones. *The Myth of Capitalism* should be required reading by regulators, students, and anyone with a stake in America's future."

—**J. Kyle Bass**, Chief Investment Officer, Hayman Capital Management

"As we face concerns about the power of companies like Amazon, Facebook, and Google, we would be wise to arm ourselves with a knowledge of history. This breezy, readable account of the theory and practice of monopoly, duopoly, and oligopoly provides a solid foundation for the argument that many of the ills of today's economy can be traced to the concentration of power in fewer and fewer large firms."

—**Tim O'Reilly**, founder and CEO of O'Reilly Media

"A sweeping and thought-provoking treatise on the past, present and future of competition. The forces at play in fairness, inequality, consolidation and dispersion shape the great game as it shapes us from markets to geopolitics."

—**Josh Wolfe**, Founding Partner &
Managing Director, Lux Capital

"We are barreling towards an economy with few lords and millions of serfs. Tepper's *The Myth of Capitalism* fiercely articulates the raw, hard truth behind the monopolistic behaviors of today's corporations driving inequality, endangering the consumer, and eroding what American Capitalism used to mean."

—**Scott Galloway**, Professor of Marketing and
Serial Entrepreneur

"A takedown of what we now call 'capitalism' - by and for people who are true believers in it. Tepper and Hearn have written a love letter for a (free market) romance, scorned. As a person who has the word 'capitalist' in his job title, I believe we need to reverse the many-decades trend of falling entrepreneurship if we want to provide more opportunity for more people and better products and services for all of us. This book may give you a way to rekindle your love for markets, by proposing fixes for all the ways they've broken us."

—**Roy Bahat**, Venture capitalist, head of Bloomberg Beta

"Jonathan Tepper and Denise Hearn have stated, 'While many books have been written on capitalism and inequality, the left and right don't even read the same books. Researchers have analyzed book purchases, and there is almost no political or economic books that both sides pick up and read.' They hope that *The Myth of Capitalism* will bridge the divide and find common ground between the left and right. I strongly endorse that goal. At a time of extraordinary partisanship in the U.S. Congress and legislative bodies all over our country, the need for some common grounds of public policy is imperative to create new jobs, new industries, new standards of economic and political freedom, and new leaders who will provide a more stable base for American and world peace and justice. I salute the wisdom and vigor with which the authors have supplied thoughtful critiques of past economic policies and excellent prescriptions for the future."

—Senator Richard Lugar (retired)

"This is a brilliant, clear work of political economy in the classical sense: a rigorous analysis of how government action benefited monopolistic firms, which have used their profits to procure even more governmental favors, which in turn entrench their position at the top of the economic food chain. Even more importantly, Tepper connects his expertise to our everyday experience. If you have ever been strong-armed by an airline, ignored by a cable company, or cheated by a bank, you'll see the roots of your misfortune in the dynamics of lax antitrust enforcement and absentee regulators so capably chronicled here. This book should be required reading in introductory economics courses, to understand the true nature of the contemporary economy."

—Frank Pasquale, Professor of Law, University of Maryland

"If you want to start a business in America today, or just want to know what's gone wrong with our country, *The Myth of Capitalism* is a great place to start. Tepper and Hearn provide a highly readable and very useful guide to America's monopoly problem, and to the many great and growing harms of economic concentration. Inequality, political disfunction, the choking off of opportunity, the rise of too-big-to-fail, the book shows how all stem largely or mainly from monopolization. Best of all, the authors make clear this concentration is not the inevitable result of any natural force within capitalism, but of political decisions that we can begin to reverse today."

—Barry C. Lynn, director of Open Markets Institute,
author of *Cornered: The New Monopoly Capitalism
and the Economics of Destruction*

"A deeply insightful analysis of the rapidly creeping tentacles of the corporatocracy and the devastating impacts of a predatory form of capitalism. By discouraging competition, empowering the very few — the very rich oligarchs — and demolishing the very resources upon which it depends, predatory capitalism has created a failed global economic system, a Death Economy. This book helps us understand the importance of replacing it with a system that is itself a renewable resource, a Life Economy."

—**John Perkins**, former chief economist and author of
New York Times best-selling books including
Confessions of an Economic Hitman and
The Secret History of the American Empire

THE MYTH OF
CAPITALISM

THE MYTH OF CAPITALISM

Monopolies and the Death of Competition

JONATHAN TEPPER
with **DENISE HEARN**

WILEY

Published by John Wiley & Sons, Inc., Hoboken, New Jersey.
Published simultaneously in Canada.

Library of Congress Cataloging-in-Publication Data:
Names: Tepper, Jonathan, 1976- author. | Hearn, Denise, 1986- author.
Title: The myth of capitalism : monopolies and the death of competition /
   Jonathan Tepper with Denise Hearn.
Description: Hoboken, New Jersey : John Wiley & Sons, 2019. | Includes index.
   | Identifiers: LCCN 2018038947 (print) | LCCN 2018041857 (ebook) | ISBN
   9781119548171 (Adobe PDF) | ISBN 9781119548140 (ePub) | ISBN 9781119548195
   (hardcover)
Subjects: LCSH: Monopolies—United States. | Capitalism—United States.
Classification: LCC HD2757.2 (ebook) | LCC HD2757.2 .T46 2018 (print) | DDC
   330.973—dc23
LC record available at https://lccn.loc.gov/2018038947

Cover Design: Wiley
Cover Image: ©iStock.com/simon2579

Printed in the United States of America.

V10005141_101118

Contents

Introduction

On April 9, 2017, police officers from Chicago's O'Hare Airport removed Dr. David Dao from United Express Flight 3411. The flight was overbooked, but he refused to give up his seat. He had patients to treat the next day. Fellow passengers recorded a video of him being dragged off the plane. You could hear gasps of disbelief from fellow passengers: "Oh, my god!" "No! This is wrong." "Look at what you did to him." No one could believe what they were seeing.

In the video he could be seen bleeding from the mouth as police dragged him down the aisle. The video quickly went viral. United's CEO, however, did not apologize and instead blamed the passenger for being belligerent. Eventually, the outrage was so great that the CEO apologized and the airline reached an undisclosed settlement with Dr. Dao.

Dr. Dao's lawyer Thomas Demetrio told journalists that Dr. Dao "left Vietnam in 1975 when Saigon fell and he was on a boat and he said he was terrified. He said that being dragged down the aisle was more horrifying and harrowing than what he experienced when leaving Vietnam."[1]

Years ago, such a public relations disaster would have caused United's stock to stumble, but it quickly recovered. Financial analysts agreed that it would have no effect on the airline. For all of 2016, the company reported full-year net income of $2.3 billion. The results were so good that in 2016 United's board approved a stock buyback of $2 billion, which is the financial equivalent of spraying yourself with champagne. Research analysts dismissed the incident, saying "consumers might not have much choice but to fly UAL due to airline consolidation, which has reduced competition over most routes."[2] Online news sites helpfully explained to readers what had happened with headlines like, "Airlines Can Treat You Like Garbage Because They Are an Oligopoly."[3] Once investors started focusing on United's dominant market position, the stock price in fact went *up*.

The analysts were right. The American skies have gone from an open market with many competing airlines to a cozy oligopoly with four major airlines. To say that there are four major airlines overstates the true level of competition. Most US airlines dominate a local hub, unironically known as "fortress hubs," where they face little competition and have a near monopoly. They have the landing slots, and they are willing to engage in predatory pricing to keep out any new entrants. At 40 of the 100 largest US airports, a single airline controls a majority of the market.[4] United, for example, dominates many of the country's largest airports. In Houston, United has around a 60% market share, in Newark 51%, in Washington Dulles 43%, in San Francisco 38%, and in Chicago 31%.[5] This situation is even more skewed for other airlines. For example, Delta has an 80% market share in in Atlanta and 77% in Philadelphia, while in Dallas-Fort Worth it has 77%.[6] For many routes, you simply have no choice.

The episode became a metaphor for American capitalism in the twenty-first century. A highly profitable company had bloodied a consumer, and it didn't matter because consumers have no choice.

When consumers see a man bloodied by a big company or see a suffering patient gouged by a hospital, they get the sense that something is profoundly wrong with companies.

All around the world, people have an overwhelming sense that something is broken. This is leading to record levels of populism in the United States and Europe, resurgent intolerance, and a desire to upend the existing order. The left and right cannot agree on what is wrong, but they both know that something is rotten.

Capitalism has been the greatest system in history to lift people out of poverty and create wealth, but the "capitalism" we see today in the United States is a far cry from competitive markets. What we have today is a grotesque, deformed version of capitalism. Economists such as Joseph Stiglitz have referred to it as "ersatz capitalism," where the distorted representation we see is as far away from the real thing as Disney's Pirates of the Caribbean are from real pirates.

If what we have is a fake version of capitalism, what does the real thing look like? What *should* we have?

According to the dictionary, the idealized state of capitalism is "an economic system based on the private ownership of the means of production, distribution, and exchange, characterized by the freedom of capitalists to operate or manage their property for profit in competitive conditions."

Parts of this definition have universal appeal today. Today, for example, we take private property for granted in the world. Communism defined itself in opposition to private property. Karl Marx wrote in *The Communist Manifesto*, "The theory of Communists may be summed up in the single sentence: Abolition of private property." After the fall of the Berlin Wall in 1989, Communism collapsed and was widely discredited as a miserable failure. The battle for private property had been won.

The harder part of the definition follows: capitalism is "characterized by the freedom of capitalists to operate or manage their property for profit in competitive conditions." The battle for competition is being lost. Industries are becoming highly concentrated in the hands of very few players, with little real competition.

Capitalism without competition is not capitalism.

Competition matters because it prevents unjust inequality, rather than the transfer of wealth from consumer or supplier to the monopolist. If there is no competition, consumers and workers have less freedom to choose. Competition creates clear price signals in markets, driving supply and demand. It promotes efficiency. Competition creates more choices, more innovation, economic development and growth, and a stronger democracy by dispersing economic power. It promotes individual initiative and freedom. Competition is the essence of capitalism, yet it is dying.

Competition is the basis for evolution. An absence of competition means an absence of evolution, a failure to adapt to new conditions. It threatens our survival.

There are fewer winners and many losers when there is less competition. Rising market power by dominant firms has created less competition, lower investment in the real economy, lower productivity, less economic dynamism with fewer startups, higher prices for dominant firms, lower wages and more wealth inequality. The evidence from economic studies is pouring in like a flood.

Competition remains an ideal that is receding further from our reach. Don't take our word for it, though. According to the *New York Times*, "Markets work best when there is healthy competition among businesses. In too many industries, that competition just doesn't exist anymore."[7] *The Economist* warns that "America needs a heavy dose of competition."[8]

If you believe in competitive free markets, you should be very concerned. If you believe in fair play and hate cronyism, you should be worried. With fake capitalism CEOs cozy up to regulators to get the kind of rules they want and donate to get the laws they desire. Larger companies get larger, while the small disappear, and the consumer and worker are left with no choice.

Freedom is essential to capitalism. It is not surprising then that Milton Friedman picked *Free to Choose* as the title of his extremely popular PBS series on capitalism, and *Capitalism and Freedom* was the title of his book that sold over 1.5 million copies. He argued that economic freedom was "a necessary condition for political freedom."[9]

Free to Choose sounds great. It's a bold statement and a really catchy title, yet Americans are not free to choose. In industry after industry, they can only purchase from local monopolies or oligopolies that can tacitly collude. The United States now has many industries with only three or four competitors controlling entire markets. Since the early 1980s, market concentration has increased severely. As we'll document in this book:

- Two corporations control 90% of the beer Americans drink.
- Four airlines completely dominate airline traffic, often enjoying local monopolies or duopolies in their regional hubs.

- Five banks control about half of the nation's banking assets.
- Many states have health insurance markets where the top two insurers have an 80–90% market share. For example, in Alabama one company, Blue Cross Blue Shield, has an 84% market share and in Hawaii it has 65% market share.
- When it comes to high-speed Internet access, almost all markets are local monopolies; over 75% of households have no choice with only one provider.
- Four players control the entire US beef market and have carved up the country.
- After two mergers this year, three companies will control 70% of the world's pesticide market and 80% of the US corn-seed market.

The list of industries with dominant players is endless.

It gets even worse when you look at the world of technology. Laws are outdated to deal with the extreme winner-takes-all dynamics online. Google completely dominates internet searches with an almost 90% market share. Facebook has an almost 80% share of social networks. Both have a duopoly in advertising with no credible competition or regulation.

Amazon is crushing retailers and faces conflicts of interest as both the dominant e-commerce seller and the leading online platform for third party sellers. It can determine what products can and cannot sell on its platform, and it competes with any customer that encounters success. Apple's iPhone and Google's Android completely control the mobile app market in a duopoly, and they determine whether businesses can reach their customers and on what terms.

Existing laws were not even written with digital platforms in mind. So far, these platforms appear to be benign dictators, but they are dictators nonetheless.

It was not always like this. Without almost any public debate, industries have now become much more concentrated than they were 30 and even 40 years ago. As economist Gustavo Grullon has noted, the "nature of US product markets has undergone a structural shift that has weakened competition." The federal government has done little to prevent this concentration, and in fact has done much to encourage it.

It is difficult to overstate the stakes for the economy and politics from industrial concentration. One of the great mysteries of the past few years is why economic growth has been so poor and why so many men and women with broken hopes have simply given up and dropped out of the work force. To give a sense of the crisis, in 2016, 83% of men in their prime working ages that were not in the labor force had not worked in the previous year. That means 10 million men are missing from the workforce.[10] These are not purely statistics; they are our fellow sons, brothers, and fathers.

Economic growth has been poor despite the trillions of dollars of liquidity the Federal Reserve has pumped into the economy and despite trillions of dollars of government debt. After the global financial crisis, the United States has experienced high levels of long-term unemployment, stagnant wages, dismal numbers of new startups, and low productivity growth.

These problems, though, have deeper roots. After the dot-com bust, the economy rebounded but growth was more anemic than during the 1980s or even 1990s. After the financial crisis, growth was even more pathetic. Each expansion has experienced lower growth than the previous one. There is not one variable that answers all questions, but a growing mountain of research shows that less competition has led to lower wages, fewer jobs, fewer startups, and less economic growth.

Broken markets create broken politics. Economic and political power is becoming concentrated in the hands of distant monopolists. The stronger companies become, the greater their stranglehold on regulators and legislators becomes via the political process. This is not the essence of capitalism.

Capitalism is a game where competitors play by rules that everyone agrees. The government is the referee, and just as you need a referee and a set of agreed rules for a good basketball game, you need rules to promote competition in the economy. Left to their own devices, firms will use any available means to crush their rivals. Today, the state, as referee, has not enforced rules that would increase competition, and through regulatory capture has created rules that limit competition.

Workers have helped create vast wealth for corporations, yet wages barely kept up with the growth in productivity and profits. The reason for the large gap is clear. Economic power has shifted into the hands of companies. Income and wealth inequality have increased as companies have captured more and more of the economic pie. Most workers own no shares and have barely benefited from record corporate profits. As G.K. Chesterton observed, "Too much capitalism does not mean too many capitalists, but too few capitalists."

When the Left and Right speak of capitalism today, they are telling stories about an imaginary state. The unbridled, competitive free markets that the Right cherishes don't exist today. They are a myth.

The Left attacks the grotesque capitalism we see today, as if that were the true manifestation of the essence of capitalism rather than the distorted version it has become.

Economists like Thomas Piketty even see within capitalism itself a logical contradiction that "devours the future," rather than locating the problem in a lack of competition. But what we see today is the result of the urge to monopolize, where big companies eat up the small, and government is captured to rig the rules of the game for the strong at the expense of the weak.

While many books have been written on capitalism and inequality, the left and the right don't even read the same books. Researchers have analyzed book purchases, and there are almost no political or economic books that both sides pick up and read. Likewise, if you look at Twitter debates, the data shows that the left and the right don't even share ideas with each other or debate. Neither side speaks to the other, much less listens.

Supporting capitalism has been identified with being pro-big business rather than being pro-free markets. This book is unabashedly pro-competition. Big business is not bad, but too often size has come through mergers that have destroyed competition and subverted capitalism.

We hope this book will bridge the divide and find a common ground between the left and right. Both sides may prefer different tax rates or have different views on social policy, but left and right should agree that competition is better for creating better jobs, higher pay, greater innovation, lower prices, and greater choice.

A book that merely analyzes the problems without offering solutions is not particularly useful. In this book we'll present solutions. We end the book with thoughts on how to reform and fix the economy and political system.

We do hope you're outraged after reading this book, but more important, we hope that you come away knowing that consumer and voter anger can be harnessed for good.

In 1776 Adam Smith wrote *The Wealth of Nations*, and the Continental Congress declared independence from Britain. Smith complained bitterly about monopolies. He wrote of the East India Company: ". . . the monopoly which our manufacturers have obtained . . . has so much increased the number of some particular tribes of them, that, like an overgrown standing army, they have become formidable to the government, and upon many occasions intimidate the legislature."

That same year, among the reasons the American Continental Congress cited for separating from Britain in the Declaration of Independence was, "For cutting off our Trade with all parts of the world: For imposing Taxes on us without our Consent." The Boston Tea Party was in response to the East India Company's monopoly on tea. *The Wealth of Nations* and the Declaration of Independence were bold statements against the abuses of monopoly power. Americans wanted entrepreneurial freedom to build businesses in a free market.

Today, we need a new revolution to cast off monopolies and restore free trade.

Chapter One

Where Buffett and Silicon Valley Billionaires Agree

There's class warfare, all right, but it's my class, the rich class, that's making war, and we're winning.

—Warren Buffett

Warren Buffett is an icon for Americans and capitalists everywhere. For decades, his annual letters have taught and educated Americans about the virtues of investing. In many ways, Buffett has become the embodiment of American capitalism. He's called the annual meetings of his investment firm Berkshire Hathaway a "Celebration of Capitalism" and has referred to his hometown of Omaha as the "cradle of capitalism."[1] Yet Buffett is the antithesis of capitalism.

He has become a folk hero because of his simplicity. Even as he became America's second wealthiest man, he has lived in the same home and avoided a lavish lifestyle. He makes billions not because of dirty greed but because he loves working. Books about him, such as *Tap Dancing to Work*, capture his jaunty ebullience.

As a person he is remarkably consistent. His daily eating includes chocolate chip ice cream at breakfast, five Coca-Colas throughout the day, and lots of potato chips. His investing is as consistent as his eating. For decades, he has recommended buying businesses with strong "moats" and little competition.

The results have shown how right he is. Warren Buffett gained control of Berkshire for around $32 per share when it was a fading textile company, and turned it into a conglomerate that owns businesses with little competition. The stock is now worth about $300,000 per share, making the entire company worth more than $495 billion.

For decades, Americans have learned from Buffett that competition is bad and to avoid companies that require any investment or capital expenditures. American managers have absorbed his principles.

Buffett loves monopolies and hates competition. Buffett has said at his investment meetings that, "The nature of capitalism is that if you've got a good business, someone is always wanting to take it away from you and improve on it." And in his annual reports, he has approvingly quoted Peter Lynch, "Competition may prove hazardous to human wealth."[2] And how true that is. What is good for the monopolist is not good for capitalism. Buffett and his business partner Charlie Munger always tried to buy companies that have monopoly-like status. Once, when asked at an annual meeting what his ideal business was, he argued it was one that had "High pricing power, a monopoly."[3] The message is clear: if you're investing in a business with competition, you're doing it wrong.

Unsurprisingly, his initial business purchases were newspapers in towns with no competition. According to Sandy Gottesman, a friend of Buffett, "Warren likens owning a monopoly or market-dominant newspaper to owning an unregulated toll bridge. You have relative freedom to increase rates when and as much as you want."[4] Back in the days before the Internet, people got their news from their local paper. Buffett understood that even a fool could make money with a monopoly, "If you've got a good enough business, if you have a monopoly newspaper. . . you know, your idiot nephew could run it."[5] With that line of reasoning, in 1977 Buffett purchased the *Buffalo Evening News*. He bought this newspaper and then launched a Sunday edition to drive his competitor, the *Buffalo Courier-Express*, out of business. By 1986, the renamed *Buffalo News* was a local monopoly.[6]

In many ways, Warren Buffett is like Steph Curry of the Golden State Warriors. Curry is the master of the three-point shot. But if you look more closely at his record, you'll see that he mainly shoots *uncontested* three-point shots. He'll regularly stand several feet behind the three-point line. At first, defenders didn't even defend. Who would shoot from that far away? At one point in 2016, he made 35 out of 52 shots from between 28 and 50 feet. Scoring is a lot easier without competition.[7]

Over the years, Buffett followed his philosophy of buying into industries with little competition. If he can't buy a monopoly, he'll buy a duopoly. And if he can't buy a duopoly, he'll settle for an oligopoly.

His record speaks for itself. Buffett was one of the biggest shareholders in Moody's Corporation, a ratings agency that shares an effective duopoly with Standard & Poor's. (You might remember they rated the toxic subprime junk bonds that blew up the economy as AAA gold). He and his lieutenants bought shares in DaVita, which has a price gouging duopoly in the kidney dialysis business. (They have paid hundreds of millions to resolve allegations of illegal kickbacks.) He's owned shares in Visa and MasterCard, which are a duopoly in credit card payments. He also owns Wells Fargo and Bank of America, which dominate banking in many states. (Wells Fargo recently created millions of fraudulent savings and checking accounts in order to charge more fees to depositors.) In 2010, he fully acquired railroad Burlington Northern Santa Fe, which is a local monopoly at this stage. He has owned Republic Services Group, a company that bought its largest competitor, to have a duopoly in waste management. He has owned UPS, which has a duopoly with FedEx in domestic shipping. He bought *all* four major airline stocks after they merged and turned into an oligopoly. Lately he's been buying utility companies that are local monopolies.

We could go on listing Buffett's investments, but you're probably noticing a pattern here. He really doesn't like competition. By all accounts, he's a fine human being, but he's a monopolist at heart.

Buffett has found his soul mates with 3G Capital Partners, a Brazilian investment firm that controls 50% of the US beer market. The US beer sector has now become a duopoly. Now they're trying to dominate the packaged food sector. In 2013 Buffett partnered with 3G to buy the H.J. Heinz Company, which two years later he merged with Kraft Foods to become Kraft Heinz. This gave them complete dominance in many areas of the supermarket shelf like ketchup. They tried to buy Unilever in 2017, which would have given them even more ownership of dominant brands, but Unilever turned them down. Alas, Kraft Heinz Unilever was not meant to be.

If Warren Buffett is the embodiment of American capitalism, then billionaire Peter Thiel is Silicon Valley's Godfather.[8] They could not be more different. Where Buffett is folksy and simple, Thiel is distant and philosophical. Buffett quotes the actress Mae West, while Thiel quotes French intellectuals like Jean-Jacques Servan-Schreiber. Buffett is a dyed-in-the-wool Democrat, and Thiel is a libertarian who has procured a New Zealand passport so he can flee when the peasants with pitchforks come for Silicon Valley monopolies.

Buffett and Thiel have nothing in common, but they can both agree on one thing: competition is for losers.

Thiel founded PayPal and has funded a legendary roster of businesses like LinkedIn and Facebook, which now has a monopoly on the key social networks and has a duopoly with Google on online advertising. He dislikes competition and redefines capitalism by turning it on its head, "Americans mythologize competition and credit it with saving us from socialist bread lines. Actually, capitalism and competition are opposites." In Thiel's view, without fat profits, you can't fund innovation and improve. Thiel supported the Trump campaign, presumably because if you're running a monopoly it is good to know your potential regulator. He wrote an entire book, titled *Zero to One*, praising creating businesses that are monopolies and defiantly declared that competition "is a relic of history."[9]

Competition is a dirty word, whether you're in Omaha or Silicon Valley.

Praising monopolies has a long tradition in the United States. Joseph Schumpeter, an Austrian-born economics professor at Harvard, is generally remembered for coining the phrase "gale of creative destruction," in praise of competition. It is ironic that economists and consultants see him today as the champion of disruptive startups, when in Schumpeter's view, if you wanted to search for progress, it would lead you to the doors of monopolies. Much like Peter Thiel, Schumpeter thought that perfectly competitive firms were inferior in technological efficiency and were a waste. Monopolies were more robust because, "a perfectly competitive industry is much more apt to be routed—and to scatter the bacilli of depression—under the impact of progress or of external disturbance than is big business."[10]

Buffett and Thiel love monopolies, because when you're a monopolist, you become what economists call a "price maker." That means you can set the price of your goods near the highest amount that consumers would be willing to pay for them, unlike in more competitive industries, where competition encourages innovation and drives down prices. Typically, monopolists raise prices and restrict the supply of goods.

The problem of raising prices and restricting supply is not a distant, theoretical issue. For example, cable companies in the United States possess a local monopoly and have been using their market power to overcharge the typical household about $540 per year, according to the nonprofit Consumer Federation of America.[11] Not only are prices high, but cable companies also have long history of throttling sites and content they don't like to restrict use of the internet.[12] Comcast has throttled peer-to-peer services like Bitorrent under the guise of managing bandwidth.[13]

Buffett and Thiel's thinking has not gone unnoticed. Investment banks like Goldman Sachs (also known as the Vampire Squid of Wall Street due to its business attitude) have recommended to clients that they should welcome oligopolies and buy them. Oligopolies may have a bad reputation for pillaging consumers, but they are attractive because in Goldman Sach's view they have "lower competitive intensity, greater stickiness, and pricing power with customers due to reduced choice, scale-cost benefits including stronger leverage over suppliers, and higher barriers to new entrants all at once." Investors could read that loud and clear: oligopolies can squeeze workers and suppliers, hike prices on consumers, and that makes oligopoly stocks attractive buys.

Popular investment books openly recommend monopolies. Before the financial crisis, you could find a book titled *Monopoly Rules: How to Find, Capture, and Control the Most Lucrative Markets in Any Business*. It offered advice to young entrepreneurs, "you probably learned that monopolies are unnatural, illegal, and rare. Wrong! Wrong! Wrong! In fact, monopolies are often natural, usually legal, and surprisingly common." Just in case the government held a different view, it advised earmarking part of the very high profits "for top-flight anti-trust attorneys."[14]

Many economists now openly praise monopolies as a more enlightened form of capitalism. Robert Atkinson and Michael Lind wrote a book titled *Big Is Beautiful*. They write, "In the abstract universe of Econ 101, monopolies and oligopolies are always bad because they distort prices. . . . In the real world, things are not so simple." And to enlighten us, they continue, "Academic economics includes a well-developed literature about imperfect markets. But it is reserved for advanced students," and these lessons are unavailable to the poor, benighted souls who don't have PhDs.[15]

It is ironic that the champions of monopolies are essentially aligning themselves with neo-Marxist economists who think that in capitalism the big inevitably eat the small. As the eminent Polish economist Michał Kalecki wrote, "Monopoly appears to be deeply rooted in the nature of the capitalist system: free competition, as an assumption, may be useful in the first stage of certain investigations, but as a description of the normal stage of capitalist economy it is merely a myth."[16] Kalecki would have felt at home in Omaha and Silicon Valley.

Buffett and Thiel's views on competition capture the contradictions of capitalism. Thiel's idea that innovation comes only from large monopolies ignores his own personal history at PayPal. He was David creating a startup from nothing and competing against financial Goliaths. Today, little David has joined the Philistines.

Unfortunately, capitalism in the United States and many developed economies is not marked by competition and entrepreneurial drive. Many industries really have very few players that matter. Americans have the illusion of choice, but are not free to choose.

Many large companies have captured their regulators, and regulation exists largely to keep out new entrants. For example, top Comcast employees have gone over to the FCC in droves, and then left government to go back to Comcast and regulated firms. When it came time for Comcast to buy NBCUniversal, Comcast had 78 former government employees registered as Comcast lobbyists.[17] Unsurprisingly, despite ample antitrust concerns, the deal went through. Even more nauseating was that Meredith Attwell Baker, a key commissioner of the FCC who had approved the deal, was immediately hired by Comcast. There isn't even a thin line separating regulators from the regulated.

Markets are not black and white and are rarely entirely monopolistic or perfectly competitive either. Just as villains in movies are rarely pure evil (great directors know villains are much more frightening when they have just a touch of evil), it is extremely unusual to find a company that is a monopoly and has 100% market share. That would be too obvious and would arouse the wrath of regulators.

In general, we do not have a monopoly problem; we have an oligopoly problem. Americans have been trained to fear national monopolies, but they have given little thought to duopolies or oligopolies. Many industries are duopolies with only two major players controlling the entire market, while others are oligopolies with only three or four main competitors. Few are complete monopolies, so when you read headlines about the monopoly problem in the United States, as Professor Tim Wu has noted, "the press is sounding the wrong alarm. We know how to fight monopolies, but regulators are confused when it comes to duopolies and oligopolies."[18]

You won't find the words duopoly or oligopoly in Adam Smith's *The Wealth of Nations* or in any of the antitrust acts, such as the Sherman Act of 1890 or the Clayton Act of 1914. The word oligopoly was not even created until the 1930s by the Harvard economist Edward Chamberlin. The word oligopoly comes from Greek and means "few sellers." It has the same origin as the word oligarchs. Today's oligopolists are our oligarchs.

While the term oligopoly is more correct than monopoly, we hope you will forgive us if we use them interchangeably in this book. As the economist Milton Friedman wrote, a monopoly is any concentration of power by a firm that "has sufficient control over a particular product or service to determine significantly the terms on which other individuals shall have access to it." Today, oligopolies are monopolies under that definition.

Oligopolies often act like monopolies. While collusion and cartels between different players are illegal, tacit collusion is normal and rational. The investment firm Marathon Asset Management noted this in their wonderful book *Capital Returns*, "A basic industry with few players, rational management, barriers to entry, a lack of exit barriers and noncomplex rules of engagement is the perfect setting for companies to engage in cooperative behavior. . . . and it is for this reason that the really juicy investment returns are to be found in industries which are evolving to this state."[19]

It doesn't matter how you look at it, competition is dying in the United States.

The collapse in competition is happening across most of the economy. Work by *The Economist* found that over the 15-year period from 1997 to 2012 *two-thirds* of American industries were concentrated in the hands of a few firms.[20]

One of the most comprehensive overviews available of increasing industrial concentration shows that we have seen a collapse in the number of publicly listed companies and a shift in power towards big companies. Gustavo Grullon, Yelena Larkin, and Roni Michaely have documented how despite a much larger economy, we have seen the number of listed firms fall by half, and many industries now have only a few big players. This is translating into higher profits, lower wages, and less competition. They noted, "Firms in industries with the largest increases in product market concentration have realized higher profit margins, positive abnormal stock returns, and more profitable M&A deals, which suggest that market power is becoming an important source of value."

A couple of charts will be helpful to visualize the stunning concentration we've seen in the United States and the decline in the number of companies in most industries. The boom in mergers and acquisitions over the past 30 years is unprecedented and surpasses the original merger mania at the peak of the Gilded Age when we had robber barons. You can see that mergers tend to move in waves, except that the most recent merger waves have all happened quickly and back to back. We've seen three separate peaks in mergers since 1980. One was at the height of the late 1990s bull market, another at the peak of the market before the financial crisis in 2007–2008, and we're currently living in another great merger wave (Figure 1.1). We have yet to see how crazy things can get this time around.

Today, we're in a second Gilded Age.

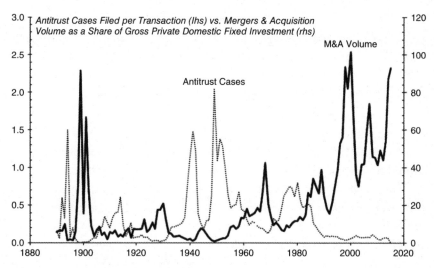

Figure 1.1   Merger Manias: 1890–2015
SOURCE: Taylor Mann, Pine Capital.

The scale of mergers is so extreme that you would almost think American capitalists were trying to prove Karl Marx right. In Marx's view, capital generally grew via the absorption of capital of one company by another. In this struggle, he wrote, "the larger capitals," as a rule, "beat the smaller . . . Competition rages in direct proportion to the number, and in inverse proportion to the magnitude of the rival capitals. It always ends in the ruin of many small capitalists, whose capitals partly pass into the hands of their competitors, and partly vanish completely."[21] As Marx often said, one capitalist kills many. Marx wanted to replace the monopoly of the fat robber baron with the monopoly of the state. Both of those are wrong. We need real, lively competition.

(For the record, even though Marx was one of the most influential writers on economics ever – to the great misfortune of anyone who ever lived in a communist country – he was a disaster with money and the last person anyone should ever listen to. He was typically penniless and his friend Friedrich Engels stole money from his father's factory to give to Marx. Furthermore, we don't know of any communist countries that are not abject failures. But on the point of large capitalists swallowing the small, he was right.)

This extreme corporate cannibalism where the big eats the small has huge implications for the number of firms in the economy. Companies are simply vanishing – to borrow the term from Marx – and being swallowed up by their competitors. It is nothing short of a collapse in public companies. *Over half of all public firms have disappeared over the past 20 years.* Astonishingly, according to a study by Credit Suisse, "between 1996 and 2016, the number of stocks in the U.S. fell by roughly 50%— from more than 7,300 to fewer than 3,600—while rising by about 50% in other developed nations."[22] It is not lower growth or the global financial crisis that caused fewer IPOs. The collapse in listed stocks is happening in countries where industries are becoming more concentrated.

The decline in listed companies has been so spectacular that the number is lower than it was in the early 1970s (see Figure 1.2), when the real GDP in the United States was just one third of what it is today.[23] America's economy grows every year, but the number of listed companies shrinks. On this trend, by 2070 we will only have one company per industry. Or we may get social revolution.

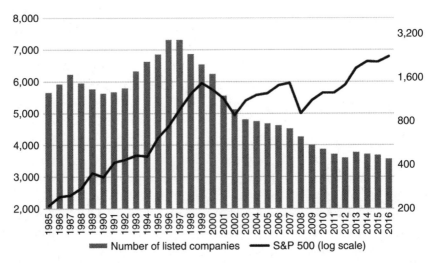

Figure 1.2   Collapse in the Number of US Public Companies Since 1996
Source: Data from Charles Schwab.

Not only are the big companies gobbling up the small, but we have not seen a new wave of startups coming in to compete with the Goliaths. Notice that as merger waves have happened, we've seen far fewer initial public offerings (IPOs) (see Figure 1.3). The lack of new companies trading on the NYSE or Nasdaq exchanges is historically very unusual given how much markets have risen. Normally, during stock market rallies lots of new companies go public. CEOs take advantage of rising stock markets to sell shares to the public. In the boom years of the 1990s there were an average of 436 IPOs per year in the US. In 2016, we saw only 74 IPOs.[24] The great American economic machine is slowly grinding to a halt.

Given the lack of any new entrants into most industries, it should be no surprise that companies are getting larger and older. The average age of public companies in the United States is currently 18 years old, up from 12 years old in 1996. In real terms, the average company in the economy has become three times larger during the past two decades.[25] Not only do we have fewer, older companies, but they are also capturing almost all the profits. In 1995 the top 100 companies accounted for 53% of all income from publicly traded firms, but by

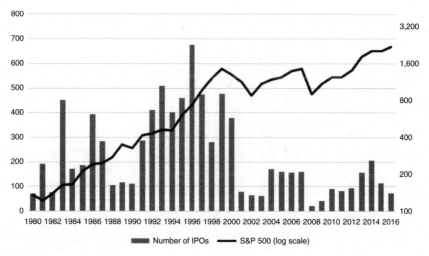

Figure 1.3 Collapse in Initial Public Offerings (IPOs)
SOURCE: Barrons.

2015, they captured a whopping 84% of all profits.[26] Like Oliver Twist asking for more, there is little left for smaller companies after the big ones eat their fill.

All the mergers and acquisitions have killed competition. Every year companies write an annual report that shareholders can consult. They have to discuss their business, their competitors, and the risks to their business. *The Economist* looked at how often companies mentioned the word "competition" and the chart (see Figure 1.4) is astounding. We've seen a collapse in the use of the word competition in annual reports, and this has coincided with the increasing concentration in the economy. CEOs no longer even need to write about competition because so little remains.

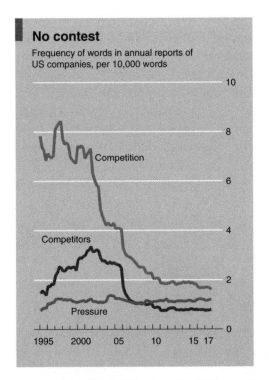

Figure 1.4   Frequency of the Words "Competition," "Competitors," and "Pressure" in Annual Reports
SOURCE: The Economist.

The lack of competition is not due to a few industries; *almost all* industries are becoming more concentrated. In a landmark study, titled "Are US Industries Becoming More Concentrated?," Gustavo Grullon, Yelena Larkin, and Roni Michaely showed that over the past 20 years over 75% of US industries have experienced an increase in concentration levels. In almost all industries, the top four firms had significantly increased their market share, as smaller rivals disappeared. Much more disturbingly, they noted that the companies in industries that had become the most concentrated had the highest profit margins and the highest stock returns.[27] They used information from publicly listed companies, but they also looked at the census data for private companies, and the message was the same. The key conclusion from their study was alarming: "Overall, our findings suggest that the nature of US product markets has undergone a structural shift that has weakened competition."

When Grullon and his colleagues analyzed industries by size, they found that the more concentrated the industry, the higher the return on assets. They wanted to see if that was simply because larger firms might be more efficient and better run, but instead, what they found was that almost all the return came because "the higher returns on assets are mainly driven by firms' ability to extract higher profit margins." The effect was huge and highly correlated with the size of the companies. You really can hike prices and get higher profits when you have little competition.

Buffett was on to something. Grullon's study found that a strategy of buying the most highly concentrated industries and shorting the least concentrated industries outperforms the market.

No study is perfect, but the overall message is unmistakable: the United States has become a lot less competitive. Recently John Kwoka, one of the great authorities on industrial economics, antitrust, and regulation offered a damning assessment based on all of the available research: the "totality of this body of work provides a compelling portrayal of rising concentration throughout large segments of the U.S. economy over the past 20 years."[28]

Dozens of studies are now showing that higher industrial concentration leads to higher profits for firms, higher prices for consumers, fewer startups, lower productivity, lower wages, and greater inequality. Yet CEOs keep gobbling other companies up.

On the surface, our current problems would appear to be a case of greedy CEOs and investors without ethics ruining the economy for their own benefit, but something deeper is happening.

Edward Queen, director of Emory's Turner Program in Ethics and Servant Leadership, found that when business students are presented with an ethics case, 20% to 30% of the students cannot find or identify the ethical issue. In Queen's view, "far too much of the world's corporate leadership is driven by moral midgets who have been educated far beyond their capacities for good judgment." Queen argues that for the past six decades the disciples of Nobel Prize–winning economist Milton Friedman have been emphasizing that the only duty of a corporation is to generate profits and a return on investment.[29] These lessons that were drilled into generations of business school graduates are now playing out on a grand scale.

Headlines of high-profile CEOs and managers who have been convicted of crimes reinforce the view that MBAs lack ethics. Jeffrey Skilling was Harvard Business School class of 1979 and he brought an army of McKinsey MBAs to Enron. The head of McKinsey Rajat Gupta was convicted of insider trading, and he also had a Harvard MBA. Headlines from Duke University seem to confirm the problem. MBA candidates at Duke are required to take "Leadership, Ethics, and Organizations" but close to 10% of first-year students in Duke's business program were suspected of cheating on a take-home examination.[30]

The answer is not so neat and tidy as saying that evil CEOs without ethics are choking the US economy.

Every MBA has learned Michael Porter's Five Forces of management. Porter taught at Harvard, and his book *Competitive Strategy* is now the bible for managers and investors. MBAs are trained to analyze the level of competition within an industry and avoid industries with high competition.

Among Porter's Five Forces are the threat of established rivals and the threat of new entrants. For a Five Forces–trained MBA, the worst industry you can find yourself in is one where your competitors are strong and anyone can enter the industry and compete. If a CEO can find ways to keep out rivals, they are trained to do so. That is why mergers are so typical to eliminate established rivals. It is also why companies will do all they can to erect regulatory and legal barriers to entry in their industries. This is the MBA gospel.

Over the past few decades, MBAs have also learned to specialize and dominate markets. Jack Welch taught managers at General Electric that they should not be third- or four-place players in industries. Only first or second place would do. Since the cult of Welch and GE has taken over, managers have sold smaller competitors to the biggest rivals, and the top firms have gobbled up any small competitor.

In the investing world, hedge fund managers are trained to invest in companies that have absorbed Porter's Five Forces and have established moats to protect against new entrants. Buffett has said, "In business, I look for economic castles protected by unbreachable moats." Pension fund managers and investors need to find the stocks that produce high long-term returns. They would be failing, in a way, if they did not chase the monopolies, duopolies, and oligopolies. Yet in order to generate returns, in the words of one manager, they have to look for "corporate killer whales that can feast on baby seals."

Libraries of books at business schools are devoted to explaining different kinds of moats. Investors search for companies that achieve such scale that they become the "Low-Cost Producer." Investors try to find firms with "High Switching Costs" that lock clients into a relationship. They try to find businesses with "Network Effects" where you win by being the only system people can use to call or pay each other, for example. They also look for industries with "Intangible Assets" such as patents that keep your competitors out by law. In the medical industry, in particular, patents allow companies to charge astronomic prices because, by law, no other companies can compete with them while they hold a patent.

Company CEOs and investors are all behaving in a perfectly rational way when they buy competitors and find ways to monopolize their industries. They are reducing the threat of established rivals as well as the threat of new entrants. They are following Porter and Buffett and widening their moat every day.

Almost all big companies are not bad. The paradox is that what is good, right, and logical for the corporation is not good, right, or logical for the economy as a whole. The growth of monopolies does not lead to growth for the economy.

Every company that is a Goliath starts out as David and tries to increase its dominance and market share. That is what MBAs are taught with Porter's Five Forces and what they learn from Buffett by "increasing the moat" around their businesses. Every manager tries to do this, and investors are trained to reward companies that reduce competition. This system of incentives is a Monopoly Machine.

This drive to monopoly works at the micro level, but not at the macro level. What is good for the CEO to do for his company is not necessarily good for the whole economy. In the economy, it is logical for big companies to try to seek efficiencies, acquire competitors, pay lower wages, and increase their own income, but when all companies try to do this at the same time, everyone is worse off. The paradox is that as every company does this, it leads to lower wages, higher inequality, lower growth, less investment, and we're all worse off. Growth for the monopolist does not mean growth for the economy.

After the financial crisis Walmart's CEO Mike Duke said, "Our customers are running out of money, buying smaller pack sizes and less discretionary items near the end of the month. It shows greater pressure on consumers."[31] Yet in no way did he connect the low pay of his own employees to the lack of consumer income and demand.

The squeeze on workers brings to mind G.K. Chesterton's observation: "Capitalism is contradictory as soon as it is complete, for the master is always trying to cut down what his servant demands, and hence is cutting down what his customer can spend. He is asking the same person to act in contradictory ways. He wishes to pay him as a pauper, but wants him to spend like a prince."

Record high corporate profit margins are merely the other side of the coin of suppressed wages.

Long gone are the days when Henry Ford could double his workers' wages and do so happily. As Ford explained, "Unless industry can keep wages high and prices low it destroys itself, for otherwise it limits the number of customers." Ford understood that the economy was not a zero sum game between himself and his workers.[32]

During the Great Depression, the British economist John Maynard Keynes was trying to figure out why the economic collapse was so severe. He realized that in downturns, it is logical for each household to demand more cash and save money on a precautionary basis to put itself on a better footing. However, when all households do it at the same time, the economy contracts, the demand for goods falls, workers are fired and all households are worse off than if none of them did it. Your spending is someone else's income; if you don't spend, someone else doesn't get paid. It is illogical for each household not to save and look after itself, yet it is illogical for all households to do that at the same time. The paradox that what is true for the part is not true for the whole is one of the key problems in economics and is at the heart of *The General Theory* by Keynes.

In logic, this is called the fallacy of composition. If you are at a football game and stand to see the game better, you might get a better view. But if everyone stands, no one has a better view and everyone is worse off. Again, what is true for the part is often not true for the whole.

Once you start looking, you'll find the fallacy of composition everywhere in economics.

During the euro crisis, the Germans seemed completely oblivious to the logical fallacy. In German, *Schulden*, the word for debt, comes from *Schuld*, which also means guilt. Debt was almost evil and immoral. German Finance Minister Wolfgang Schäuble blamed the European economic crisis on smaller European countries for abandoning "long-term gains for short-term gratification," by increasing their debt load and abandoning trading competitiveness.[33] Yet just as your consumption is someone else's income, Germany's trading surplus had to be someone else's deficit. Likewise, Germany's assets were someone else's "irresponsible" loans. Not everyone can run trade surpluses at the same time, and not everyone can be a creditor at the same time. Your consumption is my income, and your borrowing is my lending.

In the summer of 2007, long lines of depositors started forming outside the bank Northern Rock in London. It was the first bank run in Britain since 1866. Ironically, the panic started when the Bank of England said Northern Rock was in fine shape and that it would stand by the bank. Problems can only be believed when they are officially denied. Immediately customers were alerted to problems and demanded the return of their deposits.[34] Every depositor was behaving in a perfectly rational way, yet when all of them showed up to get their cash at the same time, they were causing the very bankruptcy they sought to avoid. (A bank run happens when customers try to withdraw more money from the bank than the bank can provide. Banks do not keep all customer deposits available in cash for immediate withdrawal, and instead the money is lent out.)

Mervyn King, governor of the Bank of England, once noted that it may not be rational to start a bank run, but it is rational to participate in one once it has started. It is illogical for you not to pull your money out of a bank when you're worried about the bank's solvency, but it is also illogical for everyone to pull their money at the same time, as that itself brings the bank down.

The idea of the fallacy of composition applies in the field of energy as well.

Coal was the main energy source in Victorian England. Charles Dickens had described the skies of industrial towns as "black vomit, blasting all things living or inanimate, shutting out the face of day, and closing in on all these horrors with a dense dark cloud."[35] In 1865, the English economist William Stanley Jevons published *The Coal Question*. He set out to establish the size of England's coal reserves. During his research, he stumbled upon a surprising paradox. As steam engines became more efficient, coal consumption overall went *up*, rather than down. Jevons concluded, in italics, "It is wholly a confusion of ideas to suppose that the economical use of fuel is equivalent to a diminished consumption. The very contrary is the truth."[36] What was true for each individual steam engine was not true for the whole of England. This insight is known as Jevon's Paradox: make something more efficient, and people will use more, not less of it.

Jevons Paradox is the reason why expanding freeways in Los Angeles, Houston, and other concrete jungles only leads to more cars, less carpooling, and worse traffic. When people can drive more easily, they can live further away. Suddenly, much larger, more affordable homes are in commuting distance from cities. In an attempt to keep traffic moving by adding more lanes, city planners have made room for more cars and encouraged driving. What is true for the efficiency of the individual lane in a freeway is not true of the efficiency of the whole of Los Angeles. In 1990, British transportation analyst Martin Mogridge observed it as a more general characteristic of highways, and his insight is known as the Lewis-Mogridge Position: the more roads that are built, the more traffic grows to fill the roads. It holds everywhere from Nairobi to Beijing to Los Angeles.

When CEOs are presented with the choice of maximizing efficiency for the overall economy or behaving like a monopolist, the answer is obvious. It is perfectly logical for them to behave like monopolists. Most CEOs don't sit down and consider the effects their individual decisions have on society at large. That is not the way they are trained or what is logical for them.

The logical choices to reduce competition and dominate industries creates a natural cycle in business where the Davids in business always try to become Goliaths and kill off all threats.

When you look at the history of large monopolies in telecommunications and media, they started out by trying to provide a better product to the mass market. Initially hobbyists built telegraph lines between towns, but there was no way to reliably connect all of the United States until Western Union pieced together regional networks. Western Union went from a small upstart to the dominant monopolist of its day, much like Facebook went from a website at Harvard to a network that connects over two billion people. Likewise, AT&T started out as the little David. The quality of phones was terrible, and you couldn't really call many people, so it was viewed as little more than a toy. However, soon the telegraph and telephone competed head on and were in a patent war. Eventually, Western Union settled. The telegraph company sold its telephone network to Bell in exchange for 20% of Bell's telephone rental revenue. AT&T built a formidable monopoly that completely eclipsed Western Union's previous control over American life.[37]

This cycle of David turning into Goliath is told in Professor Tim Wu's dazzling book *The Master Switch*. In "The Cycle" businesses go "from somebody's hobby to somebody's industry; from jury-rigged contraption to slick production marvel; from a freely accessible channel to one strictly controlled by a single corporation or cartel – from open to closed system. It is a progression so common as to seem inevitable, though it would hardly have seemed so at the dawn of any of the past century's transformative technologies."[38]

It is not only telecommunications or media where you see the cycle. We've seen it in supermarkets, farming, insurance, and many other fields. Mom-and-pop stores have been replaced by big-box giants like Walmart, local community banks have been replaced by global banks like JP Morgan or Bank of America and small farmers have been replaced by the likes of Cargill and Tyson. Cable companies initially started out fighting the television networks to be able to transmit broadcasting, and the networks themselves were a hobby of connecting towns for shared programming. Over time, though, it has morphed into giant monopolies with no competition for high-speed internet.

Buffett is extremely smart, but his greatest advantage is the insight that monopolies, duopolies, and oligopolies face little competition and little threat of new entrants. Companies that dominate their industries represent toll roads in your daily life. Every time you do anything in your daily life, you're sending part of your paycheck to monopolists. You're making Buffett richer, and he's tap dancing all the way to the bank.

Key Thoughts from the Chapter

- It doesn't matter how you look at it, competition is dying in the United States.
- In general, we do not have a monopoly problem; we have an oligopoly problem.
- The paradox is that what is good, right, and logical for the corporation often is not good for the economy as a whole.
- Companies that dominate their industries represent toll roads on your daily life.

Chapter Two

Dividing Up the Turf

Our competitors are our friends.
Our customers are our enemies.
— *James Randall, president, Archers Daniel Midland*

Turf wars are bad for business. The Mob understands that, and businesses do as well.

In 1931, after a very bloody power struggle known as the Castellammarese War, peace came to the Italian-American mafia in the United States. The organized Mafia Commission was created to mediate conflicts and divide the territory after Charles "Lucky" Luciano ordered the killing of Salvatore Maranzano, the *capo di tutti capi* ("boss of all bosses"). As a youngster, Maranzano had wanted to become a priest and even studied to become one, but drifted into the Mob.[1] Maranzano wanted to establish peace and divide up the United States among families, but he saw himself as the master at the top. That did not suit many of the families, who wanted their territory, without a boss.

"Lucky" Luciano quickly arranged which families would share power to prevent future turf wars. He abolished the title of *capo di tutti i capi*, and instead, maintained control through the Commission by forging alliances with other bosses. The Mafia Commission divided up

21

New York among the Five Families: the Bonanno, Colombo, Gambino, Genovese, and Lucchese families.[2] As long as they stayed off each other's streets, things were fine.

The Commission was open minded and cooperative. It had representatives from the Los Angeles crime family, the Philadelphia crime family, the Buffalo crime family, and the Chicago Outfit of Al Capone. The Commission also had ties with the Irish and Jewish criminal organizations in New York, although their representatives could not vote because they were not Italian.[3]

Many industries have carved up the United States like the Mob divided the turf between families. Except in this case, there are no "made men" and only middle-aged white power brokers dividing the country. It doesn't matter where you look, competition looks fierce on paper but in reality it is often carefully orchestrated.

There is nothing new under the sun. Even in the eighteenth century, Adam Smith wrote in *The Wealth of Nations* that "People of the same trade seldom meet together, even for merriment and diversion, but the conversation ends in a conspiracy against the public, or in some contrivance to raise prices." A little later John Stuart Mill echoed the sentiment, "Where competitors are so few, they always end by agreeing not to compete." Yet these lessons are lost on us now.

When Americans think of businessmen getting together to fix prices, they generally think of Matt Damon in *The Informant*. In the movie, he played Mark Whitacre, the highest-level corporate mole in FBI history, who was spying on Archer Daniel Midland (ADM). Whitacre helped break the lysine price fixing scandal. Lysine is an essential amino acid for the development of hogs and poultry. In a market with lots of competitors, price fixing would be more difficult, but in the 1990s only three companies dominated the market.[4]

ADM never met a price it did not want to fix. Like a Mob family, they met with competitors to restrict citric acid and high fructose corn syrup as well. In documents that came to light in court, an ADM executive wrote, "Our competitors are our friends. Our customers are the enemy."[5]

The lysine price fixing scandal is not an outlier, and the dirty secret behind concentrated industries is that corporate collusion is far more widespread than you might believe. According to the Organisation for Economic Co-operation and Development (OECD), there is extensive evidence that the number, size, and impact of discovered cartels is high.[6] The most comprehensive research on this subject is by Purdue University's John Connor, who surveyed 1,040 cartels over 235 years.[7] He estimated the median price overcharge to be 25%. In the United States, for example, from 1996 to 2010 the Department of Justice convicted 128 corporations in criminal price fixing in global cartels in everything from computer screens to generic drugs to transportation contracts.[8] The number of cartels, however, is much higher. These are only the cases that regulators have *detected*. Reasonable estimates are that only 20% of collusion cases are caught, which would place the global cost from higher prices by cartels as high as $600 billion a year.[9]

Some economists sincerely believe that cartels and collusion are impossible. In particular, the ultra-free-market Chicago School of economics argued that cartels and collusion were almost impossible because it is difficult to coordinate competitors, competitors would be prone to cheat, and new entrants would come in to compete with the cartel. All of these ideas, however, were not based on any evidence and were simply conjured out of thin air by theory.

The Chicago School's view on cartels flies in the face of decades of evidence and billions of dollars of fines. According to *The Economist*, in the past few years, "international conspiracies have been busted in fields as diverse as seat belts, seafood, air freight, computer monitors, lifts and even candle wax." Cartels that fix prices and reduce supply often persist for years. Furthermore, cartels don't necessarily break down because it is difficult to coordinate price fixing. In 2006, representatives of 20 or more airlines met in airports and restaurants to fix prices of international air-cargo services. They were caught and forced to pay penalties of more than $3 billion.[10]

The move towards oligopolies is at the heart of the cartel problem. Studies indicate that two-thirds of cartels take place in industries in which the top four firms have 75% or more market share. Some highly ideological economists think cartels can't exist because they break down easily, but their views fly in the face of experience and history. Evidence shows that the median duration of cartels is five years, and some go on for decades.[11]

One cartel even lasted over a century. If you've ever bought a diamond engagement ring, chances are you bought it from a cartel that has controlled diamonds since the nineteenth century. In 1888, Cecil Rhodes set up De Beers Consolidated Mines in South Africa, and it took control of every facet of the global diamond trade. (The Rhodes Scholarship is also named after him.) In London the cartel was known as the Diamond Trading Company, while in Israel it was "The Syndicate," and in Europe it was called the Central Selling Organization. Its corporate names were endless. According to *The Atlantic*, "At its height – for most of this century – it not only either directly owned or controlled all the diamond mines in southern Africa but also owned diamond trading companies in England, Portugal, Israel, Belgium, Holland, and Switzerland."[12] The cost of diamonds went up every year, and most people assume they are beautiful, rare and precious. While they may be beautiful, they are in fact plentiful and would hardly be worth what people pay if there were no cartel.

Cartels have appeared in almost all industries and affected trillions of dollars of financial transactions. Over the past few years, as the banking sector has consolidated, we have seen cartels in foreign exchange markets and in interest rate markets.

Every day, over $5 trillion of currencies – dollars, euros, sterling, and yen – change hands in London. Almost any business deal that depends on currency exchanges will rely on what is known as "the fix." For decades, this was based on currency deals that took place at 16:00 London time. The transactions at the time then became the benchmarks for that day. Because the window of the fix was so short, big traders could manipulate the prices every day, if the regulators were asleep, and for many years they were.

British regulators caught foreign exchange traders at Barclays, Citigroup, Royal Bank of Scotland, Standard Chartered and JP Morgan all rigging the daily fix. In online chat rooms with glamorous names such as The Bandits Club, The Cartel, and The Mafia, traders colluded to distort the fix. The practice was known as "banging the close." The bankers knew that if they traded against very big clients, it could mean millions of dollars for themselves, and companies that needed to buy or sell currency for business were the losers. As in most cases of cartels, the blatant price fixing was not noticed by enterprising regulators or even bank managers but by a whistleblower.[13]

If you thought foreign exchange markets are big, consider that the Libor interest rate underpinned over $350 trillion of financial bets and investments around the world. For decades it was the benchmark rate for borrowing, and consumers, investors and businesses borrowed over Libor. The better the credit of the borrower, the lower the spread. Libor was the benchmark for all other interest rates.

Given the importance of Libor for all borrowing globally, you would think it would be impossible to game the system and screw customers. However, internal messages revealed in court documents showed how traders manipulated Libor. As the financial crisis was unfolding in 2007 and 2008, senior executives at the Royal Bank of Scotland were encouraging their employees to rig the rates. On August 19, 2007, a trader from RBS sent a message to a trader at Deutsche Bank. "It's just amazing how Libor-fixing can make you that much money or lose it if opposite," he wrote. "It is a cartel now in London."[14]

Traders were busy screwing the entire financial world and laughing while they collected their bonuses. Eventually, the British taxpayer was forced to bail out RBS at a cost of more than £40 billion.

Economists have studied cartels to try to determine what creates them and how they break apart. Economists Margaret C. Levenstein and Valerie Y. Suslow looked at over 500 cases between 1961 and 2013. They thought that perhaps cartels formed when times were bad and businesses banded together. Or perhaps they formed when authorities were lax in enforcing the rules. But those were dead ends.

After examining the evidence, Levenstein and Suslow made the unusual discovery that the most important factor in the creation and breakups of cartels was the interest rate. Cartels are more likely to break up during periods of high real interest rates, presumably because higher interest rates require higher immediate rates of return for collusion. They found the relationship was almost perfect, and observed that creating and sustaining cartels required patience. The higher the interest rates, the less likely cartels would be sustained, and the lower the real rates, the more likely cartels would cooperate and keep playing their games. They noted that there was a very close "relationship between the ability of a cartel to sustain collusion and the discount rate of its members."[15] (See Figure 2.1)

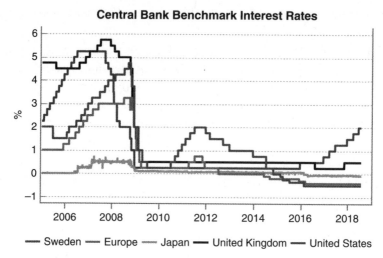

Figure 2.1   Zero and Negative Central Bank Rates Promote Cartels
SOURCE: Variant Perception.

You don't need players to talk to each other to get collusion. Game theory has shown that firms are able to reach what look like cooperative outcomes on the basis of genuinely independent decisions.[16] Many firms that have been caught continue to collude even after they no longer speak to each other.[17] Tacit collusion can lead oligopolistic firms to achieve monopolistic outcomes, leading to reduced output, higher prices, and lower consumer welfare.[18] This is known as the "oligopoly problem." By allowing extreme industry concentration, the government has essentially guaranteed oligopolies can act like monopolies and encouraged outright and tacit collusion.

Game theory applies to almost any interaction. Everyone has seen *A Beautiful Mind*. In the film John Nash, played by Russell Crowe, has an epiphany at a bar with his friends as they are trying to pick up women. There are a group of women: a stunning blonde and some average looking brunettes. All the men want the blonde woman, and one of Nash's friends remarked that Adam Smith would have encouraged competition, and the best strategy would be for them to all go and speak to her. But, Nash points out that this would be a really dumb strategy. If they did that, none of them would get the girl. She would feel pressured and then the others would be offended that they were the second choice. The optimal strategy is for the group to cooperate—no one talks to the blonde and they all talk to the less attractive friends.

Nash's key idea was that among different players, they might all choose tacit cooperation rather than face competition. The solution to the problem of competition is called "Nash Equilibrium."

Nash didn't create game theory, but he developed it. His idea was a direct descendant of John von Neumann's Minimax theory. The idea is that players of a game won't seek to achieve the highest payout but will try to minimize their maximum loss. The easiest way to understand this is the example of a mother who allows her two children to divide a cake. The most equal division will happen if one cuts the cake and the other chooses the first piece. Each kid doesn't seek a theoretical bigger piece – he tries to minimize the chance he ends up with a really small one. Firms will often collude to avoid competition and minimize their maximum loss. That's what Nash was describing in the film with the blonde.

There is much more to game theory than walking into a bar to talk to a blonde or dividing a cake.

The most famous example in game theory is The Prisoner's Dilemma. If two prisoners are caught by the police and interrogated separately, they each have a difficult choice to make: to snitch or not to snitch. They can both be silent and not rat on each other. That is the best outcome for both. However, if one of them wants to improve his own lot, he might talk to the police and betray his friend. He might walk, and his friend will serve a longer sentence.

There is no right answer to the Prisoner's Dilemma. If you play the game only once, you are highly motivated to betray your partner. However, completely different solutions begin to emerge if you play the game many times.

In 1984 Robert Axelrod invited mathematicians, economists, and computer scientists to submit strategies for playing Prisoners' Dilemma. What he found surprised him.

Strategies in the competition could either cooperate with each other or try to punish each other, but rather than play once, they had to play repeatedly until a victor emerged. The computer programs could not speak to each other or know each other's intentions. All they could do was observe what the other program did in the previous games. Most strategies were sneaky and tried to get away with punishing their partners any chance they got. Other strategies economists submitted were very complicated with all sorts of rules for cheating or cooperating.

It was completely counterintuitive, but none of the complicated strategies won. The simplest, least elaborate strategy emerged victorious; the strategy was Tit for Tat. If the opponent cheated, Tit for Tat cheated. If the opponent cooperated, Tit for Tat cooperated. It was that simple. The program generally elicited cooperation, yet if others cheated, it punished the opponents and didn't let them take advantage of Tit for Tat's kindness.

If you play only one game, punishing your partner might make sense. You can get away with it once. If you're in a repeated game, things work differently. The dominant strategy of any repeated interaction is tit for tat, which leads to cooperation.

The lessons from Tit for Tat for industries is that if you're in a cozy enough industry with very few players, selling to the same customers day in and day out over many years, the optimal strategy is always to cooperate.

Hostage negotiators know the lessons of game theory. The FBI hostage negotiators goal is not to end a hostage negotiation as quickly as possible. What they want is cooperation, and it takes time to build trust. Trust requires repeated interactions. It should be no surprise that *Stalling for Time* is the title of a book on hostage negotiation by Gary Noesser, a former FBI negotiator.

On April 9, 1988, Noesser got a call in the middle of the night. The FBI asked him to go to Sperryville, Virginia, where Charlie Leaf was holding his former common-law wife and their son captive. Leaf told the police that he planned to kill both of his hostages. Without the patience of the negotiater, Leaf might have killed his wife and son. Instead, the FBI was able to save them while marksmen put a bullet through Leaf's head.[19]

A cardinal rule of hostage negotiations is to make the criminal work for everything he gets by extracting a concession in return, no matter how small. Through repeated interactions, you get cooperation. Giving Leaf food and clothes, Noesser was able to get him to agree to leave the house.

Most industries are involved in repeated "games" where they can observe their competitors' actions, and much like the strategy Tit for Tat, the greater the number of interactions they have, the greater the incentive to cooperate. They know competition can be punished in the future with price wars, and they know that tacit collusion can lead to higher margins.

For decades Anheuser-Busch got its rivals to cooperate by not lowering prices. Generally everyone else followed, and if they didn't, Anheuser-Busch played Tit for Tat. They signaled to competitors that if they lowered their prices, they'd start an ugly price war. In 1988 Miller and Coors lowered prices on their main beers. In response Anheuser-Busch slashed prices on their key beers. As August Busch III said, "We don't want to start a blood bath, but whatever the competition wants to do, we'll do." Miller and Coors quickly abandoned their price cuts.[20]

Winning everything through competition sounds great, but it is even better not to lose everything.

Academic research on tacit collusion in oligopolies shows that in highly concentrated markets, firms will often coordinate their behavior simply by observing and reacting to their competitors' moves. This often leads parallel price movements, and the results that you would associate with a traditional agreement to set prices, output levels, or other conditions of trade.[21] In the United States a wide variety of industries are now oligopolistic, which makes tacit collusion easy.

It is common knowledge that companies don't even need to speak to each other to collude. Hermann Simon is a recognized consultant and has worked for decades with companies on their pricing strategies. He wrote a book titled *Confessions of the Pricing Man* that explained how firms could increase their pricing and get around antitrust laws and competition policy. Simon recognized that the easiest way to fix prices would be to speak to competitors, but noted that is illegal. Instead, he suggested following a "price leader" and signaling to the market.

A widely used method in the "game" of price setting is the concept of price leadership. Companies in the US car market practiced price leadership for decades, with General Motors setting price increases.[22] The largest company in most duopolies and oligopolies functions as the price leader, and other companies tend to follow price increases in lock step. These moves are almost never prosecuted.

Another frequent method that companies use is price signaling, where CEOs will indicate to the market their desired price hikes to see what the reaction is from competitors. Before any planned hike, a company sends "signals" to the marketplace. Then the company can listen to whether competitors, investors, or regulators send signals back. Simon helpfully explained that, "Signaling is not illegal per se. As long as companies keep their communication relevant to everyone in the marketplace, including customers and investors, and do not go overboard, they are usually on the safe side."[23]

Just in case these informal methods of price fixing encountered problems, Simon advised, "Please always discuss any application of these approaches with your legal department or advisors to make sure that your company's policies comply with the law."

Tacit collusion works in practice. Despite 15 price increase announcements and numerous supply reductions by paper companies over six and a half years, in August 2017 the courts decided in favor of the containerboard oligopoly: Georgia-Pacific, Westrock, International Paper Company, Temple-Inland Inc., and Weyerhaeuser Company. The court ruled that it was not a violation of antitrust law for a firm to raise its price, hoping its competitors would do the same. The containerboard companies bet on a follow-the-leader strategy and that "gamble paid off."[24] Cooperation is rarely punished.

Insurers learned long before other industries that the key to screwing your consumer is carving up the United States and sticking to your own states. They did that thanks to the McCarran–Ferguson Act, which was passed in 1945, and allows states to regulate insurers and makes selling insurance across state lines illegal. You can sell pencils, clothes, and soft drinks across state lines, but not insurance. God forbid someone shop around and get a lower price for insurance. As a result, the market for health insurance is extremely oligopolistic. United Healthcare, Aetna, Cigna, and the Blues (Blue Cross and Blue Shield Association) have almost 90% market share nationally.[25]

Like Mob families, insurance companies completely dominate their own states. According to data from the Kaiser Family Foundation the median market share of the leading health insurer per state is 54%. There are 17 states in which a single insurer covers more than 65% of the population, and there are at least 24 states in which one insurer covers more than 55%.[26]

We also see the same tacit retreat from direct conflict with "competitors" in many agricultural activities, like meat production. Only four corporations provide 57% of all poultry, 65% produce all pork, and 79% control all beef sold in the United States.[27] Today, over 96% of chickens are raised under production contracts with large companies that set out exactly how they're raised, how they're fed, the size of facilities, and so on. The pattern of a big company dictating terms to farmers is growing. As of the 2012 Census, 34.8% of the entire value of US agricultural production was governed by production or marketing contracts, up from 11% in 1969.[28]

Purdue and Tyson have carved up their processing networks so that the farmers who raise chickens in many parts of the country have only one place to sell their birds.[29] Much like the mob, the turf is divided up among themselves. According to the US Department of Agriculture in 2011, 21.7% of contract poultry farms are located in an area with only a single integrator.[30] Growers have written to the Justice Department complaining of formal or informal arrangements between companies to blacklist growers who have ended an association with another poultry company in the region.[31] Supermarket chains have filed lawsuits alleging that the poultry producers conspired to fix the price of broiler chickens for nearly a decade.[32]

The companies put the poultry processing plants in areas where there are few other economic or job opportunities, giving farmers few options but to grow chickens for that one company. Furthermore, onerous contracts, effectively allow the companies to dictate how its contractors are run. Small farmers have to borrow over $1 million secured against their land and house to build farms for Tyson or Purdue. The debt becomes a millstone around their necks, and contractors must keep producing to service the debt. The farmers have compared this relationship to southern sharecropping or even medieval serfdom. The human cost is high; farmers have been dying from suicide at much higher rates than the average population for many years.[33]

The impact of collusion and corporations not stepping on each other's turf has meant the ruin of farmers. Astonishingly, since 1980, 40% of all American cattle farmers and 90% of all hog farmers have gone out of business while the big players have made dozens of billions of dollars of profit. In the 2000s decade, gross income for small and medium-size hog and cattle farmers declined by 32%, while 71% of all chicken farmers were estimated to be earning less than the federal poverty line.[34]

Things are not much better for the workers on the farms and processing plants. The workers at the four largest US poultry companies are routinely denied bathroom breaks, forcing some to wear adult diapers to work and others to urinate on themselves in order to avoid retribution from supervisors.[35] In 68% of the counties where Tyson operates, per capita income has grown more slowly over the last four decades than the average in that state.[36]

The problems of dividing up the turf are everywhere from cable to railroads to waste management to groceries. For example, if you look at the cable industry, it would appear that the top four cable companies are highly competitive, and they have 71.1% market share to split between them. But in fact, almost all cable and high-speed internet companies have a local monopoly and don't step on each other's turf.

The US grocery market is another industry that appears extremely competitive with a lot of players, but generally large chains seek domination of a state and expand only once they have established a high market share in their home market. If you look at maps of the United States, you'll find that there is not much head-to-head competition.[37] Albertson's has the Northwest, Aldi has the Northeast, and Publix and Winn-Dixie have Florida. Food Lion has the area just north in the mid-Atlantic. Safeway mainly operates along the West Coast. It is even worse when you look down to the town and city level. Walmart's strategy for decades was simple and wily: find towns that are too small to support two Walmarts and then drive down prices to ensure that there is not room enough for competition. That explains why the company has 50% market share of all retail in 40 separate metro areas.

Because territories have been divvied up, headline numbers are often misleading. It is difficult to comprehend how uncompetitive the US economy is unless you look industry by industry. And even then, it is worse than it appears. You have to go state by state to look at the lack of choices available to consumers.

The way economists measure market power of firms and industrial concentration is by looking at two key measures. The first is the Herfindahl-Hirschman Index (HHI). This is an elegant way of turning an industry into a number, so you can quickly get a measure of it. It squares the market share of every firm and ranges from 100 to 10,000. The score starts rising very quickly as you get fewer and fewer players. If four firms have 25% market share, then it would be ($25^2 + 25^2 + 25^2 + 25^2 = 2,500$) and that is the level that the Justice Department considers to be a concentrated industry. Over the past two decades, the measure of concentration has been increasing across almost all industries, and it has risen 90% for the average industry. Today, more and more industries are above 2,500.[38]

The other way economists look at concentration is to look at the market share of the top four players. This is known as the CR4, or the concentration ratio of the top four, and is the standard measure for oligopolies (See Table 2.1).

Looks can be deceiving, and most industries are a lot less competitive than any national figures would indicate. When you dive into the scores, you realize just how little they actually tell you. Even HHI scores and CR4 scores are practically meaningless.

Table 2.1   The Largest Highly Concentrated Industries

Segment	Market Share of Top Four Companies	Annual Revenue (2012)
Warehouse clubs and supercenters	93.6%	$406 billion
Drug wholesalers	72.1%	$319 billion
Auto and truck manufacturing	68.6%	$231 billion
Drug stores	69.5%	$230 billion
Mobile-phone service	89.4%	$225 billion
Airlines	65.3%	$157 billion
Administration of pension funds	76.3%	$145 billion
Landline-phone service	73.4%	$142 billion
Cable TV	71.1%	$138 billion
Airplane manufacturing	80.1%	$113 billion

SOURCE: Data from 2012 Economic Census.[39]

Some industries are shaped like an hourglass with millions of producers at one end and hundreds of millions of consumers at the other
end, connected through a few large companies. This is true for agriculture in particular. The United States has about 2 million farmers and
300 million consumers. If you saw those numbers you'd think agriculture would be extremely competitive, but it is in fact one of the most
concentrated industries. The "Big Four" – ADM, Bunge, Cargill, and
Louis Dreyfus – control up to 90% of the global grain trade. They're
right at the middle of the hourglass connecting farmers and consumers, and they're like a toll road collecting money every time you touch
any grain.

In meat processing, four firms also sit at the middle of an hourglass
between over 65,000 hog farmers and millions of consumers.[40] Consumers go to the supermarket and see many bacon brands on the shelf,
such as Armour, Eckrich, Farmland, Gwaltney, and John Morrell, but
Smithfield owns them all.[41]

Everywhere we look, we see the illusion of competition, but very
little of it is real.

Key Thoughts from the Chapter

- Many industries have carved up the United States like the Mob
  divides the turf between families.
- Firms will often coordinate their behavior simply by observing and
  reacting to their competitors' moves.
- By allowing extreme industry concentration, the government has
  essentially guaranteed oligopolies can act like monopolies and
  encouraged outright and tacit collusion.

Chapter Three

What Monopolies and King Kong Have in Common

I have never known much good done by those who affected to trade for the public good.

—Adam Smith, The Wealth of Nations

In 2007 Rosemary Alvarez, a young woman in Arizona, went to the Barrow Neurological Institute at St. Joseph's Hospital because she had balance problems, difficulty swallowing, blurred vision, and numbness in her left arm.

It was her second visit to the emergency room. Strangely, her earlier tests had come back as normal. Doctors could not explain her symptoms until they saw something deep in her brain. An MRI scan revealed what looked like a brain tumor near her brain stem. Dr. Peter Nakaji, a neurosurgeon, was worried: "Ones like this that are down in the brain stem are hard to pick out, and she was deteriorating rather quickly, so she needed it out."[1]

Alvarez was prepared for surgery, and Dr. Nakaji and his colleagues went into the operating room, expecting to remove a tumor. What

35

they found, however, was bizarre; Alvarez had a worm in her brain.[2] A worm was an unpleasant finding, but they were relieved it was not a life-threatening tumor.

Worms have become a lot more common in the United States in recent years. According to Raymond Kuhn, professor of biology and an expert on parasites, "Upwards of 20 percent of neurology offices in California have seen it."[3] However, the pork tapeworm is not new and has afflicted people for thousands of years. The parasite lives in undercooked pork tissue, and is likely the reason why Jewish and Muslim dietary laws ban pork. Normally, the tapeworms are small and live inside the small intestine of humans, but they can reach up to a record 37 feet long.[4] The main symptom that people complain about is strange stomach sensations and a general lack of energy.

Most people are surprised to find out that parasites rarely kill their hosts. The reason is that they require a living host to feed on, in order to thrive, and reproduce. Parasites live off their host organisms and suck away nutrients and energy to sustain their own existence.

Much like Rosemary Alvarez, the US economy is suffering from unexplained symptoms, and economists and policymakers cannot figure out what the problem is. The Federal Reserve pumped trillions of dollars into the economy as a giant dose of medicine, but over $2 trillion sits unused as excess reserves at the central bank. Government debt has increased by over $10 trillion since the financial crisis, yet GDP growth has been anemic, at best. Large corporations have been hoarding almost $2 trillion dollars, primarily offshore, yet corporate investment levels are dismal by historical standards. Corporations prefer share buybacks to raising wages or investing. Economists cannot figure out what ails the patient.

Finding the source of our ills is critical. The stakes for the health of the US economy could not be greater. Why has the rate of startup creation declined? Why are wages not rising? Why is productivity low and not rising? Why has inequality been increasing?

Many politicians and economists think the problem is the tumor of income inequality, but the answer, much like in Alvarez's case, is that the US economy has large parasites that are sapping nutrients and robbing the country of its energy. Monopolies and oligopolies won't kill the economy, but they can cripple it.

It may seem strange to think some companies are sapping our economic strength when the stock market is at all-time highs and corporations are raking in cash. Is it really so awful that companies are gobbling each other up? How could anyone dislike profits and people getting rich? Surely a rising stock market is as American as motherhood and apple pie. How bad could economic concentration really be for the economy?

The damage to the economy is far worse than you could imagine. The evidence is overwhelming that higher economic concentration has created a toxic cocktail of higher prices, less economic dynamism, fewer startups, lower productivity, lower wages, greater economic inequality, and damage to smaller communities. Competition has not so much declined as thudded into the abyss.

The only people who should be happy with the situation we have today are people who own shares in monopolies. Egalitarians should be appalled by higher inequality. Free market conservatives should be horrified by less competition, economic stagnation, lower productivity, and less investment. Everyone should be concerned about the concentration of economic and political power in the hands of very few.

In the following pages, we'll review the consequences of concentration in turn: higher prices, fewer startups, lower productivity, lower wages, higher income inequality, less investment, and the withering of American towns and smaller cities.

Lower Wages and Greater Income Inequality

Almost all the focus in industrial concentration has been on profits, productivity, and investment, but the biggest impact has been on wages. Workers have systematically lost power versus large companies that now dominate industries.

Dozens of studies now document how industrial concentration is driving income inequality. The smoking gun, however, has been missing. Researchers had the intuition but could not prove that monopsonies, particularly at the local level, affected consumer wages.

In a *monopoly*, one company is the only seller and can hike prices as it likes. In a *monopsony*, one company is the only buyer and can pay whatever prices or wages it likes. For example, Amazon has become the monopsonist in the book industry, as the main buyer from publishers, and it sets the price at which books are sold. For some professions, one company can set wages.

Markets have shifted to monopolies and oligopolies when it comes to selling goods, but it is just as bad when you look at the power of companies as buyers. When workers have fewer employers to choose from in their line of work, their bargaining power disappears. Corporate giants can squeeze their suppliers, but the main things companies buy is labor, and they have been squeezing workers. If Adam Smith's invisible hand required many buyers and sellers to find the right price, then the invisible hand has gone missing as we have moved toward oligopolies.

Many markets are monopsonies. Monopolies are rare, and so are monopsonies. However, oligopolies are very common across almost all US industries. Consumers can choose from only a very few companies when it comes to buying, and likewise when it comes to finding a job. Likewise, workers are finding they have very few companies in their line of work that they can turn to for employment. If oligopolies behave the same way, then they function just like monopolies.

Buffett praises pricing power, where companies can raise prices on consumer. If companies have that kind of market power over consumers, do they also have the power to lower wages for workers? The answer is now clear.

Recently, economists have begun to look into the problem of labor market monopsony to find out just how bad the situation is.

The evidence is depressing. Economists Marshall Steinbaum, Ioana Marinescu, and José Azar looked at job markets across the United States to see how concentrated employers were. They found that most commuting zones where workers would search for a job were highly concentrated, and this dragged down wages.[5] The results of wage decreases were extremely troubling. They showed that going from a very competitive to a highly concentrated job market is associated with a 15–25% decline in wages.

The research explains why the average worker feels screwed. Workers' options in industry after industry are limited, and they are bargaining against monopolists and oligopolists when it comes to getting paid. It also helps explain the growing urban rural divide in the United States. The market for goods is national, while job searches happen locally. This helps explain why ideal, perfectly competitive markets are in fact a myth. Steinbaum's study shows that this insight is correct. He and his colleagues note, "The most concentrated labor markets, and the ones where the effect of concentration on wages is largest, are the rural ones."[6]

If the situation is so bad for workers in any town, why don't they pack their bags and go to towns with more opportunity? Many people have relatives and high school friends they don't want to leave behind. They may not know people in the new town that could help them find a job. They also might not be able to uproot their husband or wife and kids to go find a job. All of these factors mean that labor markets are not as perfect as they are portrayed to be in college economics textbooks. Wages and prices don't magically adjust higher.

Companies can pressure workers in many ways to drive down pay. Economists Jason Furman and Alan Krueger have shown that many firms are able to suppress wages through monopsonistic behavior, such as collusion, noncompete agreements, and barring employees from class action lawsuits. In 2015, Jonathan Baker and Steven Salop identified market power as a likely contributor to the growth in US wealth inequality. Lina Khan and Sandeep Vaheesan have noted how monopoly pricing is a form of regressive taxation that turns the disposable income of the many into capital gains, dividends, and executive compensation for the few. "Evidence across a number of key industries in the United States indicates that excessive market power is a serious problem."[7]

Some monopolies pay very well for the lucky few. Pay tends to increase with size of the firm. Professor Holger M. Mueller of New York University and his colleagues found that wage differences between high and low-skill jobs increase with firm size. They also demonstrated that there is a strong relation between the change in firm size and rising wage inequality for most developed countries. They note that what many interpret as a broad move toward more wage inequality may be driven by an increase in employment by the largest firms in the economy.[8]

At monopolies like Google, the caste system is immediately visible. At Google, workers operate under a color-coded caste system.

Employees wear white badges, interns wear green badges, and contractors wear red badges to indicate their inferior status. (From 2007 to 2008, contractors wore yellow badges. It is not clear whether Google discontinued yellow badges for the *Untermenschen* because of historic connotations of Jews wearing yellow badges on their clothing, but contractors now wear red.[9])

The trend toward larger companies is driving a wedge between the few at the top dominant companies who are paid spectacularly well and the majority of Americans whose wages are stagnant. Economist David Autor and his colleagues concluded in a recent paper that the rise of "superstar" firms with high profits and relatively small workforces has contributed to the shrinkage in workers' share of national income and a corresponding increase in the share of profits.

Higher Prices

The primary reason why regulators have allowed an orgy of mergers and acquisitions is that the combined companies, the "NewCos" in investment banking speak, are supposedly more efficient and can provide lower prices for customers via economies of scale. Allegedly consumer welfare is enhanced when two or three companies completely dominate an industry. As payrolls are slashed and companies achieve the holy grail of "synergies," reducing duplicate accounting, legal, and HR functions between companies, these savings are magically passed on to buyers.

Passing on cost savings to consumers is a wonderful story that has no basis in reality. Dozens of economic studies have shown that businesses don't get more efficient after a merger. The simple truth is that they make more money because they gain market power and can get away with higher prices. Professor Rodolfo Grullon found in his major study on industrial concentration that there is no clear relation between the efficient use of assets and concentration. The main reason companies made money was because they had market power.[10]

A recent paper by economists Justin Pierce of the Federal Reserve Board of Governors and Bruce Blonigen of the University of Oregon shows that mergers cause higher prices with little evidence of greater productivity and efficiency. They also looked in great detail at whether mergers increased efficiency through reductions in administrative costs and greater asset productivity, but again find little evidence for these grand claims.[11] This corroborates the work of the economists Jan de Loecker and Jan Eeckhout who charted a rise in corporate mark-ups from 18% in 1980 to 67% today.[12] In plain English, companies' profit margins go up because they can raise prices, not because they're more efficient.

When companies merge, they announce the dazzling, stupefying cost savings they'll be able to share with clients. These projections are meant to please regulators, who mistakenly believe that efficiencies improve consumer welfare. To give you a sense of how absurd the estimates are, at the peak of the most recent M&A boom in 2015, the accounting firm Deloitte calculated that the savings companies said they would deliver amounted to $1.9 trillion.[13] That would be equal to the size of Canada's GDP or $205 per person on the planet. The claims do not so much border on the ridiculous as run straight into fantasyland, complete with unicorns, elves, and forests of candy canes.

Companies tout synergies and cost cuts when they merge, but do they share any of these supposed savings with customers via lower prices? The evidence, again, is that they don't.

The proof is so overwhelming that it begs the question why antitrust authorities have allowed firms to merge. Firms always lobby to plead their case with regulators and legislators, arguing they will exercise their market power responsibly. Firms use economists for hire to create models "proving" that mergers will lower prices. But once mergers go through, prices mysteriously go up. These remind us of New Year's resolutions to lose weight. They sound great at the time but quickly fade away as soon as donuts and pizza show up.

If you torture an economic model long enough, it will tell you what you want. Financial models rely on very questionable assumptions of demand, costs, and the way firms will behave in the future. Numerous studies show that these assumptions turn out to be incorrect, and merger simulations do not accurately predict actual post-merger prices.[14] In layman's terms, the problem of incorrect assumptions in financial models is known as "garbage in = garbage out." If we were charitable, we would say economists were bad at their jobs. If we were being mean, we might compare promerger economists to paid prostitutes, but that would be grossly unfair to prostitutes.

It doesn't matter what period you look at, the evidence is abundant: increasingly concentrated industries with less competition cause higher prices.

In 2007 the economist Matthew Weinberg undertook a comprehensive study of mergers between competitors over the previous 22 years. He documented what every consumer intuitively knows already. He found that the majority of deals "resulted in increased prices for both the merging parties and rival firms." But he also found that many firms increased prices even *before* a merger went through.[15] Perhaps it was a case of premature inflation, and they were so excited they couldn't even wait for the merger to close.

Professor Weinberg and his colleagues followed up his study seven years later and the results were the same. Weinberg looked at 49 different studies in 21 industries over the last 30 years. The industries covered included airlines, banks, hospitals, and many others. Of the 49 studies surveyed, 36 find evidence of merger-induced price increases. His conclusion was devastating: "The empirical evidence that mergers can cause economically significant increases in price is overwhelming."[16]

Mergers raise prices and harm consumers, even mergers in industries that are only moderately concentrated. That is the definitive finding of John Kwoka, a competition policy expert who recently wrote a book titled *Mergers, Merger Control, and Remedies*. He created the most detailed, comprehensive study available of mergers and antitrust enforcement by the Department of Justice and Federal Trade Commission over the previous 20 years.[17] He found almost 50 studies covering more than 3,000 mergers. By creating his database, he was able to see what actually happened versus what economists and lawyers said would happen.

Kwoka's damning conclusion was that reducing the number of competitors raised prices. He found that in mergers that led to six or fewer significant competitors, *prices rose in nearly 95% of cases.*[18] On average, postmerger prices increased 4.3%. Despite this devastating evidence, antitrust authorities have done nothing while mergers and price increases were happening. Of all mergers that resulted in price increases, the agencies failed to act in 60% of cases. The conclusion is clear: authorities do not diligently enforce antitrust laws.

The evidence is overwhelming. In study after study and industry after industry, mergers lead to higher prices. Here are a few highlights of what mergers to do prices:

- **Hospitals.** Local monopolies raise prices for consumers. One study has shown that prices are 15% higher in markets with one hospital as compared to markets with four or more hospitals, a cost differential of $2,000 per admission.[19] Other studies place price increases even higher, at 20%.[20] In California, the average price for hospital admissions increased 70% from 2004 to 2013, but the spike was even bigger for the most concentrated hospital chains, where the price for average admissions increased 113%.[21] The evidence is devastating: concentration is bad, yet the Affordable Care Act has encouraged more and more mergers. It is the triumph of hope over experience.
- **Cable.** 46 million American households are served by only one fast-broadband provider who exercises market power to overcharge. According to *The Economist,* American consumers would gain $65 billion a year if they paid the same as Germans do for mobile-phone contracts.[22]
- **Airlines.** In the 1980s the General Accounting Office found fares were 27% higher in concentrated hubs versus nonconcentrated hubs.[23] It is still the case today. Overall, the 10 most expensive airports for air travel include six "fortress" hubs dominated by one airline and four small cities without much fare competition. You would not be surprised to know that in most years the highest airfares in the United States are in Houston, where United has almost 60% market share.[24]
- **Concrete.** A study by Robert Kulick found that after mergers the pattern of price increases is accompanied by decreased output, which is precisely what would be expected as a result of the creation of additional market power. He found significant price increases due to horizontal mergers after a relaxation in antitrust enforcement standards in the mid-1980s.[25]
- **Beer.** After InBev acquired AB in 2008, they raised prices, and in 2011 increased them again. MillerCoors quickly matched the price increases in a clear case of tacit coordination.[26] In an oligopoly, frequently tacit collusion is called "price leadership," where the

biggest company hikes prices and the rest follow. The government accused AB InBev of doing just that when it tried to prevent AB InBev from buying Modelo,[27] although it later allowed the merger in 2013 as well as allowed it to merge with SAB Miller. As the *New York Times* wrote after the merger, "The immediate result was a 6 percent increase in beer prices and the end of a decades-long decline in beer prices."[28] Even as beer volumes have declined, AB InBev has raised prices on its beers, and euphemistically refers to price increases as "premiumization" of its beers.[29]

The list of industries with higher prices is almost endless.

The main reason offered for mergers and greater industrial concentration was the promise of greater efficiency and lower prices, yet neither materialized. Instead we got higher prices, bankrupted and squeezed suppliers, and more concentrated industries.

If higher prices were the only negative side effect of mergers, our book would be unnecessary. It would be overkill to dedicate page after page to price gougers. The reason industrial concentration is so deadly is that a few dominant players in most industries are choking the life out of the economy and sapping American strength. When concentration rises, the average American – instead of merely being worse off – is deprived of the opportunity to be better off.

Many economists reading the previous pages will wonder: if bigger firms lead to higher prices, why has the overall inflation rate in the economy been close to 2% for years? Shouldn't it be higher, if mergers lead to higher prices?

Not all mergers necessarily raise prices, and many are intended purely to squeeze workers, suppliers, and business partners.[30] By crushing their counterparties, they transfer wealth to themselves. This is most evident when you look at the profitability of agricultural giants as farm incomes have fallen and bankruptcies increased. In other cases, mergers are a direct response to a competitor's merger. Companies are in an arm's race to get bigger and bigger. It is a game of mutually assured destruction, where fewer smaller companies survive.

Walmart's rise as a grocer triggered two massive waves of industry consolidation in the late 1990s and early 2000s. The first was a wave of mergers by Walmart competitors, for example, Kroger and Fred Meyer.

The second wave of consolidation came as meatpackers, dairy companies, and food processors merged to avoid being crushed by Walmart and supermarkets. The squeeze on suppliers was intense. Of Walmart's top 10 suppliers in 1994, four have sought bankruptcy protection.[31] For example, Tyson bought IBP, the nation's largest beef processor, in order to gain more power against Walmart and the big supermarkets. A similar dynamic has played out in nearly every segment of food manufacturing, where bigger companies beget bigger mergers. Prices may not rise, but almost all the gain is captured by Walmart and the middlemen, while the amount paid to farmers has steadily declined.[32]

Fewer Startups and Jobs

America is supposed to be a land of economic dynamism filled with disruptive companies, but the reality is very different. Everyone knows the inspiring stories of companies starting in garages in Silicon Valley from Hewlett Packard to Google. The popular press focuses on the big success stories we all know: Dropbox, AirBnB, Tinder, Nest, Fitbit, and so on. However, the overall numbers tell a different story. Recent research shows that the rate of new business formation in the United States has slowed dramatically since the late 1970s. The decline affects almost all sectors of the US economy, even high technology, which has such a powerful impact on all of our lives. The lack of economic vitality is deeply troubling.

In a growing, healthy economy new businesses are starting every day, and older businesses fail and die. New restaurants like Chipotle open, while older ones like Chevys Fresh Mex go bankrupt. Start-ups like Netflix launch new media offerings, and older businesses like Blockbuster go bust. This process of creative destruction is how the economy moves forward as consumer wants and needs change. Much like children are born every day and grandparents die, this is a natural, vital part of economic life. Over time, as the economy grows, the overall population of businesses should grow too, creating more new jobs.

Unfortunately, this process of creative destruction has been steadily slowing over the past 30 years, and has worsened in the past few years. If America were a movie, it would be *Children of Men*, a dark, futuristic movie where children are not born and only the old remain.

The decline in entrepreneurial activity is not due to the recent financial crisis or the cyclical ups and downs of the economy; it is structural. The economist Robert E. Litan of the Brookings Institute has found that "Business dynamism and entrepreneurship are experiencing a troubling secular decline in the United States."[33] What is most troubling is that the decline in economic health is not confined to one sector but is widespread across all industrial sectors and has been nearly universal geographically, reaching all 50 states. From the late 1970s to today, we have seen a steady decline in the creation of new firms (Figure 3.1). In fact, we have seen more firm exits than entries. This is dire for the health of the US economy.

The collapse of startups should be no surprise. Ever since antitrust enforcement was changed under Ronald Reagan in the early 1980s, small was bad and big was considered beautiful. Murray Weidenbaum, the first chair of Reagan's Council of Economic Advisors, argued that economic growth, not competition, should be policymakers' primary goal. In his words, "It is not the small businesses that created the jobs,'

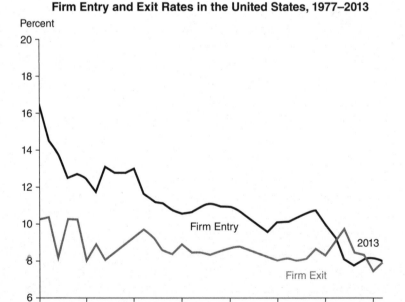

Figure 3.1   The US Economy Has Become Less Entrepreneurial over Time
SOURCE: "Beyond Antitrust: The Role of Competition Policy in Promoting Inclusive Growth," Jason Furman, Chairman, Council of Economic Advisers.

he concluded, 'but the economic growth." And small businesses were sacrificed for the sake of bigger businesses.[34]

Ryan Decker, an economist at the Federal Reserve, found that the decline is even infecting the high technology sector. Americans look at startups over the years like PayPal and Uber and conclude the tech scene is thriving, but Decker points out that in the post-2000 period, we have seen a decline even in areas of great innovation like technology. Over the past 15 years, there are not only fewer technology start-ups, but these young firms are slower growing than they were before. Given the importance of technology to growth and productivity, his findings should be extremely troubling.

The decline in firm entries is a mystery to many economists, but the cause is clear: greater industrial concentration has been choking the economy, leading to fewer startups.

Firms are getting bigger and older. In a comprehensive study, Professor Gustavo Grullon showed that the disappearance of small firms is directly related to increasing industrial concentration. In real terms, the average firm in the economy has become three times larger over the past 20 years. The proportion of people employed by firms with 10,000 employees or more has been growing steadily. The share started to increase in the 1990s, and has recently exceeded previous historical peaks. Grullon concluded that when you look at all the evidence, it points "to a structural change in the US labor market, where most jobs are being created by large and established firms, rather than by entrepreneurial activity."[35] The employment data of small firms supports Grullon's conclusions; from 1978 to 2011, the number of jobs created by new firms fell from 3.4% of total business employment to 2% (Figure 3.2).[36]

Lower Productivity

One of the big puzzles for economists has been why productivity has been so low over the past decade. Many economists have traced the collapse to a broad slowdown in innovation, others to a switch toward low-end service sector jobs, and some question whether we can even measure productivity properly.

New firms play a decreasing role in the economy

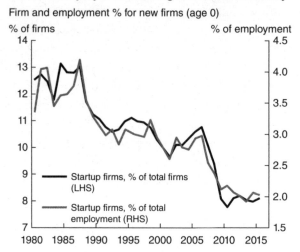

Older firms now account for a large amount of activity

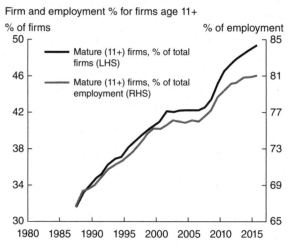

Figure 3.2   New Firms Play a Decreasing Role in the Economy
Used with permission from Nomura.

If productivity is low, then it has an enormous impact on the ability for the US economy to grow and for our standards of living to rise. The arcane question is even arousing popular concern, and the *Wall Street Journal* devoted a series of front page articles to the question.

Large companies argue that big is beautiful, due to economies of scale, where being a gorilla is better than being a chimpanzee. Some industries can't be small because the technology dictates the size of manufacturing plants. The airplane industry's scale is such that only Boeing and Airbus can compete globally. Each of these, in turn, employs dozens of companies to build subcomponents. For example, the latest Boeing 787 costs over $200 million and has parts from 45 separate companies.[37] For other industries, the scale of research and development is now so great that no startup could ever compete. For example, given the complexity of microchips few companies can spend what Intel does. Intel's latest chip will have the equivalent of over 100 billion synapses.[38] And finally, for some businesses network effects create winner-takes-all outcomes that favor vast size. In social networks, everyone wants to be on the network with the highest number of users, which is why Facebook has over two billion users. Yet not all industries fall into these categories.

When it comes to productivity, small is often good. Sometimes scale does not necessarily help. For some industries, throwing more people at a problem is not an answer. Nine women cannot produce a baby in one month, and eight musicians cannot play a Mozart quartet in half the time.

While Hollywood loves movies like *King Kong* and *Godzilla*, there is a good reason these fantastical creatures don't exist in real life. As J.B.S. Haldane put it in his classic essay, "On Being the Right Size," "You can drop a mouse down a thousand-yard mine shaft; and, on arriving on the bottom, it gets a slight shock and walks away . . . A rat is killed, a man broken, a horse splashes." This is the key to the problem of scaling.[39]

The size of an object determines its structure. The biological principal is referred to as the square-cube law. As a shape grows in size, its volume grows faster than its surface area. As an animal's size increases through evolution, their structure has to strengthen more than proportionally. This explains why it is so difficult to build ever-taller skyscrapers and why King Kong would shatter his thighbone if he tried to walk. Big animals like hippos need much fatter legs than dogs do.

The square-cube law produces strange things when you scale down. Children marvel when they see ants pick up breadcrumbs that are many times their size. The reason is that the strength of muscles depends on their cross-sectional area, which is proportional to the square of height. If you were shrunk to 1/10th your height, your muscles would be 1/100th as strong, but you'd weigh only 1/1000th of what you weigh now. That is why almost all creatures can jump the same height. Believe it or not, a flea can jump as high as Kobe Bryant.[40]

There isn't a formal square-cube law in economics but the general idea holds. Companies scale much like organisms do. Small, rapidly growing businesses are the most productive, and giant businesses are less nimble than startups. It should not be surprising that when Louis V. Gerstner Jr. wrote about turning around IBM, he titled his book *Who Says Elephants Can't Dance?* The book became a best seller, precisely because businessmen know that big companies are lumbering giants.

Economists in the area of growth theory have found that new companies are like little ants, carrying far more than their weight. They are responsible for innovations, opening new markets, and creating economic growth. The work of John Haltiwanger is critical to understanding the causes of job creation and economic performance. Haltiwanger's book *Job Creation and Destruction* was a landmark book that showed that it was "young, high-growth startups – the ones that are experimenting, innovating new products and services and trying to figure out new business models that are disproportionately responsible for the great majority of new job creation." Even though many young firms do not succeed, they contribute to economic vitality through a churning effect.[41]

Ever since the time of Thomas Jefferson, Americans have idealized the yeoman farmer and the small business. While family neighborhood restaurants and stores are a critical part of the economy, it is important to make a distinction between small businesses and the young, high-growth startups that Haltiwanger describes.

Small-scale businesses like restaurants, barbershops, and dry cleaners create most jobs, but they also destroy most jobs. They create the most new businesses, but they have the highest rate of business failures. They are a dynamic part of the economy, but they don't drive productivity. It is the small companies that become big, like the next Starbucks, Costco, Southwest Airlines, or Celgene. All of these started small.

Nature teaches us other lessons on why small is good. Robin Dunbar, a primate expert, was studying the connection between the size of a primate's brain and the size of their social group. He stumbled on a far more intriguing application for his research.[42] He realized that the insight from monkeys applied to humans and created Dunbar's Number. The theory holds that any one person can maintain stable relationships with a maximum of 150 individuals.[43] Sure, the average Facebook user has 338 "friends,"[44] and the average LinkedIn user has over 500.[45] But these are not friends you see or interact with regularly. Numbers larger than 150 generally require more bureaucracy and rules to maintain cohesion; for example, think of the army or any large company. Dunbar focused on companies, but he also found similar results in other communities, such as Native American tribes, military units, and Amish communities.[46]

The bad news for productivity is that as older companies employing 10,000-plus employees now predominate employment, we're seeing the drags of exceeding the Dunbar numbers. Huge companies require increasing bureaucracy and rules to enforce cohesion. They tend to employ more people to manage the increasing number of people.

Geoffrey West, in his masterful book *Scale*, showed that companies are like living organisms, which has profound implications for profitability and growth. Just like in the animal world, many startups die when they are very young, but those that survive and grow quickly tend to grow exponentially, which leads to higher profitability and economies of scale. As they get older, their growth slows and they become less innovative. Large firms spend the most on R&D (after all they are much larger), but the relative amount allocated to R&D systematically decreases with their size. The funding for innovation lags the spending on bureaucratic and administrative expenses as companies expand. Much like human beings, the limited energy of companies is used for the internal repair of cells rather than for growth.

When West examined the data for large companies, he found that they appear to settle down toward a slow, steady rate of growth, but reality is slightly trickier. Continuous growth sounds wonderful, but the truth becomes clear when the growth of each company is measured relative to the growth of the overall market (Figure 3.3). When you adjust for inflation "and the overall growth of the market has been factored out, *all large mature companies have stopped growing.*"[47]

Unlike humans, large companies don't simply die; they use the Monopoly Machine to buy smaller, fast-growing rivals.

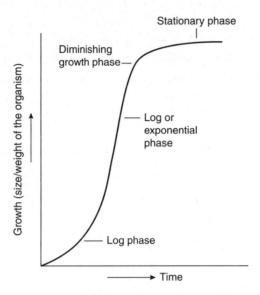

Figure 3.3   Growth Phases of Organisms and Companies

In an influential paper, Titan Alon, David Berger, and Robert Dent found that the age of a company plays a key role in shaping the dynamics of labor productivity growth. If new companies can survive their startup phase, they show cumulative productivity growth of roughly 20% in the first five years of operation. When monopolists stamp out startups, they kill productivity in the economy. In fact, if you look at the decline in high-growth entrepreneurship in high tech, it coincides with the decline in aggregate productivity growth in high tech (Figure 3.4).[48]

The battle lines are drawn in the battle of productivity as big companies face off against the small. The truth is far more interesting. In their book *Big is Beautiful* Robert Atkinson and Michael Lind show that large companies spend the most on research and development. Historically, giants like AT&T or IBM could pay for large research centers like Bell Labs or Yorktown, but not all big companies are alike. Today, large companies are still the biggest spenders; DuPont and Google can dedicate a lot of money to R&D. But this is only half the story.

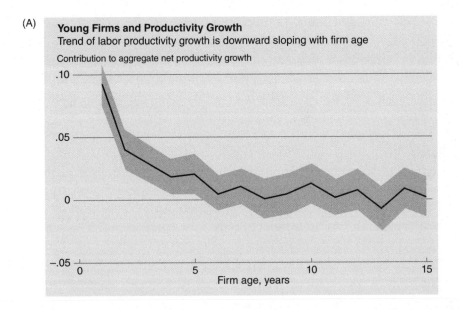

Figure 3.4   Lower Productivity Growth as Fewer Firms Enter
SOURCE: (A) Courtesy of Dr. Titan Alon, (B) Courtesy of Jason Furman.

Not all large companies are the same. In a major study, Zoltan Acs and David Audretsch looked across firms; they discovered that companies in highly concentrated industries spent less on R&D. They found that "the total number of innovations is inversely correlated with concentration[49] and that *monopoly power deters innovation*. They concluded, "Innovation falls as industrial concentration increases."[50]

Not only are we getting fewer startups, big companies are also gobbling up small ones and ruining them. Today, many of the new tech startups never get the chance to compete with the established companies, because as soon as they prove their technology, they are acquired. Between Google, Amazon, Apple, Facebook, and Microsoft more than 500 companies have been bought out in the past decade.[51] These giants are looking for the younger fast growers.

You can see how big companies kill productivity by looking at Google and the field of robotics. In 2013 Google acquired Boston Dynamics, as well as eight other robotics companies, to create a new robotics division called Replicant, named in honor of the cyborgs in *Blade Runner*. The robotics industry was excited that the 800-pound gorilla in technology was throwing money at research. However, it turned into a disaster.

Over time, Google shut many of the companies down and many of the top researchers left. Jeremy Conrad, a partner at hardware incubator Lemnos Labs, said, "These were some of the most exciting robotics companies, and they're just gone."[52] Google faced internal fears of being associated with terrifying machines that may take over human jobs, and Boston Dynamics was not part of its key search ad business.[53] In June 8, 2017, Google announced the sale of the company to Japan's SoftBank Group.

The phenomenon is not new. We've seen giant monopolies throw away innovation before. During the 1960s and early 1970s, Xerox had a monopoly on its copying technology, protected by its patents. Xerox's Palo Alto Research Center basically invented the modern computer and internet, yet failed to profit from it. Anything besides copying was simply not of interest.

The list of Xerox's inventions is extraordinary: the graphical user interface, computer-generated bitmap images, WYSIWYG (What You See Is What You Get) text editors, object-oriented programming,

Ethernet cables, and workstations for DARPAnet.[54] Yet the company did little with these innovations. It took Steve Jobs and Apple to license them and bring products to the public. Likewise, AT&T and RCA were extremely innovative companies, but other companies ultimately developed their key technologies, such as the transistor. AT&T and RCA stuck to phones and radio, and became the antithesis of originality.[55]

There is a reason why big companies are so bad at implementing new ideas. Steve Jobs rarely recommended books, but he liked *The Innovator's Dilemma* by Clayton Christensen. His 1997 book was embraced by Silicon Valley and called one of the six best business books ever by *The Economist*.[56] Christensen's theory was that because successful companies cannot disrupt themselves; they leave themselves vulnerable to competition from upstarts because they abandon the lower end of the market. Smaller companies are willing to pursue niche markets, and produce cheaper, lower-quality products. Over time, though, the market gets bigger and quality improves. Eventually David crushes Goliath – the nimble boy with a sling beats the lumbering giant.

If you doubt that creativity can stagnate when businesses become monopolies, let's look at some examples. Frederic Scherer of Harvard University has examined the patents of monopolists and shown that as firms become dominant, the number of important patents declines. Indeed, monopolists often fail to commercialize their own inventions.[57] Before Standard Oil was broken up, it invented "thermal cracking" to improve gasoline for cars, but did nothing with the technology. When the monopolist was broken up, the Indiana unit that discovered the technology commercialized it to enormous success.

The examples of mature companies failing to disrupt themselves are too numerous to recount, but a few of the most famous ones will show why bigger is not better. Kodak is often accused of failing to anticipate the shift to digital photography, but Kodak *invented* it. It simply wasn't core to selling silver halide film, which was its bread and butter.

The problem of size is acute, and companies frequently buy and then get rid of units via spinoffs. Big companies hand shares in their subsidiaries to shareholders and allow the smaller company to go its own way. Think of it like sending your kid off to college and watching him succeed. McDonalds spun out Chipotle, eBay spun out PayPal, and Sara Lee spun out Coach. These turned into phenomenal investments. It should not be surprising that all available research on spinoffs tells us that these companies vastly outperform the parent company and the market when they're freed from the shackles of the domineering or neglectful parent. Small is often beautiful.[58]

As companies get bigger and more like King Kongs, we'll never know how much productivity and how many innovations are lost.

Lower Investment

Another great mystery for economists and central bankers is why businesses are not investing more. It is a puzzle why they're returning almost all cash to shareholders rather than doing more research and development or spending it on new factories and equipment.

Larry Summers, the former Secretary of the Treasury and Harvard economics professor, shares the view with the 1930s economist Alvin Hansen that we're experiencing a "secular stagnation." Supposedly, the economies of the industrial world suffer from "an imbalance resulting from an increasing propensity to save and a decreasing propensity to invest."[59] This means that the slowdown is structural and not cyclical. He blames inequality and technology. "Greater saving has been driven by increases in inequality and in the share of income going to the wealthy."

Summers and fellow stagnation proponents do not tie the problem to monopolies and oligopolies, but the connection should be obvious. Under competitive market conditions investment will be greater than under conditions of monopoly, where the monopolist reduces investment so as to maintain high prices and profit margins. Monopoly can be a strong force contributing to economic stagnation.

New research by Germán Gutiérrez, Thomas Philippon, and Robin Döttling of New York University helps explain the lack of investment. In a paper titled "Is there an investment gap in advanced economies? If so, why?" they analyzed investment in the United

States over the past 20 years. They found that investment was lower than predicted by fundamentals starting around 2000, and the gap is driven by industries where competition has decreased over time. They looked at how much firms invest relative to the return on their assets. They found that investment relative to returns had fallen most sharply in concentrated industries. According to their calculations, if leading firms had maintained their share of overall investment since 2000, the American economy would have 4% more capital today, an amount roughly equivalent to two years' investment by nonfinancial companies (Figure 3.5).[60]

Today firms find it is more profitable to restrict production and dampen supply than it is to invest in expanding their capacity. Think of airlines who don't want more capacity, beer companies that don't expand plants, cable companies that don't upgrade infrastructure, drug companies that don't spend money on research and development, and so on.

Instead, firms take their very high profits and plough it into share buybacks and dividends. The money goes to wealthy shareholders who have a much lower level of spending relative to income than poor people. This explains why low investment and low consumption are tied together.

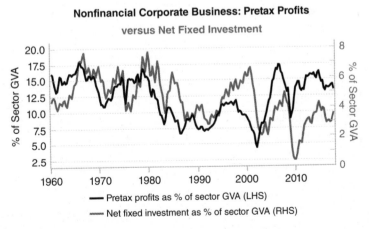

Figure 3.5 Investment Significantly Lagging Profitability
SOURCE: Variant Perception.

Localism and Diversity

Before the United States became dominated by distant oligopolies, most cities and towns had businesses with deep roots in the community, such as banks, newspapers, TV stations, factories, and drug stores. The owners and the top managers of those businesses lived in the community. The money generated by those businesses stayed local, spreading the wealth. Owners helped fund the arts, libraries, schools, and hospitals because they lived there.

Today, monopolies control large swathes of industry, and the owners and managers of companies rarely live near their businesses. As Christopher Lasch prophetically wrote in 1995 in *The Revolt of the Elites*, "The new elites are in revolt against 'Middle America,'" he warned, "imagined by them to be technologically backward, politically reactionary, repressive in its sexual morality, middlebrow in its tastes, smug and complacent, dull and dowdy."[61]

In the nineteenth century, Benjamin Disraeli wrote of two nations "between whom there is no intercourse and no sympathy; who are as ignorant of each other's habits, thoughts, and feelings, as if they were dwellers in different zones, or inhabitants of different planets; who are formed by a different breeding, are fed by a different food, are ordered by different manners, and are not governed by the same laws."

Ever since the time of David Ricardo, economists have praised specialization. Progress comes from specialization. People who oppose big business due to size are often completely impractical. In pre-industrial societies, small towns had to learn to do all the tasks necessary for life, including hunting, growing their own food, making their own tools, etc. Human progress depends on specialization. While it is appealing for every town to be self-sufficient and to buy locally, the reason people in Maine can eat bananas in the winter is that they come from somewhere else. The reason a consumer in Texas can enjoy Italian handmade shoes, French scarves, and Californian wines is that each area develops its expertise. But specialization can make cities more vulnerable to catastrophic change.

Today, we have fewer and fewer companies dominating the economy. This creates less localism and less diversity. In biology, genetic diversity is crucial for adapting to new environments. More variety leads to more individuals within a population having favorable traits to withstand harsh conditions. Although planting a single, genetically uniform crop might increase yields in the short run, low genetic diversity increases the risk of losing it all if a new pest is introduced or rainfall levels drop.[62]

The Irish Potato Famine is a cautionary tale of the danger of monocultures, or only growing one crop. The potato first arrived in Ireland in 1588, and by the 1800s, the Irish had used it to solve the problem of feeding a growing population. They planted the "lumper" potato variety.[63] And it fed Ireland for a time, but it also set the stage for human and economic ruin. All of these potatoes were genetically identical to one another, and the variety was vulnerable to the pathogen *Phytophthora infestans*. Because Ireland was so dependent on the potato, one in eight Irish people died of starvation in three years during the Irish potato famine of the 1840s. (By the way, in America the Russet Burbank potato is the American equivalent of the lumper, producing the same, homogenous fries for hundreds of millions of McDonalds customers.)

For cities to be stable, they should not be dependent on a single source of income or company. Today, American agriculture is becoming more like Ireland before the famine. We have fewer and fewer companies in each market.

The lessons from nature are dire. In the 1920s, the Gros Michel banana was almost wiped out by a fungus known as *Fusarium cubense*, and banana shortages became a growing problem (that's why we got the hit song, "Yes! We Have No Bananas"). Today, everyone eats one type known as the Cavendish, and the same thing may happen again due to a pathogen known as Panama Disease.[64] The widespread planting of a single corn variety contributed to the loss of over a billion dollars worth of corn in 1970, when a fungus hit the US crop. In the 1980s, dependence upon a single type of grapevine root forced California grape growers to replant approximately two million acres of vines when the pest *phylloxera* attacked.

Monopoly is the last stage of capitalism, according to Lenin. Yet it was the Soviet Union that achieved a total monopoly in industries. When the Cold War ended, Moscow residents rioted because cigarettes were unavailable; the filter tips that were only produced in war-plagued

Armenia had run out.[65] We are approaching the Soviet stage in some industries, and the monopoly ownership of many industries is rapidly accelerating.

Americans are not rioting over cigarette filters. They are meekly accepting far worse shortages. In 2017, when Hurricane Maria hit Puerto Rico, the United States faced a severe shortage of intravenous-solution bags. Baxter and Hospira have an effective duopoly on IV bags, and their production facilities were in Puerto Rico.[66] (They had chosen the island due to its lower tax rates.) Even before the hurricane, price hikes were a problem. Prices in the United States have more than doubled in the past few years. A saline bag that cost $1.77 in 2012 is now more than $4, whereas the price has increased to only roughly $2 in the United Kingdom.

Saline solution is water and salt, so it may come as a surprise that something so simple is in the hands of only two companies. It is even more appalling that such a vital medical supply could be in such short supply. Yet that is the story of America: high profits due to offshored production, and artificial scarcity at the hands of private monopolists.

The United States needs growth, productivity, and diversity in business. A Harvard Business School study that analyzed the community involvement of 180 companies in Boston, Cleveland, and Miami found that locally headquartered companies do most for the community on every measure. They had the "most active involvement by their leaders in prominent local civic and cultural organizations."[67] Locally owned businesses are better for communities. They hire more local workers, they buy from local suppliers, and the revenue they receive is recycled locally. Today, though, even large local champions have been acquired, and their headquarters moved to major US metropolises.

According to research on the effects of mergers on communities, local owners and managers have more ties to the local community than distant owners. By contrast, studies of mergers show that "branch firms are managed either by 'outsiders' with no local ties who are brought in for short-term assignments or by locals who have less ability to benefit the community because they lack sufficient autonomy or prestige or have less incentive because their professional advancement will require them to move."[68]

Today, the owners and top managers have moved on. Like parasites sapping energy and nutrients, they soak up local earnings, turning them into share buybacks and dividends. They retreat to the Upper East Side and the Hamptons while the body politic suffers from lower investment, lower productivity, lower wages, and greater inequality.

Small towns across America have been discovering how deadly it is to become monocultural when it comes to business.

In early 2016, Walmart announced that it was closing 154 stores in the United States. In the grand scheme of things, this matters little to the nation, but for the tiny coastal town of Oriental, North Carolina, it was devastating news. Renee Ireland-Smith's family grocery store was forced to close in October 2016 after 45 years because it could not compete with Walmart. Walmart was finally the only game in town. But two weeks later, Walmart announced it was closing in Oriental. At the same time, Walmart announced a $20 billion share buyback to send money to shareholders.

"This town was fine before," Ireland-Smith said. "Now it's broken."[69]

Key Thoughts from the Chapter

- The evidence is overwhelming that higher economic concentration has created a toxic cocktail.
- Innovation falls as industrial concentration increases.
- Today, we have fewer and fewer companies dominating the economy. This creates less localism and less diversity.
- The consequences of concentration: higher prices, fewer start-ups, lower productivity, lower wages, higher income inequality, less investment, and the withering of American towns.

Chapter Four

Squeezing the Worker

No society can be flourishing and happy, of which the far greater part of the members are poor and miserable.
—*Adam Smith, The Wealth of Nations*

This book started out as a simple detective story: Who killed your paycheck?

When we're not writing books, we spend our hours looking at economic charts of leading economic indicators. Sometimes, we even think about them when we shave or are in the bath, where we hope for a eureka moment. Our clients pay us to tell them where the economy is heading and how they should invest. They want to know answers to important questions like: Will the United States go into a recession? Will China experience a big debt crisis? Will Italy leave the euro? Will US wages rise?

Our clients are not economists. They are entrusted with the savings of pensioners and the insurance premiums families have paid. They're investors managing people's savings, and it matters to them whether inflation is rising, whether unemployment is falling, and whether profits are rising. These factors affect the investments of pension funds, insurance companies, and mutual funds. They want to avoid major market crashes, and benefit when markets are good.

Most of the charts we use to advise our clients go back decades and are based on sound fundamental relationships, so they never need changing. If building permits are strong, the housing sector will flourish, and the economy will be strong. If the People's Bank of China is hiking interest rates, the Chinese economy will likely slow down. If the unemployment rate is falling, it is likely that wages will go up, as companies must competitively bid for workers.

Once in a while, the tools and charts we use to infer future trends will appear "broken" and will stop working. Either something has changed in the world, or we need to figure out why we're wrong.

One chart in particular was bugging us. At meetings with money managers in mid-town Manhattan, we would present our reports while they flicked through our charts. We would stare out at Central Park while they scoured the lines that moved up and down. They would scroll through the pages, but they always stopped at the page with our chart of US wages (Figure 4.1). It had barely gone up in the past nine years.

Our US Wages Leading Indicator is supposed to lead wages very closely and tell us whether US workers will get a raise or not. It gathers data on how tight the labor market is, how low initial unemployment claims are, and other factors affecting a worker's ability to get a raise. Across half a dozen business cycles, it has told us when workers would be paid more and when corporate profits would be crimped.

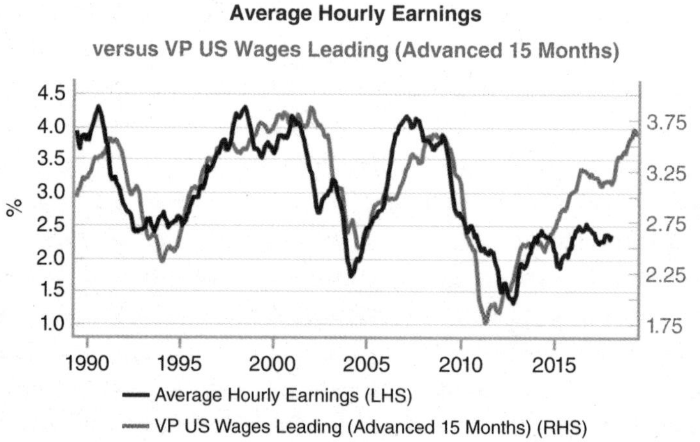
Average Hourly Earnings
versus VP US Wages Leading (Advanced 15 Months)
4.5
4.0
3.5
3.0
2.5
2.0
1.5
1.0
%
3.75
3.25
2.75
2.25
1.75
%
1990
1995
2000
2005
2010
2015
Average Hourly Earnings (LHS)
VP US Wages Leading (Advanced 15 Months) (RHS)

Figure 4.1 Variant Perception US Wages Leading Indicator
SOURCE: Variant Perception.

Back in Manhattan, our client questioned us: "Why is your indicator telling me that wages are going up, when I don't see that in the data? It looks broken," our client said. "Why are you wrong?"

"Trust me, wages will turn up. Just wait a big longer. The lead time is very long."

The first time this happened, we genuinely thought wages would rise and our indicator would be right. After all, if the job market is tight businessmen say they will increase wages. Yet workers' pay barely went up.

This leading indicator had worked flawlessly for decades, but over the past few years it started to behave in a strange way. Our index kept moving higher, yet workers' pay never budged. Meanwhile, corporate profits were rising to all-time highs and stayed there. In fact, corporations have never had it so good.

If capitalism were a game, it would be: Workers 0 – Corporations 1.

As months passed and the wage data came out, it became clear. Our indicator was not working. Corporate profits seemed to be defying the gravity of competition. We had missed something very big happening in the economy, and we had no idea what was causing wages to stay so low.

Something was very broken. The rules of the game had changed for American workers. This book became our attempt to answer why.

Today everyone in the world thinks of Silicon Valley as the cradle of technology, but in the 1950s, people would have thought you were crazy if you set up a tech company in California. Santa Clara County was little more than apple trees.[1] Most renowned technology companies had headquarters in Massachusetts along Route 128, near the research hubs of MIT and Harvard.

William Shockley was as close to a rock star as it got in the science world. He was a Nobel Prize winner who had coinvented the transistor. When he moved to Palo Alto to found Shockley Semi-Conductor Laboratory, people thought he had gone mad. It was far removed from Route 128, but he had his reasons. He had grown up in the area, and he wanted to return home to help his ailing mother.

Shockley hired an all-star cast to join him. They were all experts in physics, metallurgy and mathematics, and they abandoned the East

Coast to work with Shockley to commercialize the transistor. Robert Noyce, one of the hires, said getting the call from Shockley was like picking up the phone and talking to God.

Shortly after arriving, however, they discovered that Shockley was an erratic and difficult boss. He was a genius, but a jerk, and not just your ordinary, run-of-the-mill jerk. He was an epic egomaniac. When his colleagues at Bell Labs discovered the transistor, he tried to claim sole credit. Later in life, he spent his time espousing a racist eugenics agenda, promoting a high-IQ sperm bank, and losing all contact with his children. He was, by most accounts, a horrible boss.

Within a year of joining Shockley, the new hires sat around a breakfast table at the Clift Hotel to plot their escape. Although they were America's most brilliant scientists and engineers, they were distinctly unhappy working for Shockley. In a brazen display of disloyalty, they decided to leave and found a new company: Fairchild Semiconductor. Later dubbed the "Traitorous Eight," they signed dollar bills in place of formal contracts – a symbol of non-conformity.

Many consider this act of employee treachery as the definitive moment of Silicon Valley's creation, though the term would take another 10 years to enter the public lexicon. The defection set a precedent of 'can-do' entrepreneurialism and loyalty to lofty ideas, rather than individual firms and egos.[2]

The ringleader was Noyce, only 29 at the time, and the group's resident transistors expert. Even he had abandoned "God." Eventually Noyce and his colleague Gordon E. Moore outgrew Fairchild, and again poached employees to start Intel. In 1971, only three years after founding Intel, Noyce made history yet again with the invention of the Intel 4004, the world's first microprocessor. He had invented the beating heart of the modern computer.

Silicon Valley owes its success to many things – access to capital, proximity to Stanford (one of the best universities in the world), and being close to a vibrant city like San Francisco. But what helped make it the innovation capital of the world is rarely discussed: California is one of the few states where noncompete clauses in work contracts are completely nonenforceable. In other words, employees have full rights to leave and work for a competitor.

In many other states, when employees join a firm, they may be asked to sign a noncompete agreement as a condition of their employment. The terms vary considerably, but the basic idea is that if you are fired or quit your job, you cannot work for a competitor within the same industry for a certain period of time – which can range from a few months to years. These clauses deprive workers of their livelihoods if they make it difficult for them to leave jobs and bargain for higher wages elsewhere.

In 1872 California made it illegal for employees to be bound to a specific employer, allowing them to move freely between jobs and firms. This state law is still in effect nearly 150 years later. The lack of noncompetes is a primary reason why the Valley achieved such tremendous success. To this day, Boston continues to lag Silicon Valley in the commercialization of new technologies.

Imagine where the Valley would be today if Noyce were prevented from defecting and founding a new firm with his colleagues. What if Wozniak had never left Hewlett Packard to join Steve Jobs? Think of the history of technology. Imagine where we would be today if Nikola Tesla were prevented from leaving Thomas Edison.

Silicon Valley's history demonstrates that respect for worker talent was prized above strict company loyalty. This lead to a malleable ecosystem, where good ideas spread quickly from company to company and innovators were free to choose their own fates. Professor AnnaLee Saxenian, author of many books on the tech industry, points out that, "In the early days engineers would say, 'I work for Silicon Valley.' And the idea was that they were advancing technology for a region, not any single company's technology. We often think in the U.S. that people or companies create success, but what Silicon Valley shows us is that often it's communities of people across a region."[3]

If Noyce thought Shockley was God in the early 1950s, Steve Jobs idolized Noyce in the 1970s. When Apple was starting, Noyce was already a legend with Intel. "Bob Noyce took me under his wing," Jobs said. "He tried to give me the lay of the land, give me a perspective that I could only partially understand." Jobs continued, "You can't really understand what is going on now unless you understand what came before."[4]

Although Jobs worshipped Noyce, he failed to give his own Apple employees the same freedoms that allowed Noyce's best innovations to flourish. In 2014 it came to light that Jobs had been preventing employees from moving to other companies. Silicon Valley was founded on freedom of mobility for workers, but the tech giants – Apple, Facebook, Google, Adobe and many others – were caught in "gentlemen's agreements" to not poach each other's employees. Staff brought the case forward claiming that these pacts made it difficult to market their skills and that they also suppressed their salaries.

As part of the lawsuit, emails came out in court between Steve Jobs and Eric Schmidt, the CEO of Google, "I am told that Google's new cell phone software group is relentlessly recruiting in our iPod group. If this is indeed true, can you put a stop to it? Thanks, Steve." In another email, Larry Page from Google sent a distressed message saying Steve Jobs had threatened war if a single one of his staff were hired.[5]

In the end, the agreement not to poach went out across Silicon Valley. Google, Adobe, and others developed *Do Not Hire* lists. This was clear collusion, and the tech firms were forced to pay a $324.5 million fine for their illegal noncompete pact.[6]

Some readers may find it hard to feel sorry for highly paid software engineers, but the problems of noncompetes do not end there. What is particularly insidious is that these contractual arrangements are creeping into the entire economy and hurting the poorest the most.

These restraints on trade have spread like an epidemic. Today noncompetes cover almost 18% of the entire American workforce.[7] Nearly 40% of workers have signed one in previous jobs.[8] Only California and three other states (Montana, North Dakota and Oklahoma) totally ban noncompete agreements in the United States.

Lawyers sometimes argue that noncompete clauses help protect trade secrets, which help companies to innovate. While it might be understandable for firms that earn most of their revenue from intellectual property to ask key employees to sign noncompetes, is there any good reason to ask camp counselors, janitors, and personal care workers to sign these agreements? There are already federal laws dedicated to protecting IP[9] and, today, even those who clearly do not possess trade secrets are made to sign them, including 15% of workers without a four-year college degree and 14% of people earning less than $40,000 (Figure 4.2).[10]

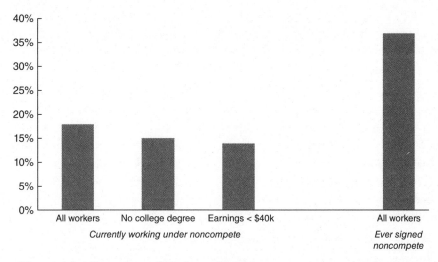

Figure 4.2   Percentage of Workers with Noncompete Agreements, by Group
NOTE: These estimates are preliminary and may differ from subsequent versions of the cited page.
SOURCES: US Treasury; Data: Evan Starr, Norman Bishara, and J.J. Prescott, "Noncompetes in the U.S.
Labor Force," working paper, November 10, 2015.

These employment clauses are found in a staggering percentage of America's largest fast-food chains with minimum wage employees. Chains like Burger King, Carl's Jr., Pizza Hut, and, until recently pressured in 2017 to drop them, McDonald's. These no-hire rules affect more than 70,000 restaurants – more than a quarter of the fast-food outlets in the United States – according to Alan B. Krueger, who is an economist at Princeton University.

The fast-food industry has been one of the biggest sources of job growth since the recession. More than 4.3 million people are now dipping fryer baskets, which is a 28% increase since 2010. The growth in fast food employment is almost double the increase in the overall labor market, according to the most recent data from the Bureau of Labor Statistics.

Arguments about protecting intellectual property are outlandish, given there are relatively few trade secrets in flipping burgers or taking orders. Furthermore, what does Pizza Hut have to lose if one of their store workers decides to work for another Pizza Hut across town? There are no corporate secrets to be lost. The answer is simple: the fewer options workers have, the less freedom they have to find a company that might pay a higher wage. The only function of these rules is to limit worker mobility and diminish their ability to bargain for wage increases. This is modern-day feudalism, and workers have become vassals to corporate lords.

The truth is that noncompetes help firms that want tight control over employees. They offer little for a given industry at large or for the economy. Worst of all, they harm workers and are disastrous for workers' wages.[11] Noncompetes are not unique to the fast food industry, but are also frequent in maintenance, health, and food services where employer concentration is high. You can see in Figure 4.3 that wages are much lower in states that enforce noncompetes and wages are much higher in states that do not enforce them. It is clear to see that noncompetes depress hourly wages (Figure 4.3).

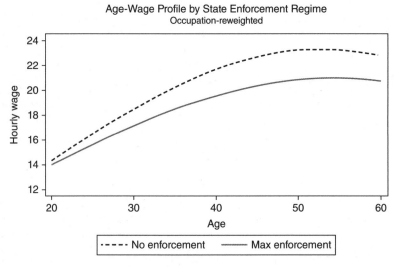

Figure 4.3   States That Do Not Enforce Noncompetes Have Higher Wages
SOURCE: US Treasury; Data: Evan Starr, Norman Bishara, and J.J. Prescott, "Noncompetes in the U.S. Labor Force," working paper, November 10, 2015.

Why do workers sign such terrible contracts in a supposedly open and free market? Often employees do not realize they are signing away their right to work somewhere else, as firms are not legally obligated to disclose noncompete clauses in almost all states. According to a study by economists Matt Marx at MIT and Lee Fleming at Harvard University, barely 3 in 10 workers were told about the noncompetes in their job offer, and in 70% of cases, they were asked to sign them after they had already accepted the offer and turned down any alternatives. Half of the time, noncompete agreements were presented to employees on or after their first day of work.[12] It goes without saying that this hardly represents a true choice for workers.

Barring workers from moving in search of better opportunities works only in an environment where firms have all the power. Because of industrial concentration, a number of firms now have monopsony power – that is, they are the only buyers of labor. A monop*oly* means there is one *seller*, and a monop*sony* means there is only one *buyer*.

In a monopsony, workers have little choice in where they work and have little negotiating power for wages with employers. In a healthy economy, many firms would be competing equally for workers and would be incentivized to entice new hires with higher wages, better benefit packages, and few restrictions on their next career moves. But monopsonies make it easier for firms to depress worker wages. The classic example of this is a coal-mining town, where the coal plant is the only employer and only purchaser of labor. Today, in many smaller towns, Walmart is the new coal plant – and is the only retail company hiring.

Today, the story of America is largely the story of two economies – rural and urban. It was not always this way. The antitrust movement of the 1940s not only targeted giant corporations, but was also an attempt to weaken regional centers that had amassed too much power. This largely worked and, by the mid 1970s, there was a fairly uniform American standard of living – being middle class in the Mideast was pretty much the same as being middle class in New England. America had achieved an incredible feat – a stable majority middle class that was largely consistent across the nation.

In the 1980s, however, many of the policies that had helped ensure this regional equality were neglected or reversed. A great divide formed between rural and metropolitan areas in the United States. Rural towns were left behind, as gleaming centers of industry increasingly attracted talent by offering high-paying jobs.

The divergence are now alarming. In 1980, if you lived in Washington DC, your per-capita income was 29% higher than the average American; in 2013 you would be 68% above. In New York City, the income was 80% above the national average in 1980 and skyrocketed to 172% above by 2013.[13] Power and money began concentrating in urban centers across the country as a rural "brain drain" occurred.

Major cities attract diverse talent and many corporations, which must bid competitively for workers. Workers living in these cities make significantly more money than workers elsewhere (Figure 4.4). There is power in numbers, and nurses who have five metropolitan hospitals to choose from will make more money than those who work in a town with only one hospital.

A recent study by the Marshall Steinbaum, José Azar and Ioana Marinescu shows that labor monopsony is not only pervasive across the United States, but is especially so in nonmetropolitan areas (Figure 4.5). Again, this makes intuitive sense – smaller towns have fewer employment options. Figure 4.5 represents commuting zones that have a few dominant companies in each industry and very concentrated labor markets.[14] Only the major cities are exempt from this high degree of concentrated employers.

The labor market outside of big cities has been co-opted by a few large players in each industry. Research by Nathan Wilmer of Harvard University shows that pressure from large corporate buyers decreases wages

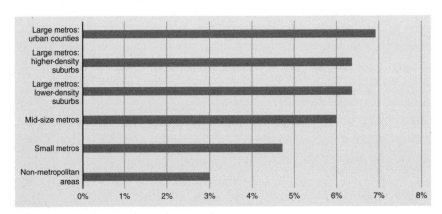

Figure 4.4 Rural Areas Are Lagging (aggregate wage growth, year-over-year, third quarter 2016)
SOURCE: Indeed Analysis of BLS Data. © 2018 Indeed, Inc.

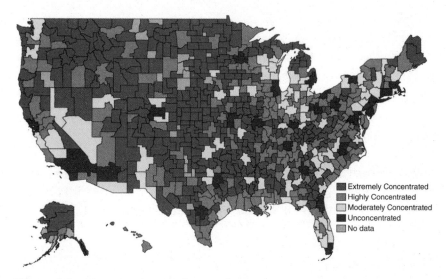

Figure 4.5   Monopsonies in Labor Markets: Commuting Zones with High
Labor Concentration
SOURCE: José Azard, Ioana Marinescu, and Marshall Steinbaum, "Labor Market Concentration"
(December 15, 2017). Available at SSRN: https://ssrn.com/abstract-3088767 or http://dx.doi.
org/10.2139/ssrn.3088767.

among their suppliers' workers. When Walmart or other large buyers
demand lower prices, suppliers end up taking it out of their employees' paychecks. Wilmer found that the squeeze on suppliers accounts for around
10% of wage stagnation since the 1970s. Increases in industrial concentration have shifted market power and lowered workers' wage growth.[15]

Monopsony for workers explains the curious Trump phenomenon.
While almost all political analysts doubted that a real estate developer
and reality show star could become president, his success almost seems
inevitable when you look at where his votes came from.

The overlap of Trump votes with concentrated counties is very
high. Trump knew how to connect with voters, when he spoke about
rigged markets. He spoke to the average worker's fears. In the 2016
election Hillary Clinton won 472 counties that represented 64% of US
Gross Domestic Product, compared to the 36% for the 2,584 counties
that voted for Donald Trump. In many small towns, a single meat pack-
ing company, insurer, hospital system, or big box store owned by a distant company has now replaced locally owned businesses. Trump was
tapping into a profound, justified anxiety across the country.

The wage squeeze is even greater if you are in a small town, with a small labor market facing off against corporations. Monopsony means workers have little choice and little power. In Ohio, Amazon is one of the state's major employers and 10% of Amazon workers are on food stamps.[16] Walmart and McDonald's are also major culprits with 10,000-plus workers at each firm also relying on food stamps, according to the same study by Policy Matters Ohio.[17]

The increasing imbalance of power that firms have as sole purchasers, explains not only why harmful noncompetes are more prevalent, but also why wages are dangerously low, why workers accept forced arbitration against employers, and why they waive rights to class-action lawsuits. Workers on their own are in no position to bargain against monopolists and oligopolists.

The weakness of workers relative to large, concentrated employers is most evident in the massive shift toward temporary work. An overwhelming 40% of American workers fall into the category we call *precarious*.[18] Work is considered precarious if any of these descriptions apply:

- You are not paid if you miss work.
- You are not in a standard employment relationship.
- Your weekly income and hours are unstable.
- You work on call or your work schedule is unknown in advance.
- You get paid in cash.
- You are in temporary employment.
- You do not have benefits.
- You have a weak voice or little bargaining power at work.

Full-time, reliable work with benefits is becoming a relic of history. This is attributable to many interwoven factors like globalization, offshoring, the rise of the "gig economy," and others. But understanding the factors does not change the fact that the number of temporary workers in the United States is at an all-time high.[19]

America has been creating more jobs, but most of these have been temporary. Temporary jobs are a normal part of the economy, but record numbers tell us something else is going on.[20] Research conducted by economists Lawrence Katz at Harvard and Alan Krueger at Princeton shows that almost all of the 10 million jobs that were created since 2005 are temporary.[21] The overall number of temp workers (including independent contractors, freelancers, and contract company workers) increased from 10.7% to 15.8%.

Temporary work can be empowering when you have the luxury of choice, but it is disempowering when you can't negotiate wages or benefits. Most people think of companies such as Uber, with an estimated seven million drivers worldwide, when they think of part-time and contracted work. The company is constantly in the headlines, facing a barrage of lawsuits aimed at reclassifying drivers as employees, rather than contractors, and at providing full-time benefits, overtime pay, and collective bargaining.

Uber is only the tip of the iceberg when it comes to contract work. In many other industries, the trend to seek cheap, no-strings-attached employees also applies. Every day we see workers dressed in bright, colored uniforms with corporate logos; but the people who are valeting cars at a hotel, acting as concierge, and cleaning your room do not work for Hilton, instead they are contracted through a third party. The FedEx delivery person, cable box technician, and the security guard at a local office building do not have allegiances to the companies they appear to represent; they are subcontracted.

Tech companies like Apple, Google, and Facebook are known for their extravagant perks and how they look after employees. The reality is very different. A growing number of workers at the large tech firms also fall into contract work. Apple, with a market capitalization of over $900 billion as of December 2017, directly employs only 80,000 workers in the United States. Apple stopped reporting their number of contracted workers in 2015 but, according to their own job creation website, they claim responsibility for two million jobs in the United States. That means only a fraction of their workforce are full-time employees.

Contracted positions create a lack of stability and benefits for workers. Many temporary workers struggle to stay above the poverty line. A Bloomberg study examining changing work trends showed that almost 50% of workers had variable incomes and didn't know what they would earn in a given week or month. Even small, unexpected economic setbacks could cause financial trouble. An astonishing 28% of those surveyed said they would worry about a $10 surprise expense, and 62% couldn't handle anything over $500.[22]

Fervor for hiring contract workers is not limited to the United States but is widespread globally. In the UK, the number of people employed on zero-hours contracts since 2011 has increased fivefold, and two in every five people are precariously employed, according to the New Economics Foundation. These statistics help explain why two-thirds of children in poverty in Britain come from working families.[23]

Max Weber, the author of *The Protestant Ethic and the Spirit of Capitalism*, argued that low wages were bad for the economy because they inhibited a worker's ability to take pride in their work. He argued that "low wages do not pay, and their effect is the opposite of what was intended." If workers spent their hours worried about how little they were being paid, they would not work well. "Labor must, on the contrary, be performed as if it were an absolute end in itself, a calling."

A recent Bloomberg investigation of American workers found that people valued security and stability of their income more than large salaries or even doing fulfilling work. If we look at Maslow's hierarchy of needs, most workers are not asking to find their true calling at their jobs, as Weber suggested, but are simply asking to get paid a living wage and have certainty they'll have a job next week. Workers are asking for their most basic needs to be met; they're not asking for Porsches or even personal enlightenment (Figure 4.6).

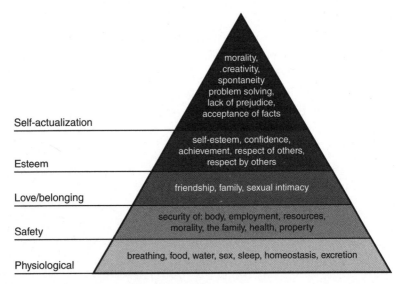

Figure 4.6   Maslow's Hierarchy of Needs

SOURCE: Wikimedia Commons, https://commons.m.wikimedia.org/wiki/File:Maslow%27s_Hierarchy_of_Needs.svg. Used under CC BY-SA 3.0.

One company that understands the needs of workers is Costco. Costco continuously ranks among the world's most beloved companies – and not only because of the free samples. They continue to outperform industry competitors, pay workers well, offer great benefits to close to 90% of staff, and have very low turnover as a result. Costco workers are paid more than $20/hour and as a result have only 5% employee turnover for those who have been with the company for over a year. Costco's CEO, Craig Jelinek puts it this way: "I just think people need to make a living wage with health benefits. It also puts more money back into the economy and creates a healthier country. It's really that simple."[24]

Stagnant and insecure wages are a problem for all of society. If your restaurant workers cannot afford to eat in your restaurants, or your retail employees cannot afford to buy your clothes, the entire economy breaks down. In some cases, people cannot even afford to live in the places where they work.

The *New York Times* recently chronicled the story of Sheila James, a 62-year-old woman who wakes at 2:15 a.m. every day to commute three hours into downtown San Francisco by taking two trains and a bus. As sky-high housing prices have pushed her out of living closer to her US Department of Health and Human Services job, she now loses six hours of her day to commuting.[25] People can't even live where the new economy is creating jobs. Something is seriously wrong.

In the no-strings-attached labor world, workers shoulder a disproportionate amount of personal responsibility for their success: workers are forced to pay for their own up-skilling (vs. company funded training), must figure out their own pension plans and benefit schemes (if available to them at all), and insurance. This makes it incredibly difficult, if not impossible for people to get ahead. A health setback, road accident, funeral of a loved one, or any number of normal life surprises can be devastating and compound an already bad economic situation.

Not only are wages low, but workers are sometimes cheated out of them entirely. Low-wage workers are routinely the victims of wage theft, and it is becoming an increasingly common problem. Companies will fail to pay overtime, comply with minimum wage laws, or pay a worker for the total amount of hours she has worked. Claims that workers have been insufficiently paid have quadrupled over the past decade. A 2009 survey of over 4,000 low-wage workers in three major US cities found that 76% of full-time workers had been unpaid or underpaid for overtime hours, and 26% were paid less than minimum wage.[26]

In Seattle, home to two of the world's richest men – Bill Gates and Jeff Bezos – some companies can't be bothered to pay their employees minimum wage. SkyChefs, a company that puts together airplane food trays, was fined $335,000 in 2017 for violating Washington State's $13.50/hour minimum wage laws.[27] The city later settled privately with the company for 40% less than the original fine at $190,000. As we write this book, employees are still complaining that they have yet to receive compensation for their lost wages. Some workers were owed up to $7,000 in stolen pay. This happens all too frequently. A study by the Economic Policy Institute found that 2.4 million workers lose $8 billion annually (or an average of $3,300/year per worker) due to minimum wage violations alone. This is a quarter of their earned wages.

When worker's rights are violated, what mechanisms do they have to challenge employers? To understand current power dynamics, it is useful to look to history. After the Great Depression in the early 1930s, tensions had escalated between workers and firms due to deteriorating working conditions. Enter Roosevelt's New Deal. It made a host of sweeping reforms aimed at strengthening the battered economy and providing basic working conditions guidelines. The New Deal helped to restrengthen unions, which had waned through the roaring 1920s. Unions are divisive, and considered a bad word in certain circles today. But, at this point in history, they were seen as a necessary force to balance power dynamics between employers and employees.

Unions maintained an important part in American working life for decades, but then declined again. In 1983, about one in five Americans were part of a union; today, only 6.4% of private sector workers in America are unionized and less than 11% of total workers.[28] This represents a considerable decline in the ability of workers to organize. Unions, though controversial, provided a needed forum for workers to band together and advocate for their collective rights.

Inequality is inversely related to union membership. If you plot the percentage of national income going to the top 10%, as you can see in Figure 4.7, it is almost the perfect mirror image. When union membership is low, a higher percentage of income goes to the top 10%. This may help, in part, to explain recent trends in income inequality.

Managers collectively represent thousands if not millions of shareholders. Union leaders may likewise represent thousands if not millions of workers. The strength of unions, however, does not come merely from concentrating forces but from the real threat of strikes. There is an extremely high correlation historically between the index of the number of strikes in the United States and the wage growth of workers (Figure 4.8). Today, strikes are extremely rare, and this in part explains why wages are so low.

In today's climate of minimal union participation, companies have capitalized on the fact that workers are isolated and dispersed. This brings us to another hidden force, largely ignored when talking about declines in worker power – forced arbitration.

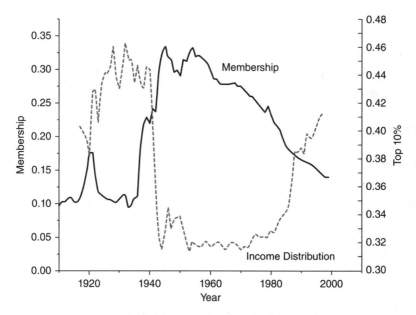

Figure 4.7 Union Membership versus Income Distribution to Top 10%
Source: Emin M. Dinlersoz and Jeremy Greenwood.[29]

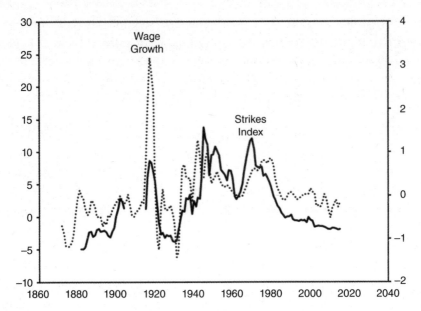

Figure 4.8   Wage Growth Closely Associated with Strikes
SOURCE: Taylor Mann, Pine Capital.

Increasingly, workers are unable to bring lawsuits against their employers because of clauses hidden within their initial employment contract. The Federal Arbitration Act gives companies the right to avoid the court system when an employee has a grievance. If you were sexually harassed at work, or were cheated out of full wages, or feel you were racially discriminated against, these class action waivers prevent you from pressing charges publicly in a state or federal court. You are instead forced to negotiate a settlement privately with the company.

Take the 69,000 women who, since 2008, have filed claims against Sterling Jewelers, the multibillion-dollar conglomerate behind Kay Jewelers and Jared the Galleria of Jewelry. Female employees allege that they were often coerced into having sex with managers to be promoted, and had to attend mandatory annual manager's meetings that were no-spouses-allowed sex parties.[30] This gives new meaning to "every kiss begins with Kay." Only in 2015, seven years later and with resolution still pending, were the women allowed to bring their case forward collectively as a class action suit.

When workers lose the ability to sue as a group, they lose all power for a better outcome. Forced arbitration has been called a "harasser's best friend," as it means the harasser will not be publicly exposed in court, and often leaves the victim suffering in isolation. Additionally, when a company mistreats its employees just a little bit – say it steals a small sum of money from their paycheck each month – it's unlikely that an individual would spend hundreds of thousands of dollars on legal fees for their personal case. This is the purpose of class action suits: regular people can pool their small claims and collectively take on the company.

Going to arbitration instead of the courts has some benefits, like faster and cheaper settlement of disputes and the ability for companies to keep slanderous claims out of the media spotlight. However, workers lose important rights in arbitration. There is a very limited evidence process, and they lose the right of appeal if they lose.

The real reason companies force workers into arbitration is not saving money on an expensive court case. Unsurprisingly, firms win significantly more often in arbitration than in court cases, and damage amounts awarded tend to be lower in arbitration.[31] Arbitrators feel pressured to rule in a company's favor when they are likely to be rehired by the same firm in the future.[32]

Workers are not the only losers here, and consumers frequently agree to arbitration without even realizing. Over 50% of credit card contracts and 99% of cell phone contracts have mandatory arbitration clauses included upon sign up, preventing you from ever suing the company if you are not protected by their services. You might even be subject to forced arbitration claims before getting a chance to read them. If you buy a product (like a phone), and the contract is wrapped inside the packaging, simply by purchasing the product you have legally bound yourself to the terms of the agreements inside.

The worst, most darkly comical example of this was the Equifax security breach in July 2017. Equifax is a credit monitoring company that collects data on consumers and judges their creditworthiness to buy a house, get insurance, or open a line of credit. Considering their entire business is collecting and protecting consumer data, you would think that they would take extra cybersecurity precautions. No, that would be asking too much. Equifax admitted it was hacked, with over 143 million people affected. That is almost half the country. The worst part is that it was entirely preventable if they had only bothered to update their software platform. Worried consumers who wanted to find out if their data was stolen were required to waive their right to a class action suit when logging into the Equifax online system.[33]

We would not need to sound the alarm on forced arbitration, if only a small segment of companies were using this tactic. In 1992, right after the Supreme Court made arbitration permissible under the Federal Arbitration Act, only 2% of companies were using it. Today 56% of private sector nonunionized workers are forced into mandatory arbitration and of those, 23% are also denied any access to class action lawsuits. This means that nearly a quarter of working Americans in the private sector do not have the basic legal right to sue their employer.[34] Another study found that 80% of America's 100 largest companies use mandatory arbitration clauses in employment contracts.[35] If firms had to compete for labor, and workers had more bargaining power, these kinds of legal moves would be highly unlikely.

It was a scene right out of a Hollywood movie. On August 21, 2010, after more than a month of planning, teams from the Orange County Sheriff's Office descended on multiple target locations. They blocked the entrances and exits to the parking lots, while police dressed in ballistic vests and masks, with guns drawn, rushed into the buildings — and demanded to see their barbers' licenses[36]

More raids followed in September and October. The police raided a total of nine shops and arrested 37 people. Supposedly, the SWAT raids were drug sweeps. But when the police failed to find drugs, 34 of the 37 arrests were for "barbering without a license," a misdemeanor in Florida.[37]

Most employees don't face SWAT teams if they do their jobs without a license, but it doesn't mean they are not breaking the law. Occupational licensing laws have been spreading across the United States, even for the most menial professions. Workers must pay fees, pass exams, be of a minimum age, and/or have a certain level of experience in order to work. It is essentially a permit from the government to be able to do your job.

In some industries where consumers need to be protected, licensing is important – like healthcare and education. But the state of Louisiana makes hair braiders undergo 500 hours of training for a hair-braiding license. Cosmetologists, on average, are required to complete more than a year of education or experience, whereas emergency medical technicians (EMTs) need only about a month of training. In fact, according to a national study by Dick M. Carpenter II, Lisa Knepper, Kyle Sweetland, and Jennifer McDonald, 73 occupations have a greater average training burden than EMTs (examples include: bartenders, massage therapists, and tree trimmers).[38] It is harder to become a barber than it is an EMT. Interior designers have the most burdensome licensing requirements of all – they are subject to more regulation than elementary school teachers and midwives.

Seventy years ago in the 1950s, around 1 in 20 American workers needed an occupational license. Today, it is one in four. And licensing requirements vary vastly between states, in terms of what level of education or training is required. This makes it very difficult for families who move and their partners. And there is no clear link between improved quality of service and licensing – which means that workers are excluded from work and consumers are receiving no discernable improvement in their services.

Excessive occupational licensing tends to affect the most economically challenged, making starting work in a chosen occupation extremely cumbersome. Even for higher-paid professionals like lawyers or doctors, licensing boards that regulate those industries become gatekeepers for keeping new workers out. They determine how many can be welcomed into their elite circle and maintain a monopoly on a worker's ability to practice.

Maureen K. Ohlhausen, Acting Chairman of the Federal Trade Commission, speaking to this problem states, "too often, the members of an occupation gain effective control over the quasi-public board that regulates their profession. Once this happens, private actors wield their government-granted power to block potential competitors from entering "their" market."

With this increased bureaucracy, workers are left to navigate confusing legal processes alone. Unionization has collapsed while occupational licensing has grown exponentially (see Figure 4.9). While unions are imperfect and can, themselves, become powerful barriers to entry for people on the outside, workers have little to no collective bargaining power without them.

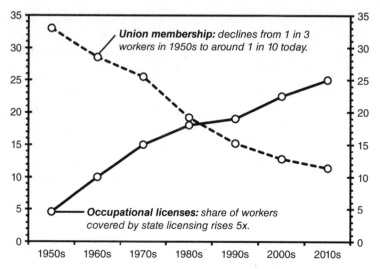

Figure 4.9   The Great Suppression: Falling Unions and Increasing Licensing, 1950s–Today
Source: Taylor Mann, Pine Capital.

Workers are now faced with pressure on all sides – governments that require excessive licensing to work, and corporates that require workers accept onerous employment terms. Those terms include: non-compete agreements, forced arbitration, stagnating wages, and burdensome occupational licensing.

Without any form of countervailing power, American workers are left to fight alone. It is a toxic cocktail for the average American. The hangover from increased corporate power is real, with many struggling to meet basic needs. This is not the free capitalism we need or the hope that drove the "traitorous eight" in Silicon Valley decades ago. Workers deserve better.

Key Thoughts from the Chapter

- In a monopsony, workers have little choice in where they work and have little negotiating power for wages with employers.
- Noncompetes have spread like a plague. These restrictive clauses cover almost 18% of the entire American workforce.

- Because of rising industrial concentration, a number of firms now have monopsony power – that is, they are the only buyers of labor.
- Increasingly, workers are unable to bring lawsuits against their employers because of clauses hidden within their initial employment contract.

Chapter Five

Silicon Valley Throws Some Shade

Who will guard the guardians?

—Juvenal, Satire VI, lines 347–348

A dam Raff and Shivaun Moeran were the founders of the most promising startup you've never heard of.

In the late 1980s, Raff was studying programming at the University of Edinburgh, while Moeran was focused on physics and computer science at King's College London. Even though they grew up half a mile apart, they had not met. Friends thought they would get along, given their science and engineering backgrounds. Their friends were right; they met and married soon after.

The pair spent their careers working in technology. Shivaun managed software projects for Boots and General Motors, while Adam looked after the supercomputers for the European weather-forecasting service.

The idea came to Adam one day as he had a cigarette outside his office: What if you could create an engine to find the best price for products? In 2006 the couple started Foundem, a website for finding cheap online prices. Adam and Shivaun's technology was very good and could figure out which websites charged hidden shipping fees and which had the lowest prices. The Raffs quit their jobs and launched Foundem.com to beta testers. They thought they were onto a big winner.

Once Foundem.com was available to the entire world, the excitement faded quickly. At first, users were rushing to use the site, but then suddenly after the second day, visitors left and never came back.[1]

The Raffs were startled. They checked every possible reason for the drop in traffic, wondering what happened. The answer was clear: they had simply disappeared from Google. During the beta testing, Foundem had been appearing near the top of Google's search results, but suddenly it was missing. It was as if someone had blacklisted them.

When people search on Google, they generally click on the top four links. They will almost never go down the page or even to the next page. If your website is not on top of the first page, you might as well be dead. Foundem had dropped off the first page of Google, but it wasn't on the second page, or even the third or fourth. It was stuck on the 15th or even 170 pages down. The practical effect was the same as if Google hadn't linked to it at all.

On other search engines such as Yahoo, Foundem ranked very well, but it didn't matter. Given Google has a global market share of over 85% of searches, it was a death sentence for Foundem to disappear.

It was clear Google had shut them out. Not only were they removed from Google's organic search results, but the company was prevented from purchasing ad placement via Google AdWords. Like in Stalinist Soviet Union, Foundem's face had been blotted out from photographs. Its annoying existence had been erased from memory.

It was not hard to see why Google would behave differently from Yahoo and other smaller search engines. The reason Foundem was demoted was that Google had its own product search site that it wanted to promote. While no one could find Foundem, Google Product Search appeared right at the top of all searches.

It turns out that Google was doing this to many other sites as well that were potential competitors. While Google is known as a universal search site, it also wanted to get business from what are known as "verticals" that do searching only in very specialized areas, like real estate listings, local business directories, legal filings, price comparisons images, and so on.

When Google started favoring its own Product Search, Google's comparison shopping service increased its traffic 45-fold in the United Kingdom, 35-fold in Germany, 19-fold in France, 29-fold in the Netherlands, 17-fold in Spain, and 14-fold in Italy. Meanwhile, the traffic for other competitor vertical search sites collapsed 85% in the United Kingdom, 92% in Germany, and 80% in France.[2] The problem, though, was not only European.

Yelp was for many years the most popular website for rating local businesses in the United States. The site was so good that Google tried to buy it, but Yelp turned them down. Google then took revenge. They started scraping Yelp's website, so the information appeared on Google without searchers ever visiting Yelp. Google took almost 386,000 images from Yelp per hour, and then used some of the photos in business listings in Google Maps.[3] Then Google also started offering its own reviews of local businesses, competing with Yelp.

The list of sites Google "disappeared" is very long. Getty Images was the leading photography library in the world and had long been a go-to place for designers and editors looking for stock photographs. Yet in 2013, Google decided that they themselves would be the place to find images rather than Getty, and they scraped Getty's images to resurface them on Google Images. Like Foundem, Getty's traffic fell 85%.[4]

CelebrityNetWorth.com launched in 2008 because Brian Warner, a former finance major working at a digital media company, wondered what Larry David was worth. The results he found were "garbage," so he decided to start his own website. People surfing the web had an insatiable desire to know how much their favorite stars were worth. The site became the most popular place to find what actors and actresses were worth. He started employing staff, and the ad money flowed in.[5]

Then Google came after it. In 2014, Warner got an email from Google asking if he would be interested in giving the company access to his data for free. He declined. He didn't see why he should practically give them something that had taken years to create and cost millions of dollars to make. Google took the data anyway.

In February 2016, Google started displaying a Featured Snippet for each of the 25,000 celebrities in the CelebrityNetWorth database. People viewed the net worth numbers on Google but stopped visiting the actual site. Like Getty Images and Foundem, the traffic collapsed and fell by 65%.[6] Warner had to lay off most of his staff.

When Google disappeared Foundem, it was abusing its market position to crush a competitor, but when it cut snippets, it was effectively killing the web by accelerating their stranglehold on search and search advertising and doing so at the at the expense of content creators.

Given that Google is the doorway through which people enter the internet, the search engine can effectively shut out competitors by demoting them or by taking their data. Google is using its dominance in one product area – universal search – to move into other markets. Economists call this "bundling," which historically has been illegal.

Google's power over what consumers see on the internet is vast and extends far beyond the desktop search function. Its Android mobile operating system powers most smartphones in the world with a whopping 85% market share.[7] It has tied the Android operating system to its own search engine, and it has tied Android to its own app store, effectively becoming the gatekeeper to what apps and companies consumers can access.

It uses its dominance in browsers to its own advantage as well. Its Chrome browser has 60% market share globally.[8] Google's Chrome browser will block certain types of online advertisements. It is also now effectively the gatekeeper to what kind of ads consumers can see. Mysteriously, the ads that are blocked are the kinds its competitors use, but not its own.

Google argues its new ad blocking is the work of a collective, industry-wide effort to get rid of annoying ads. However, through its dominant position with Chrome browsers, Google can block competitor ads and allow its own. They are creating a standard that doesn't apply to them.[9]

As we write this book, the top technology companies in the United States now have a market capitalization that exceeds the Gross Domestic Product of Germany, France or Italy. The $4 trillion price tag places them among the most valuable in history, alongside Standard

Oil, which controlled the US oil market. Perhaps only the East India Company, which had its own army and controlled half the world, was a bigger monopoly.

Google now controls nearly 90% of search advertising, Facebook almost 80% of mobile social traffic. The two companies captured almost 90% of the digital advertising growth last year. An astonishing 45% of Americans get their news from Facebook. When you add Google, over 70% of Americans get their news from the two companies.[10] The two companies have more information on their users' likes, preferences, political beliefs, and personal relations than any government spying agency, and they track users across the web with a complete history of what people see and search for.

In e-commerce, Amazon is by far the largest player, with an estimated share of 43%. Last year, Amazon accounted for 53% of all the incremental growth of online shopping. One study indicates that more than half of all product searches start on Amazon.[11] They are already in a monopoly position in book sales. Amazon gets about 75% of e-book sales.

Google, Facebook, and Amazon have great technology, but much of their current status and financial success comes from regulatory and antitrust mistakes. Amazon was allowed to buy dozens of e-commerce rivals and online booksellers to give it a monopsony position in the book industry. Google was able to buy its main competitor Doubeclick and vertically integrate online ad markets by buying advertising exchanges. Facebook was able to buy Instagram and Whatsapp with no regulatory challenges.[12] In no small degree, nonexistent antitrust has allowed them to achieve their dominance.

The scale of digital platforms puts them in a completely different category to the companies they compete against. Frank Pasquale, a professor of law and expert on digital platforms, has noted the tech behemoths are essentially functioning as governments now. "They are no longer market participants. Rather, in their fields, they are market makers, able to exert regulatory control over the terms on which others can sell goods and services. Moreover, they aspire to displace more government roles over time."[13]

Apple and Google determine what apps can be sold through the app stores on iPhones and Android, effectively regulating billions of phones. Facebook has over two billion people and its completely opaque algorithm determines what posts are viewed and which are not. Google's YouTube has restricted the speech of prominent conservatives and had their content censored or demonetized. In most cases they are not even given grounds for their punishment or a means of appealing it.[14] Facebook's Community Standards project puts the company in the position of deciding arbitrarily what speech is acceptable and what is not.[15]

We may fool ourselves into thinking that Facebook and Google use fair, impersonal algorithms to monitor speech. But algorithms are programmed by people, and people are imperfect and have biases. The left may be happy that conservatives are censored today, but who will control these platforms in 5 to 10 years? And who will prevent these giants from cooperating with countries that censor their own citizens?

Outright censorship is not so outlandish. According to the *New York Times*, Mark Zuckerberg has been learning Chinese. More important, the social network has quietly developed software to suppress posts from appearing in people's news feeds in specific geographic areas. "The feature was created to help Facebook get into China, a market where the social network has been blocked."[16] Mr. Zuckerberg has supported and defended the effort. In 2014 Facebook has complied with a Russian government demand to block access to a page supporting Russian opposition leader Alexei Navalny.[17]

These companies are effectively a government unto themselves. In legal circles, the term private government is most commonly associated with Robert Lee Hale. "There is government," he wrote, "whenever one person or group can tell others what they must do and when those others have to obey or suffer a penalty."[18] Under Hale's definition, the tech giants are effectively governments unto themselves.

In tax matters, the companies stand effectively beyond the laws of national governments, playing one country against another in a race to the bottom. Their arrangements mock national governments. Facebook, Google, and other tech companies have used arrangements known as a "Double Irish" and a "Dutch Sandwich," to shield the majority of their international profits from the taxman. They shift revenue from one Irish subsidiary to a Dutch company with no employees, and then on to a Bermuda mailbox owned by another Ireland-registered company.[19] It is a farce, and it is all perfectly legal.

The ultimate loss from unpaid taxes is an estimated 60 billion euros a year for the weakest members of the European Union.[20] While individuals and small businesses pay high levels of taxes, the share of corporate profits that multinationals have reported in tax havens has increased tenfold since the 1980s; much of this is coming from the large tech companies.[21]

The tech giants increase income inequality, because the losers are the people and small businesses who do pay taxes and the winners are the shareholders of the companies that use them to dodge taxes.[22]

The tech giants preach social solidarity and not being evil (Google recently decided to drop their motto "Don't be evil," as it seemed out of fashion), while they funnel billions into offshore havens and channel their European operations through tax-friendly Ireland. While preaching the values of freedom and independence, they collect untold amounts of information on their users in vast spying operations. Not only do they avoid paying taxes in the democratic states where they have their headquarters, they have allowed themselves to become tools against these very states.

Today, the tech behemoths are in many ways more powerful than most large developed nations, and they have far more power as regulators and market arbiters than government. Yet no governments are exercising their power to rein them in.

No one is guarding the guardians.

It is not the first time we have seen a dominant company use its position in one area to control another. Google uses universal search to dominate vertical search areas like price comparisons, and it uses its browser to further dominate the ad industry.

Twenty years ago, Microsoft had a total monopoly of desktop operating systems through Windows. When the little upstart Netscape introduced its Mosaic Browser, Microsoft feared that it might be left behind in the internet boom. It pre-installed its own browser Internet Explorer in its Windows operating system to crush Netscape, even though Netscape was in many ways superior and had 80% market share.

The fight was never even. Because over 90% of new computers had the Windows system, almost all ran Explorer by default. Through the operating system, they owned the users. To make matters worse, they embedded Explorer deeply into Windows so that if you tried to uninstall it, you messed up all of Windows. Financially, there was no contest either. Netscape's total revenue never exceeded the interest income generated by Microsoft's cash on hand. Within a few years, Microsoft had effectively crushed Netscape and gained over 90% market share.

In a rare display of caring about competition, on May 18, 1998, the US Justice Department and 20 state Attorneys General filed an antitrust suit against Microsoft. The government showed scores of emails from Microsoft with phrases like "take away their oxygen supply" and "crush them."

A little over a year later, Judge Thomas Penfield Jackson ruled that Microsoft had used its monopoly power to harm rivals and consumers. The judge agreed with the government's recommendation that the company be broken up into the two companies. One would be an "Operating System" company, and the other would be Applications, including the web browser or the Office suite of tools.

Microsoft barely avoided being broken up, but it had a powerful effect in favor of competition. Brad Smith, Microsoft's general counsel, recognized the importance of the trial. "It was clear that the industry, the government, the world at large expected us to step forward and assume more responsibility without appearing to quibble with whether that responsibility was required by the law itself."[23]

In one of the great ironies of history, Google and other tech giants only exist because Microsoft was reined in and was unable to use its monopoly in desktops after the settlement. There had been informal conjectures about reprogramming Microsoft's web browser, the popular Internet Explorer, so that anytime people typed in "Google," they would be redirected to MSN Search, according to company insiders.[24]

"Because of antitrust enforcement, that's why we have Google," says Gary Reback, a lawyer who represented Netscape in the '90s. "There is no other reason."[25]

Today's Federal Trade Commission and the Department of Justice have little in common with their former selves decades ago. When the Raffs met the FTC officials, they found out that the staff was very interested in Google's effects on competition. But as time passed, they did not hear back from the FTC and they got the feeling that nothing would happen.

When the FTC's political appointees reviewed the complaints from the Raffs and Google's competitors, they decided to do nothing at all.

The FTC's commissioners voted unanimously in early 2013 to end the investigation after Google agreed to some voluntary changes to its practices. Jon Leibowitz, the FTC Chairman announced that, "While not everything Google did was beneficial, on balance, we did not believe that the evidence supported an F.T.C. challenge."

It remained a mystery why the FTC did not charge Google as it had Microsoft. The missing piece of the puzzle finally emerged in 2015 through a memo that accidentally made its way to the *Wall Street Journal* via a Freedom of Information request. The 160-page FTC report concluded in 2012 that Google used anticompetitive tactics and abused its monopoly power. It argued that Google's "conduct has resulted—and will result—in real harm to consumers and to innovation in the online search and advertising markets." The report recommended the commission bring a lawsuit against Google.

When competitors asked Google to stop taking their content, it threatened to make them disappear completely. "It is clear that Google's threat was intended to produce, and did produce, the desired effect," the report said, "which was to coerce Yelp and TripAdvisor into backing down." The company also sent a message that it would "use its monopoly power over search to extract the fruits of its rivals' innovations."[26]

If the evidence was so overwhelming to the FTC staff, then why did the Commissioners vote against charging Google like Microsoft?

The answer is simple: politics.

While Google, Facebook, and Amazon behave in ways very similar to Microsoft, they spend a lot more time preemptively lobbying and donating to political parties. There is no way that the Obama administration would have pursued Google. It is easy to see why: the monopolist was the second-largest corporate source of campaign donations to President Barack Obama's reelection effort.

The level of contacts between the White House and Google was unprecedented. Google representatives attended White House meetings more than once a week, on average, from the beginning of Obama's presidency through October 2015. Nearly 250 people have shuttled from government service to Google employment or vice versa over the course of his administration.[27] The White House chose two Googlers as CTO and deputy CTO of the United States, where they regularly emailed their former employer.

Apple, Amazon, Facebook, and Google spent almost $50 million on lobbying in 2017. Google was the biggest spender and devoted $18 million to lobby the US government. That's more than its tech peers, not to mention much of corporate America. Amazon quadrupled its spending on lobbying, while Facebook spent a record amount.[28]

Google has every reason to defend itself. The search engine now accounts for an estimated 87% of online searches worldwide. It is essentially a global utility in private hands. Given the overwhelming dominance in terms of search, the company knows it is in the bull's-eye of regulators. Answering whether Google was a monopoly in 2011, Eric Schmidt, Google's CEO, had a slip of the tongue and said, "I would agree, sir, that we're in that area." And then as he caught himself, he began to hedge, "I'm not a lawyer, but my understanding of monopoly findings is this is a judicial process."[29]

Not only does Google lobby, but it also has a large network of academics who will write reports on demand. Some of them are laughable. In one, Geoffrey Manne argued that Foundem's real failure as a business was relying on Google for traffic: "The fact that Google creates an opportunity for companies to rely upon it doesn't mean that a company's decision to do so – and to do so without a viable contingency plan – makes good business sense."[30] It was Foundem's fault, in Manne's view, as if any website has a choice but to rely on Google given it has almost 90% market share globally. Google is essentially a utility at this stage.

It should have been no surprise that many lawyers and academics would support Google. Manne's father, Henry Manne, created the International Center for Law & Economics at George Mason University and both have received financial support from Google. As journalist David Dayen found, between 2009 and 2015 there were 66 published studies where the authors were either "commissioned by Google," "funded by Google," or "supported by a gift from Google, Inc."[31]

When think tanks and academics don't do what Google wants, the consequences can be severe. When the researcher Barry Lynn, wrote a critical piece on Google, the New America Foundation fired him. The foundation had received more than $21 million from Google's executive chairman Eric Schmidt.[32]

Bill Gates warned the new Silicon Valley giants not to be the new Microsoft. He has told the tech companies to be "careful that they're not trying to think their view is more important than the government's view"[33]

In the years that followed the Microsoft case, the tech giants learned all the wrong lessons from the Netscape and Microsoft browser wars. The lesson they learned is not "Don't be an abusive monopolist." Instead, they learned the power of *lobbying*.

The big break for Foundem did not come from the United States, but from Europe where the search giant had few friends.

In August 2014 Margrethe Vestager became the European Commissioner for Competition. She was a superstar Danish politician, and Danish television had even created a show *Borgen*, based on her. Her main interest was in the environment, and she didn't want to lead the Competition Commission. Yet despite the job being her second choice, she has become the most prominent competition policy official in the world.

After reviewing the complaints submitted by the Raffs and others, Vestager announced she would formally charge Google with competition policy violations. The Commission would find against Google and fine them almost $3 billion because of the "duration and gravity of the infringement."[34] As America has abandoned its antitrust traditions, the Europeans were reminding Americans of the road not taken.

In their decision, the EU noted the essential nature of platforms. The more people search on Google, the better the company gets at understanding what users are searching for and the better searching becomes. The more people search, the more likely advertisers will flock to Google, and the more revenue that is generated. The more advertisers there are, the more efficient ad auctions become.

Most of the tech monopolies are known as "platform" companies with strong network effects: Google, Facebook, Amazon, Uber. What these companies have in common is that they all connect members of one group, like vacationers looking for rooms to rent, with another group, like landlords with spare rooms. Traditional manufacturing businesses, for instance, buy raw materials, make products, and sell those to customers. Platform companies on the other hand take different groups of customers that they help bring together. The more vacationers search on AirBnB, the greater the incentive for landlords to put properties on the site. The more properties there are on AirBnB, the less likely people will search on other rental sites.

What would the value of Uber be if you were the only person on it? Zero. You need a buyer and a seller. With two people, the value would not be much. With 100, it gets interesting. With a million people, it is hard to compete with Uber. Sellers want to go where all the buyers are, and buyers want to be where all the sellers are. The more buyers and sellers there are, the greater the value of Uber as a platform. The same is true for Skype. If almost no one is on Skype, you can't call anyone, but the more people there are, the more you can call. PayPal doesn't work well if only a few people use it, but if everyone accepts it, you can pay for almost anything with it. The more people that use eBay, PayPal, Skype, Twitter, or Facebook, the less likely it is that they will face competitors.

Various mathematicians have come up with mathematical formulas to ascribe value to networks: Sarnoff's Law, Metcalfe's Law, and Reed's Law. They all show that the value of networks is a function number of users. The rule for analyzing networks is that with each additional person in the network, the number of potential connections in a network grows exponentially. The value isn't arithmetic ($3 + 3 = 6$), it is much more exponential ($3 \times 3 = 9$).

Bigger is not a little bit better; it means everything. For venture capitalists, "network effects" effectively means monopoly.

Given the feedback loops inherent in platforms, there is a very strong winner-takes-all dynamic. The bigger a platform is, the less likely it can be dislodged. It is no surprise that there has been no credible new search engine in years, and existing search engines like Yahoo and Ask have simply outsourced their search to Google or Bing. Google is completely, utterly dominant in online and mobile search.[35]

The power of platforms makes them a different class of companies. They set the rules that govern their world. We simply live in it.

Facebook and Google's fabulous profitability and complete power over the internet is due to the greatest arbitrage in media history. The traditional media and online publishers bear the financial burdens of analyzing, reporting, fact checking, writing, and publishing the news. Songwriters and musicians bear the burden of composing, recording, and producing their music, yet they get paid nothing by the tech monopolies. Almost all of the economics flow to the two companies.

While Facebook and Google claim not to be media companies, they act as the online gatekeepers to billions of people and collect untold amounts of personal information in the process. Through their role as middlemen, they capture all the economics and have become the most valuable companies in the world.

Facebook and Google are effectively publishers, yet they don't like to acknowledge that that's what they are. That would imply responsibility for what happens on their platforms and a need to compensate the creators of content.

On YouTube musicians are constantly filing "takedown" notices but, often, after one link is taken down, the song goes right back up at another one. In the first quarter of 2016, Google received such notices for more than *two hundred million* links. Google and Facebook don't care about creating content or rewarding the creators of content, only monetizing traffic and the data about their users.[36]

Facebook's relationship with the media has been a deal with the devil. News outlets were salivating to reach Facebook's two billion users, so they put as much of their content as they could on the social network. At first, they encouraged readers to post links that led back to their own news websites.[37] Facebook was getting so much traffic that they convinced publishers to post Instant Articles directly on Facebook so load times would be faster and the content would be tailored to Facebook's audience. Gradually, Facebook started exerting more and more control over what was being seen, to the point that they became the main publishers of everyone's content.

Mark Zuckerberg says his site is a "community," but the site is not a co-op. Facebook decides what gets views and what doesn't and captures all the profit.

As Facebook's News Feed became an incessant barrage of children's baseball games, cat memes, pratfall videos, and news articles,

Facebook started restricting what content would actually make it onto people's feed. Only the most popular memes would ever see the light of day. If news editors wanted their stories to reach their readers, they'd have to start paying Facebook so their articles would be promoted.

Today, Facebook is effectively a payola scam where you have to pay up if you want your own fans to see your content. The social network decides what articles can be published and what reaches its users. According to Matti Littunen, a media expert, Facebook "first gives lots of organic reach to one content type, then they have to pay for reach, then they can only get through to anyone by paying."[38]

Paying for reach might be humiliating enough for most publishers, but the situation is so much worse. Publishers have sued Facebook because it has misreported dozens of ad metrics.[39] It has overstated the organic reach of content posts, and the time people have spent reading articles.[40] Facebook has admitted that because of a miscalculation in the way it determined the video-ad viewership, it artificially inflated the time spent watching videos by 60% to 80% from 2014 to 2016.[41] Mysteriously, all errors in ad reporting have been in Facebook's favor, and none have been in the customer's favor.

To quote Oscar Wilde, "To lose one parent may be regarded as a misfortune; to lose both looks like carelessness." To misreport one ad metric is a misfortune; to misreport dozens is a pattern.

Ad fraud is rampant. Advertisers have becoming increasingly wary of the viewership numbers coming from the digital giants. Google also profited from inflated metrics. A recent study by comScore found that 54% of display ads paid for by advertisers never appeared in front of a live human being.[42] Google has been forced to compensate clients for the fraud.

In television and radio, Nielsen provided a check on ABC, CBS, and NBC inflating numbers of people who viewed ads. There is little oversight today at Facebook and Google. They are platforms have been a law unto themselves. It was only after dozens of errors that Facebook finally started allowing any outside verification of ad numbers.[43]

The problem is not only that Facebook has exaggerated its ad viewership, it has also exaggerated its user numbers. Australian's AdNews discovered that Facebook claims to reach 1.7 million more 16- to 39-year-olds in Australia than exist in the country, according to its census bureau. There is a similar situation in the United States, where Facebook claims a potential reach of 41 million 18- to 24-year-olds, 60 million 25- to 34-year-olds, and 61 million 35- to 49-year-olds. All of these numbers exceed US Census figures.[44]

It is not just news that is dying. Tim Berners Lee, the creator of the web, thinks *the internet itself is dying*.[45] In 2014 the web took a very dark turn. Beforehand, traffic to websites came from all sorts of places, and the web was a lively ecosystem. But starting in 2014, over half of all traffic started coming from Facebook and Google. Today, over 70% of traffic is dominated by the two sources.[46]

For websites like the comedy hub Funny or Die, Facebook ended up capturing all the economics of their content. In the end, Funny or Die eliminated its entire editorial team following a trend of comedy websites scaling back. When Funny or Die fired most of its staff, employee Matt Klinman posted on Twitter, "Mark Zuckerberg just walked into Funny or Die and laid off all my friends." He explained: "There is simply no money in making comedy online anymore. Facebook has completely destroyed independent digital comedy and we need to fucking talk about it."[47]

Today, there's no reason to go to a comedy website that has a video if that same video is right on Facebook. And that would be fine if Facebook compensated those companies for the ad revenue, but Facebook does not share its ad revenue with publishers.

The internet was meant to be open, anarchic, decentralized, and above all free. In the 1990s, America Online helped people get online and discover content, but it failed because it was a walled garden. AOL determined and curated the user experience, which was contrary to the spirit of the web. Once users started going online with their local cable company, and Google helped them find anything on the web, people never went back to AOL.

Facebook has become AOL 2.0, a centrally designed internet for its users. You discover only what the company wants. It is about as uncool as America Online, but it won't die the same death because Facebook has a lock on a user's life history, photos, friends, and family connections. Countless articles and videos appear only behind Facebook's guarded gate. Facebook has become a digital passport, and many apps and sites such as Tinder or Bumble will not even let a user join without a Facebook account.

Even Google is now eating the web through its new technologies. Pages load faster with tools like Accelerated Mobile Pages or Firebase. These technologies are like Facebook's Instant Articles. They sound great, until you realize that the faster pages sit on Google and Facebook's servers, displacing third-party ad networks and further tying the entire web into their ecosystem, where they exercise control.[48]

There is now a vast imbalance of power between individuals and private companies. The web is no longer free when two companies control most of the traffic. André Staltz, a computer programmer, has noted that the tech giants can ban users and "don't need to guarantee you access to their networks. You do not have a legal right to an account in their servers, and as societies we aren't demanding these rights."[49]

Faced with a closed web controlled by two private companies, users are demanding that Facebook and Google fix themselves. As Matt Taibbi has succinctly put it, "For Google and Facebook to be the cause of and the solution to problems tells you how irrelevant governments and regulators have become."[50]

Helena Steele founded the kitchen-apparel company Jessie Steele in 2002, and she started selling through Amazon in 2009. However, by 2014 she stopped. The counterfeits on Amazon were driving her out of business.

The products on Amazon are not genuine products, but are instead made in a Chinese factory that has stolen her trademark. Steele keeps close track of her inventory, and requires third-party sellers to sign documents saying they won't sell her products on Amazon. Yet her products are still for sale there, listed as "Ships from and sold by Amazon. com." She says that her sales have fallen by 90%. "Amazon has brought us to our knees," she told me. "It's just financially gutted us."[51]

Not only small entrepreneurs face having their brands ripped off. In 2016, Daimler AG, the parent company of Mercedes-Benz, filed a lawsuit against Amazon in US District Court in Washington State, arguing that Amazon "has gained profits" by selling wheels that violated Daimler's patents. Consumers trust items listed as "shipped from and sold by Amazon.com," Daimler says, and so Amazon should be doing more to "detect and deter" infringement of patents.

Last year, the chief executive of Birkenstock accused Amazon of "modern-day piracy" for allowing counterfeits to be sold on the site. Eventually, he yanked his brand from Amazon. But what is more, Birkenstock won't authorize third-party merchants to sell on the site. Despite the very public spat between Amazon and Birkenstock, you can still find fake listings of Birkenstocks on Amazon today in less than a few seconds of searching.

The law generally protects e-commerce sites from being responsible for what third-party actors are selling on their sites. Congress gave companies that provide online services "safe harbor" immunity from copyright-infringement liability for their users' actions in 1998 as part of the Digital Millennium Copyright Act.[52] Like Facebook's fake ad metrics, Amazon's mistakes are more than a misfortune. Amazon appears to be completely fine with the level of fakes, and it is an essential part of the business model to have as much inventory as possible.

E-commerce represents about 10% of all US retail and Amazon is by far the largest player, with an estimated share of 43%. Last year, Amazon accounted for 53% of all the incremental growth of online shopping, which means they are only growing their dominance. One study indicates that more than half of all product searches start on Amazon. Half of American households are now members of Amazon Prime due to the convenience of delivery backed by Amazon's infrastructure. Recent research found that only 1% of the people who paid for Amazon's loyalty program were likely to comparison shop when shopping online.

Already about half of US households are Amazon Prime members. And 55% of all online shopping searches started on Amazon in 2018, versus 30% in 2012. In recent months, Nike and Sears threw in the towel and agreed to begin selling their athletic shoes and Kenmore appliances on Amazon.[53]

Amazon's anticompetitive effect stems from its inherent conflict as both a direct seller and the operator of a platform that it invites other sellers to use. Amazon's dominance has exhibited how network effects can be self-reinforcing. The more merchants there are selling on Amazon, the better shoppers can be assured that they are searching all possible vendors. The more shoppers there are, the more vendors consider Amazon a "must-have" venue. As Lina Khan, a critic of Amazon, has written, "the company has positioned itself at the center of e-commerce and now serves as essential infrastructure for a host of other businesses that depend upon it."[54]

Inside Amazon, executives were worried that they would be helping competitors if they opened up their warehouses and distribution for third-party vendors and potential competitors in 2000. Bezos, though, realized that the expensive warehouses and distribution network needed more volume to succeed, and providing the infrastructure for others would give them a critical advantage. He would have complete visibility into his competitors' sales if they sold through Amazon.

Today, independents sell 44% of all items on Amazon worldwide and their sales are growing faster than those of the host site. Effectively, the company is the e-commerce equivalent of UPS or FedEx. However, unlike FedEx or UPS, they are not bound by any rules or oversight that applies to the transportation companies. According to some critics, "There is no guarantee they won't take advantage, and in some cases they probably have. They can sell on their own account and they can see what is selling and what is not and that puts [Amazon] in a powerful position."[55]

According to new research from Upstream Commerce, Amazon tracks third-party sales on its site and uses that data to sell the most popular items in direct competition with marketplace members. Upstream sampled over 850 women's clothing products initially sold by marketplace sellers and checked to see when Amazon started selling the same items. Within 12 weeks, Amazon began selling 25 percent of the top items first sold through marketplace vendors.[56]

Amazon gets big discounts from Federal Express and UPS as a high-volume customer. Amazon passes along those discounts to independent companies that use its fulfillment services. While customers cheer the convenience and low cost, companies may have no choice but to use Amazon's fulfillment services if they want to get competitive shipping rates and favorable listings.

Amazon has a clear conflict of interest when it comes to policing counterfeits and competing with its own partners. As a platform, it wants the maximum number of people selling on its site, much like Facebook and Google want the maximum number of eyeballs to sell ads against. Whether that comes from pirated content or not, the tech giants simply don't care.

Jeff Bezos, Amazon's founder, has been known to put an empty chair in meetings to remind employees of the need to focus on the customer. But Amazon puts itself first, when it comes to customer searches. A recent study by ProPublica found that the company is "using its market power and proprietary algorithm to advantage itself at the expense of sellers and many customers."[57] When they searched for hundreds of items on the site, about three-quarters of the time, Amazon put its own products above third-party products using its platform, even when competing products were cheaper. As a platform, it pays to be the regulator of your own marketplace.

With friends like this, who needs enemies?

It is normal for big companies to throw shade on their competitors, and this metaphor applies in Silicon Valley, as well.

As we were researching this book, a venture capitalist told us that the tech economy had now turned into a jungle. The metaphor of predators and prey made sense to us, but he was much more specific. Silicon Valley today resembles the deepest part of the jungle known as the triple canopy, where tall trees block out all the light and nothing can grow on the ground. Today, very little sunlight reaches the startups.

Most city dwellers think it is impossible to walk through jungles because of how dense they are, but that is only partly true. Deep in the rainforests there is a unique structure of several vertical layers of trees, each forming a canopy. The top canopy goes up to 130 feet above the forest floor. Almost all the wildlife lives in the canopy; many animals live high in the trees and never set foot on the ground below in their entire lives. Once you get inside the heart of the jungle in the triple canopy, almost nothing grows on the ground. Only 2% of sunlight reaches the ground after getting through all the leaves. All that is left on the floor is a thin layer of fallen leaves and branches that very quickly decomposes.[58]

American soldiers were very familiar with the triple canopy in the Vietnam jungle. The humidity down below was a stifling 95%, exhausting men and rotting clothing. Almost nothing could survive for long underneath. The Ho Chi Minh Trail itself was in the triple-canopy jungle, which made it almost impossible for helicopters and planes to see through the trees and support US troops below.[59] The response of the Department of Defense was to dump 19 million gallons of herbicide that poisoned the land.[60]

Between Google, Amazon, Apple, Facebook, and Microsoft, they have collectively bought over 436 companies and startups in the past 10 years, and regulators have not challenged any of them. In 2017 alone, they spent over $31.6 billion on acquisitions. Most small companies now do not expect to succeed on their own and their only goal is the "exit" to one of the big tech companies before they are crushed.

The threat of unlimited losses against a big player is reason enough for startups to sell to the incumbents. The retailer Diapers.com initially rejected Amazon's efforts to acquire it. In response, Amazon responded by slashing its own diaper prices in a clear effort at predatory pricing. The executives at Diapers.com calculated that, based on the cost of diapers from Procter & Gamble and shipping costs, Amazon was going to lose $100 million in one quarter merely in diapers. As a startup that needed venture capital funding, there was no way they could raise that amount of capital in order to compete with Amazon. In the end, Amazon made them an offer they could not refuse.[61]

It would appear irrational for Amazon to sell diapers at a loss, but Amazon is not a normal company. In their book *Matchmakers*, David Evans and Richard Schmalensee have pointed out that, "Traditional economics holds, for example, that it's never profitable to sell products at less than cost. The new multisided economics shows that even paying some customers rather than charging them anything can be profitable in theory and often is in practice."[62] Given the winner take all dynamics of being a platform company, Amazon will happily sell diapers at a loss if it can get more buyers and sellers interacting on its platform.

Either the upstarts sell out to the bigger company, or they get ruthlessly crushed. Most founders have little choice when facing bigger players but to sell. Some founders do, like Instagram and Whattsapp did to Facebook. The ones that do not accept an offer they can't refuse face brutal competition: their innovations are copied, they face patent lawsuits, and their top talent is poached.

The tech giants love startups, but in the same way that lions love feasting on lifeless carcasses of gazelles. Either they provide innovations the giants can't come up with in-house, or they pay a toll to the big tech companies for the pleasure of using their infrastructure.

There is perhaps no better example of this dynamic than what has happened to Snap, the company that makes the disappearing messaging app Snapchat. Although it is one of the most innovative consumer-focused internet companies, it has been battered by the giants. Snap raised $3.4 billion in one of the biggest Initial Public Offerings in years. After failing to buy Snap when it was a rapidly growing startup, Facebook repeatedly copied and cloned its key innovations for Instagram, another startup that Facebook bought. Snap shares are languishing below its IPO price, another road kill of the tech giants, and funding may be harder to come by for the next David to challenge a Goliath.

But Facebook isn't the only giant feeding off Snap's carcass. In January, Snap signed a cloud-hosting deal with Google. Snap agreed to pay Google $400 million a year for the next five years, which is about half its yearly revenue.[63]

Startups that receive venture capital funding from the tech giants learn things the hard way. Jonathan Frankel was ecstatic when Amazon's venture capital group invested $5.6m into his startup Nucleus, a startup that focused on communication and video. A year later, however, Frankel was furious. Amazon launched its latest voice-controlled device, the Echo Show, a clone of the Nucleus product.[64] As he told Recode, "they want to sell more detergent; we actually want to help families communicate easier."[65]

While the technical costs of building an online service are cheaper than ever, it has never been harder for startups to succeed. Online platforms control the essential infrastructure on which their rivals depend. The big tech companies run server clouds, app stores, ad networks, have venture firms, and they control the backbone of the internet.

Startups spend hundreds of millions of dollars of advertising on Facebook and Google to get their product in front of potential users. They need Apple and Google's approval to appear in the app stores. They pay Google and Amazon for their servers and pipes. Much like the medieval European peasants, the startups pay robber barons to cross their roads, hoping they will not be attacked along the way.

Google is so far ahead of competitors that no companies have even entered Google's search market since 2008. No venture capital group will ever fund a search engine.

Google's scale is staggering and impossible to comprehend, as much of its technology is still a highly guarded secret. To put things in perspective, if Google were not a search engine, it would be considered one of the top three internet service providers in the world, based on its ownership of fiber-optic cables.[66] Google has dozens of data centers scattered around the world, with at least 12 located in the United States.[67] One of the largest Google data centers in Oregon is approximately the size of two American football fields, with cooling towers four stories tall. Google has invested $30 billion in infrastructure over the past three years on cables connecting its cloud data centers.[68] There is simply no way any startup can compete with that level of capital spending.

It is not only Google that controls the fabled information superhighways that everyone's data passes through. Increasingly, the big internet monopolies are building and own the world's fiber-optic cables. Google and Facebook partnered to lay the first 8,000-mile cable that directly connects Los Angeles to Hong Kong. Facebook and Microsoft announced they would be building the Marea cable, which will offer speeds of 160 terabytes per second across the Atlantic.[69] They own the pipes of the utility on which others will have to pay tolls.

If you don't think today's companies are vicious, just ask venture capitalists. In the words of Benedict Evans, a venture capitalist, Google, Facebook, and Amazon are "aggressive street fighters. All of these companies have the benefit of 20 years more history – they saw what happened to Microsoft" and they won't let it happen to them.[70]

"If you provide great content in one of these categories that is lucrative to Google, and seen as potentially threatening, they will snuff you out," said Jeremy Stoppelman, cofounder and CEO of Yelp. "They will make you disappear. They will bury you."

The situation is very much like the late 1990s when it was widely known that venture capital funds wouldn't fund you if you were going to go into an area where Microsoft was involved.[71] If a new product or program interfered with Microsoft's objectives, Microsoft employees would use language like 'let's go "knife the baby,"' as a metaphor for killing off the small competitor.[72]

Today, the same thing is happening again. Albert Wenger, a managing partner at Union Square Ventures states, "The scale of these companies and their impact on what can be funded, and what can succeed, is massive." Wenger noted that many investors simply refuse to fund businesses that are in the "kill zone."[73]

Who knows how many good businesses are not funded because of the fear of the tech monopolies? As Stoppelman told *60 Minutes* in an interview, "If I were starting out today, I would have no shot of building Yelp."

Today's giants have created an ecosystem that enriches themselves even when they don't think of the best ideas first. For the biggest tech firms, competing against startups has become a one-way bet.

Key Thoughts from the Chapter

- The top technology companies in the United States now have a market capitalization that exceeds the GDP of all countries in Western Europe.
- For the biggest tech firms, competing against startups has become a one-way bet.
- In tax matters, the companies stand effectively beyond the laws of national governments, playing one country against another in a race to the bottom.
- The power of platforms makes them a different class of companies. They set the rules that govern their world. We simply live in it.

Chapter Six

Toll Roads and Robber Barons

I would rather earn 1% off a hundred people's efforts than 100% of my own efforts.

—*John D. Rockefeller*

Imagine a world where a giant corporation watched your daily habits and knew all your likes, dislikes, who you spoke to, what you bought, whether you paid your bills on time, and what you talked about with friends? What if this company assigned you a higher score and a higher score could get you a better house, a better car, and even a better life.

It all sounds like a *Black Mirror* episode from Netflix. In a recent episode, a fictional social media platform allowed users to rank one another like people review hotels on TripAdvisor or restaurants on Yelp. The score determined your trustworthiness and your value as a human. The better your ranking, the higher your social class. A low score could cut you off from jobs, goods, and friends.

This dark vision is already a reality in China. On June 14, 2014, the State Council of China published a document called "Planning Outline for the Construction of a Social Credit System." The title itself

sounded boring, but it proposed a revolutionary new tool to monitor and control the population. Everyone in China would have one
score that would determine their trustworthiness.[1] Private tech giants
are helping the government monitor and rate its 1.3 billion citizens.
These credit scores are being used for almost any purpose and track
everything users do online, who their friends are and what they say.
The Chinese government is pitching the system as a way to improve
because, as the propaganda tells us, "keeping trust is glorious."

China is becoming a laboratory where Big Data meets Big Brother.
Large technological monopolies work hand in hand with government.
If the original incarnations of Communism under Lenin, Stalin, and
Mao failed because central planning was a disaster, Big Data will now
come to the rescue. Last year, Jack Ma, founder of Alibaba, the online
platform with over half a billion users, argued, "Big Data will make the
market smarter and make it possible to plan and predict market forces
so as to allow us to finally achieve a planned economy."[2]

The 2013 revelations of Edward Snowden exposed the involvement of American companies and intelligence agencies in programs
that gave the government access to personal data. Americans were
briefly outraged and then continued their lives as they did before. In
fact, consumers were inviting Big Brother into their homes. Millions
of consumers now have "smart" devices like Amazon Echo or Google
Home that can accurately fingerprint voices and are always on.

Facebook and its subsidiaries Instagram and Whatsapp know your
email, your phone number, your likes and dislikes, your friends, your
family, most of your browsing history, where you've been, and what
you've done. Google has your entire search history and is quietly
recording all your travels through your IP address and Google Maps.

The tech giants want to track people offline through their faces, as
well. Through a clever app to get people to scan their face and compare it to artwork, Google has captured millions of face scans. Facial
recognition technology is now a key part of Apple's X Phone. Facebook can accurately identify a person 98% of the time.[3] You can
change your password, but not your face.

Almost no one cared about tech monopolies and their control
over our lives until evidence emerged that Russian intelligence influenced the American election and the British Brexit vote. The scale and

scope of Facebook and Google as sources of "news" and "information" emerged. Outrageous and often false articles circulating on Facebook finally caught the public's attention. Their algorithms put a premium on controversial posts that will get clicked and devalue accuracy.

Even early investors in Facebook have turned on the company. Roger McNamee has known Facebook's Mark Zuckerburg for years and advised him on strategy. Yet he now believes the tech giants have been given a green light by the government to run wild: "No one stopped them from siphoning off the profits of content creators. No one stopped them from gathering data on every aspect of every user's internet life. No one stopped them from amassing market share not seen since the days of Standard Oil."[4] McNamee went from being a Facebook promoter to calling for the breakup of digital monopolies.

Investors such as George Soros woke up to the danger and warned that the vast power of the data-rich monopolies could become part of an "unholy alliance" with authoritarian states. In the end, it "may well result in a web of totalitarian control the likes of which not even Aldous Huxley or George Orwell could have imagined."[5]

Only a decade ago, the biggest companies in the United States were a reasonable representation of the US economy – General Electric, Exxon Mobil, Microsoft, Citigroup, and Bank of America. Today, though, all the top five companies are tech companies – Amazon, Facebook, Google, Apple, and Microsoft. They now have more power over our lives than Western Union, Standard Oil, or AT&T ever had as monopolies.

The tech giants are not only taking over the United States, they're taking over the world. Over the past year, Amazon, Apple, Google, and Microsoft have added $825 billion in market capitalization. That is more than the *entire* market valuation of every company listed in Brazil, Italy, or Spain. Facebook has more users than Islam has believers, and it is quickly surpassing the number of Christians in the world. It should be no surprise that Zuckerberg has compared Facebook to a church.

As the tech monopolies have become the biggest companies in history, their executives are living in another world. Today, the suburb of Atherton in Silicon Valley is now the most expensive postcode in the United States. The homes and estates of the tech titans are rarely visible from the road. The most expensive homes sell for around $30 million while an average home costs over $9 million. Tech billionaires Eric Schmidt, Meg Whitman, and Sheryl Sandberg all have homes here.[6]

For over a century, California was the embodiment of technological and economic progress. Today, the Golden State suffers the highest level of poverty in the country, even surpassing Mississippi and Alabama. It is also now home to roughly one-third of the nation's welfare recipients, roughly three times its share as a percentage of the population.[7]

In the old days, the state's tech sector produced industrial jobs that sparked prosperity not only in Silicon Valley, but also in working class towns like San Jose. The iPhone is a metaphor for Silicon Valley. Today, when you buy an iPhone, it says designed in California, but it is manufactured in China. The manufacturing jobs for the working class are long gone.

The tech monopolies are making billions of dollars of profit, but the Silicon Valley growth engine appears to be going in reverse. In 2017 job growth began to roll over, as the Bay Area lost more jobs than it created throughout much of the year.[8] Housing costs have become prohibitively high and commutes to cheaper housing are becoming longer. Workers are noticing and voting with their feet. According to a study, the "out-migration" in the Valley was greater in 2016 than in any other year since 2006.

Like medieval serfs, the lords of the manor live behind walls while increasing numbers of Californians are downwardly mobile, and doing worse than their parents.[9] California increasingly resembles a class-bound medieval society, and the wealth at the top is not trickling down. California is the most unequal state, according to the report by Measure of America.[10] Around 30% of the households in Silicon Valley do not earn enough money to meet their basic needs without public or private, informal assistance, and this share jumps up to 59% for those in Hispanic or Latino households.[11]

People are finally waking up to the dangers of digital monopolies and the vast divide between billionaire monopolists and the serfs below. The problem of monopolies, though, is not restricted to Silicon Valley tech companies. They are merely the tip of the iceberg.

The term "robber baron" originally came from the medieval German lords, the *Rauberitter*, who charged illegal tolls on the roads crossing their lands without providing any improved roads in exchange. The tolls operated as taxes, transferring money from the common man to nobles.

As Americans go about their daily lives, they have the illusion of choice, but they spend their days paying tolls to a few companies that lack any real competition.

Late capitalism resembles Soviet logic when it comes to consumer options. When Americans wake up each day, they can get their cereal from Kellogg's, General Mills, or Post, who all together have an 85% share of the cereal market. At breaks from work, they might want a soft drink. The top three firms dominate more than 85% of the market.[12] Coca Cola is the leader, followed by PepsiCo and Dr. Pepper Snapple. If they don't like too much sugar, they might buy some bottled water, where they'll find that Nestlé, Coca Cola, and PepsiCo own 9 out of the top 10 brands. If they want a beer after work, they can choose Budweiser, Corona, Stella, or Coors Light. However, Molson Coors and AB InBev now control around 90% of the US beer market, including many supposedly "craft" beers, after the Department of Justice approved the creation of a new duopoly.[13]

Consumers might want their Cokes, Perrier, or Budweiser, so who cares if a few companies dominate soft drinks? If only it were that simple. Supermarket shelves are highly coveted real estate. Strong brands often have slotting arrangements that exclude other brands, and many supermarkets engage in "category management" where "captains," that is, strong brands, help dictate what brands appear where.[14] Effectively, this is a form of cartel, and weaker brands mysteriously always get shafted.[15] You won't find any small brands on a major retailer's shelves.

When you turn on your phone, chances are you're running Apple's iOS on an iPhone or an Android. Welcome to the Apple, Google duopoly. Your mobile phone company is an oligopoly. You may not think of it every day, but your internet is most likely coming from your local cable company, which is a complete local monopoly for 75% of Americans.

If so much talk of market concentration is giving you a headache, do not fear. You can get aspirin from CVS or Walgreen Boots, which have a duopoly in drugstores and the pharmacy benefits management (PBM) market. Walgreen tried to buy RiteAid to gain even more market share, but the Department of Justice was unusually bold. They let Walgreen buy only half of RiteAid's stores.[16] The appropriate analogy here is of disapproving parents who dislike their son's coke habit and tell him to settle for half a line.

If you feel like a heart attack is setting in while reading this, chances are you bought your health insurance from a local duopoly. According to a 2014 study by the Government Accountability Office, the three largest insurers in any state had at least 80% of the total share in 37 states.[17] If you make your way to a hospital, it might disturb you to know that 90% of American metropolitan areas are highly concentrated due to hospital mergers.[18]

The average person knows they're being screwed and feels the system is rigged against them. We hope the following pages will show exactly why they might feel this way as they go about their daily lives.

Dozens of industries are so egregiously concentrated that it begs the question as to what the authorities are doing with their time. We don't know. We know for a fact that workers at the Securities and Exchange Commission spent their time watching porn while the economy crashed during the Financial Crisis.[19] We would hate to speculate about the Department of Justice and Federal Trade Commission.

First, let's look at outright monopolies. These often come from industries that appear to be competitive but are essentially local monopolies. Then we'll look at duopolies and then oligopolies. In order not to bore the reader, we have only touched on a few. There are dozens more. If you're not outraged by the time you get to the end of the chapter, you weren't reading carefully. Most industries have carved up the United States with the sole purpose of screwing the consumer.

Monopolies (and Local Monopolies)

Cable/High Speed Internet

Three companies control 65% of the nation's cable market but this figure is meaningless. At the local level, the companies face no real competition. This matters a great deal because cable is the only real option if you want to get high-speed internet (only 25% have fiber optic, and DSL phone lines are much slower).[20] In 2011, John Malone, chairman of Liberty Global, stated openly that when it comes to high-capacity data connections in the United States, "Cable's pretty much a monopoly now." He's right. Almost all of the United States has essentially been carved up geographically.

Computer Operating Systems

Microsoft has an over 90% market share in computer operating systems and has a similar control over office programs through Microsoft Office (we're typing this book in Word). Microsoft has always used its existing products to leverage its new ones. WordPerfect, Lotus, and others didn't have access to certain APIs (application calls) built into Windows that Microsoft didn't share with the rest of the industry. As Windows kept evolving from one version to the next, Microsoft always knew about new APIs long before other developers did. They used the deep integration of Microsoft Office with Windows to get rid of Lotus Notes and WordPerfect.[21]

Social Networks

Facebook has over 75% market share in all global social media, far surpassing any rivals like Twitter, or Pinterest.[22] It also has an almost 45% share of all display advertising online.[23] Mark Zuckerberg is the emperor of the private data of 2 billion people who have handed over all their personal information, political views, likes, and preferences.

Users should be very scared. When Zuckerberg created Facebook, he wrote on his Harvard email, "The Kirkland dormitory facebook is open on my desktop and some of these people have pretty horrendous facebook pics. I almost want to put some of these faces next to pictures of some farm animals and have people vote on which is the more attractive . . . Let the hacking begin."[24] And so Facebook was born. As Facebook was growing, he could not believe how stupid his users were in handing over all their personal information, "They trust me – dumb fucks."[25] We could not put it better ourselves.

Networks tend to be winner-takes-all organizations. Everyone wants to be on the network with the most users. What would the value of PayPal be if you were the only person on it? Zero. You need a buyer and a seller. With two people, the value would not be much. With 100, the possibilities get interesting. With a million people, it is hard to compete with PayPal. With a few billion people, the networks dwarf nation states and almost all religions.

Search

Google has an almost 90% market share in search advertising. Google's entire business model is self-reinforcing. The more people search, the better search becomes. The more people search, the more advertisers there are. The more advertisers there are, the more efficient ad auctions are. Barriers to entry are significant. Building a search engine is expensive and takes a long time. There have been no effective new market entrants in over a decade. Google has abused this market power to promote its own websites and its own search results, according to the European Union, and has been fined $2.7 billion.[26] Astonishingly, Google has been allowed to buy competitors like DoubleClick, and even has reduced competition.[27]

Google and Facebook essentially have a duopoly in online digital ads, with Facebook dominating display ads and Google dominating search ads, and they are capturing all of the growth in the industry at the expense of other players.[28]

Milk

The milk market in the United States appears fragmented, but most dairy farmers sell their milk to one local buyer that is a local monopsonist. If you're a dairy farmer, you often have no choice when it comes to selling your milk. Dean Foods is the dominant player with around 40% market share and has grown through a series of acquisitions.[29] The firm has had to pay millions of dollars in price fixing and monopoly lawsuits.[30] It has also been forced to pay a settlement to make a big case go away where it was alleged that Dean Foods was price-fixing with National Dairy Holdings and the Dairy Farmers of America. Together these three firms controlled 77% of the dairy production in the South East and agreed not to compete.[31]

Railroads

While railroads may appear to be an oligopoly with a few major players, they are in fact local and regional monopolies. The freight railroad industry in the United States is highly concentrated with a handful of firms dominating the market: BNSF Railway, which Warren Buffett owns, CSX Transportation, Norfolk Southern Railway, Union Pacific Railroad, and the smallest Kansas City Southern Railway.

About a dozen of the nation's railroads had passed through bankruptcy or government-sponsored reorganization in the 1970s, and much of the nation's freight rail infrastructure was in shambles when Congress passed the Staggers Rail Act of 1980. Railroads today move twice the ton-miles they did in 1980 and do it with far fewer resources of all types.[32] After the Staggers Act, the number of Class I railroads dramatically shrank from over 30 to just four. Broadly, deregulation was a success. However, once railroads came down to the final four, prices have risen 40% in real terms as competition has disappeared.[33]

The railroad industry looks like an oligopoly, but for many captive shippers it is actually a monopoly since they are serviced by only one railroad. For example, two-thirds of coal shipped by rail is captive to a single railroad.[34] Today there are two major duopolies for grain transportation – BNSF Railway and Union Pacific Railroad serve the Western United States, and CSX Transportation and Norfolk Southern serve the East (Figure 6.1).[35]

Seeds

Today, genetically modified seeds have taken over the market. Monsanto controls 80% of US corn seed and more than 90% of US soybeans.[36] Bayer, a German company, is proposing to buy Monsanto as we write this book. Monsanto's biggest rival internationally is the Swiss company Syngenta, which has just merged with China's state-owned ChemChina. At the same time, US chemicals giants Dow Chemical

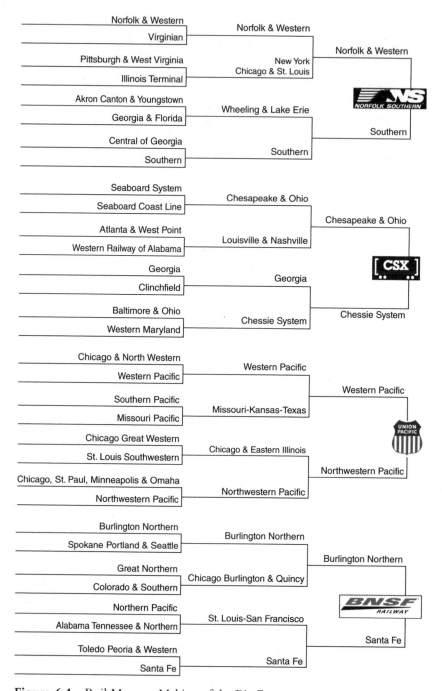

Figure 6.1 Rail Mergers: Making of the Big Four

SOURCE: Testimony of David Cleavinger, President, National Association of Wheat Growers, House Committee on Small Business, *Hearing to Review Rail Competition and Service*, May 1, 2008, p. 2.

Co. and DuPont merged and will spin off their agricultural operations. If all these deals close, three companies would control nearly 70% of the world's pesticide market and 80% of the US corn-seed market.[37] The collective power of a few companies over our entire food supply will be complete. Americans do not need to watch dystopian movies. In many ways, we already live in one.

Microprocessors

Intel dominates the market with around 80% market share, and AMD has hovered around 20%.[38] However, for much of the past two decades, Intel has had closer to 90% market share and has been a de facto monopolist. If there is one rule with monopolies it is that monopolists will monopolize. Intel has been forced to pay significant fines for abusing its market position. The European Commission found in 2009 that the company had offered rebates and incentives to computer makers to favor its products over those of a rival, Advanced Micro Devices.[39] This was after AMD has claimed that Intel engaged in unfair competition by offering rebates to Japanese PC manufacturers who agreed to eliminate or limit purchases of microprocessors made by AMD. In November 2009, Intel agreed to pay AMD $1.25 billion as part of a deal to settle all outstanding legal disputes between the two companies.[40]

Funeral Homes

The funeral industry appears highly fragmented, but generally in most towns and cities it is a local monopoly. Most people don't search further than 50 miles for a funeral home. In the anguish of losing a loved one, families aren't inclined to shop around; the opportunity for price gouging is ripe.

The 800-pound gorilla in the funeral industry is Service Corporation International (SCI). It operates over 2,000 funeral homes and cemeteries, and its market cap is over $7 billion. In 2013 the Federal Trade Commission allowed SCI to acquire its largest rival, Stewart Enterprises, despite howls of protest from consumers.

In 1960 when almost all funeral homes were small, independent businesses, funeral-related expenses averaged about $700 per person.

Today, they average more than \$8,000, and a casket alone can cost more than \$10,000.[41] Service Corporation funerals are 30–40% more expensive than independent funerals.[42] Many states have passed laws to protect funeral homes from competition, and Alabama even decided to prosecute monks for selling hand-made wooden caskets.[43] In America consumers are literally gouged from cradle to the grave, from dealing with hospitals as local monopolies when they're born, to depending on funeral homes that have no competition when they die.

Duopolies

Payment Systems

Mastercard and Visa control almost the entire market and are effectively a duopoly. American Express comes in third. The reason for such concentration is that behind the scenes on the merchant side, payments actually are an infrastructure monopoly. No matter what terminal or processor you use, your core infrastructure is still based on the "pipes" run by the duopoly MasterCard and Visa. Both companies operate a huge toll road on all credit card transactions in the United States, and this represents an invisible tax on commerce. They have been strong-arming merchants for years into paying onerous interchange fees. In 2012 Visa, MasterCard, and the nation's biggest banks agreed to pay \$7.3 billion to millions of merchants to end a seven-year dispute over credit card "swipe" fees.[44]

Beer

During an epic bout of Solitaire or porn at the Department of Justice, the great beer mergers slipped through the attention of antitrust authorities. Astonishingly, the US government has allowed the entire US beer market to be locked up by two companies. The US beer market is an effective duopoly with two players controlling over 90% of beer. Think of that every time you drink a cold one.

Recent moves have been like rearranging deck chairs on the *Titanic*, and competition has sunk to the bottom of the ocean. We have seen unprecedented consolidation in the beer industry in recent years. The first consolidation happened in 2008 when the Department of Justice approved the duopoly of a joint venture between Molson Coors and SABMiller creating MillerCoors and then a few months later the merger of Anheuser Busch and InBev. Overnight, about 90% of domestic beer production was in the hands of two companies. Then came the 2016 merger between SABMiller and AB InBev. At that stage SABMiller sold back its stake in MillerCoors, creating a new duopoly between Molson Coors and AB InBev. The deals were approved because the consumer would supposedly benefit, but the result was a 6% increase in beer prices.[45]

You might go to the supermarket or a bar and think you have choices, but you could not be more mistaken. Want an American beer like Budweiser? Prefer a craft brew instead like Keith's IPA or Blue Point? They own them too. Maybe a Hoegaarden or Leffe Blonde or maybe a German like Löwenbräu. Ditto. They're all owned by AB Inbev. They own 250 brands: Stella, Rolling Rock, Corona, Michelob, and so forth. You might as well just send them part of your paycheck whenever you order a beer.

Phone Operating Systems

Apple and Google have a duopoly where almost 99% of all global phones run Apple's iOS operating system or Google's Android system. Android takes around 80% and Apple takes the rest. However, Apple and Google don't just control your phone, they control the app stores that are billion-dollar marketplaces and tax them. As Frank Pasquale, a law professor and expert on technology notes, the tech giants "are no longer market participants. Rather, in their fields, they are market makers, able to exert regulatory control over the terms on which others can sell goods and services."[46] If they don't like your app, they can determine whether you can reach your customers via mobiles.

Online Advertising

Google and Facebook dominate the market, and each one has a monopoly in their own area. Each one has their niche. Last year, Google held 76% of the search ad market.[47] Google and Facebook are set to attract 84% of global spending on digital advertising, excluding China, in 2017.[48] In 2016 Facebook accounted for 78% of US social advertising expenditure.[49]

Kidney Dialysis

The US dialysis market is a duopoly after a series of mergers between DaVita and Fresenius. (Warren Buffett owned DaVita because he loves duopolies.) Approximately 490,000 Americans required dialysis treatment, and each company has an almost 30% market share. Much like the rest of the US healthcare industry, DaVita has screwed the government and patients. In 2014 and 2015 DaVita paid $895 million to settle whistleblower complaints that the company conspired to overcharge the US government.[50] In 2017 the company received subpoenas after being accused of steering poor dialysis patients to private insurers to inflate profits because DaVita was paid 10 times more through private insurance than Medicaid or Medicare.[51]

Glasses

Buying new glasses is extremely expensive, even though they are not expensive to make. The reason is that one company, Luxottica, completely dominates this industry. Luxottica controls 80% of the major brands in the $28 billion global eyeglasses industry.[52] They own LensCrafters, Sunglass Hut, Bright Eyes, Sunglass Icon, Cole National, which owned Pearle Vision, as well as the optical departments at Sears, Target, JC Penney, and Macy's. Luxottica also owns EyeMed Vision Care, the second-largest US vision benefits company. EyeMed steers people who need glasses to Luxottica retail outlets, angering rival frames and lens makers, according to industry sources.

In 2017 they proposed a merger with Essilor of France, which makes lenses, and the combined company will have a quarter of the global market, with Luxottica having a 14% market share and Essilor a 13% share. In the United States Luxottica has 40–50% of the US frame market while Essilor has about 40% of the US lens market. The combined companies will become the biggest US retail eyeglass sellers. Essilor is also No. 1 with Vision Source, a group of 3,300 optometric practices. This deal still has the risk of not being approved, but if it passes, it will further reduce the choice of consumers.[53]

Oligopolies

Credit Reporting Bureaus

Today, following many mergers, only three companies – Experian, Equifax, and Transunion – control the entire credit reporting market.[54]

It is not clear that these organizations are even necessary. Lenders could do their own work and access the underlying data and the Fair Isaac Corporation's (or FICO) credit-scoring formula can make the calculations. The power of these three companies is vast. They routinely commit millions of errors on these reports, harming innocent people, and it is difficult to fix your credit history if they make mistakes. Yet they screw consumers again and profit from these errors by charging customers for monitoring services and credit freezes.[55]

Most Americans were not very familiar with credit bureaus until hackers stole the Social Security numbers, birthdates, addresses, credit card and driver's license numbers of 143 million people from Equifax. Before the breach was made public, though, corporate executives found time to sell millions of dollars of stock to enrich themselves before the stock fell. After they announced the hack, the company allowed anyone to check a website where they could be screwed all over again by signing away their rights in order to find out if their information had been stolen.[56] It became a metaphor for how oligopolies treat consumers, screwing them at every step.

Tax Preparation

Taxpayers spend on average 13 hours preparing and filing their returns, and pay $200 for tax preparation services, which is about 10% of the average federal tax refund. H&R Block, TaxAct, and market leader Intuit, the maker of TurboTax, have a 90% market share when it comes to online filing of taxes. Intuit has a 65% share.[57] H&R Block tried to buy TaxAct, turning the oligopoly into a duopoly, but in a rare case of courage, the DOJ developed a spine and blocked the merger.[58]

This is a major industry that is totally unnecessary. In 1998, Congress passed the IRS Restructuring and Reform Act, which required the Treasury Department to develop, by 2008, procedures for the implementation of a "return-free" filing system that would calculate an individual's tax liability by using information already reported to the IRS each year. Yet the tax industry has successfully lobbied and killed any reform.[59] Remember this every year when you file your taxes.

Airlines

Congress deregulated the Airlines in 1978. Deregulation increased profitability, but the industry went through cycles of boom and bust, primarily due to oil prices and high fixed costs. As the *New York Times* put it, "An industry that is not naturally competitive went from being a regulated cartel, to a brief period of ruinous competition, and then to an unregulated cartel – with predictable effects on the quality of service."[60] Airlines devised frequent flier programs and "fortress hubs" to maximize their pricing power.

Carriers know to stay out of each other's hubs. Powerful airlines also buy up slots at airports to prevent new entrants, much like John D. Rockefeller bought up key swaths of land in Pennsylvania to block independent drillers from building pipelines that would enable them to escape Standard Oil's control over the railroads.[61]

Because we have little choice when it comes to airlines, they can nickel and dime us every time we fly. Extra charges will top $82 billion by the end of 2017, according to a study of global carriers by Idea-Works and CarTrawler. This is a 264% increase from the 2010 figure of $22.6 billion (Figure 6.2).[62]

Phone Companies

The US cell phone market is dominated by four firms: Verizon, Sprint, AT&T, and T-Mobile.[63] You get only a single device, one that has to be preapproved by the carrier, and it is almost always locked down. If you want to use your 3G connection as a modem for your laptop, be prepared to pay $30 extra a month. If you want to switch phones, you'll generally be forced to move to a more expensive plan, even if your

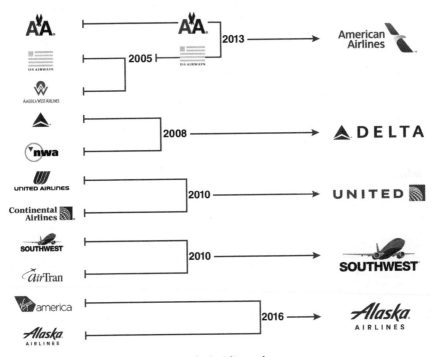

Figure 6.2   Airline Mergers in Today's Oligopoly

current plan offers unlimited data.[64] When it comes to your phone, you generally have few options.

Banks

A decade after the banking system blew up, the five biggest firms control 44% of the $15.3 trillion in assets held by US banks, according to data compiled by SNL Financial. Those banks – JPMorgan Chase, Bank of America, Citigroup, and USB – collectively held almost $7 trillion. Compare that to 1990 when the five biggest US banks held less than 10% of industry assets, but that has steadily marched higher ever since. Today, Wells Fargo controls basically the same percentage of assets that the entire top five did in 1990.

The Federal Reserve has established rules taking effective in 2015 that will prohibit mergers that result in a combined company's liabilities exceeding 10% of the industry's total. However, the damage is already done (Figure 6.3).

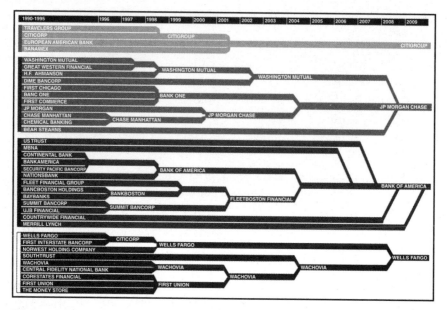

Figure 6.3 Banking Mergers in the United States

SOURCE: M. Martineau, K. Knox, and P. Combs "Learning, Lending, and Laws: Banks as Learning Organizations in a Regulated Environment," *American Journal of Industrial and Business Management* 4 (2014): 141–154.

Health Insurance

The American insurance and medical industries are closely tied together, and they're a lollapalooza of bad incentives, greedy middle-men, and powerful corporations dedicated to screwing consumers. And then there is also the more negative side. Given how opaque the industry is, outright fraud and illegality are rampant. As *The Economist* reported, in 2013 alone, federal prosecutors had over 2,000 health-fraud probes open at the end of 2013.[65] That is what happens when the entire system is designed to screw the consumer.

Earlier in this chapter we showed how the insurance market is divided up like the Mob Commission divided the United States up into territories. Insurers rarely step on each other's turf. The industry is extremely concentrated with no real competition. According to a 2014 study by the Government Accountability Office, the three largest insurers in any state had at least 80% of the total share in 37 states.[66]

Medical Care

The Affordable Care Act (ACA) has unleashed a merger frenzy, but there have been merger waves before the ACA. Nearly one half of the country's hospital markets are now considered highly concentrated.[67] There were 1,412 hospital mergers from 1998 to 2015. The number of hospitals is steadily falling due to the mergers from 6,100 hospitals in 1997 to 5,564 today, according to the American Hospital Association.[68]

Lots of mergers bring higher prices for everyone. Studies of hospital mergers in the 1990s found that prices in highly concentrated areas increased by 40% or more. More recent work found that price increases following hospital mergers in concentrated markets often exceed twenty percent.[69] The pace of hospital mergers has been accelerating. In 2015, 112 hospital mergers were announced nationwide; that's 18% more than a year earlier, and a 70% increase over 2010.[70] Hospitals have gone on a doctor-buying spree in recent years, in many areas acquiring so many independent practices they've created local monopolies of physicians. Hospitals owned 26% of physician practices in 2015, almost double from 2012.[71] It is only recently that the FTC has started getting its act together and challenging hospital mergers in West Virginia, Pennsylvania, and Illinois.[72] Unfortunately, the horse bolted the barn a long, long time ago.

Group Purchasing Organizations (GPOs)

You've probably never heard of GPOs before. While you've never heard of them, four of these groups – Vizient, Premier, HealthTrust, and Intaler – control purchasing of more than $300 billion annually of drugs, devices, and supplies for 5,000 health systems, and thousands more nonacute care facilities.[73] These secretive organizations are yet another example of how screwed up the US healthcare system is and how every step along the way is designed to rip off consumers.

The tale of GPOs is too farcical to be true, but it is. GPOs were created with the idea that if hospitals pooled their buying power, they could lower prices. Initially they might have helped, but over time they have raised prices and have become leeches on the medical system. Unbelievably, in 1986 Congress passed a bill exempting GPOs from the anti-kickback laws. Rather than collect dues from hospitals that were part of the purchasing group, GPOs could collect "fees," that is, kickbacks, from suppliers as a percentage of sales. This skewed the incentives to inflating costs, rather than reducing them. If you thought being exempted from kickback laws was bad, things became much worse in 1996, when the Justice Department and the Federal Trade Commission updated antitrust rules and granted the organizations protection from antitrust actions, except under "extraordinary circum-stances."[74] When it comes to screwing the consumer, you can always trust the government to help.

Pharmacy Benefit Managers (PBMs)

If you have drug coverage as part of your health plan, you probably carry a card with the name of a PBM on it. These organizations are gigantic middlemen, and as of 2016, PBMs manage pharmacy benefits for 266 million Americans.[75] Today's "big three" PBMs – Express Scripts, CVS Caremark, and OptumRx, a division of large insurer UnitedHealth Group – control between 75% and 80% of the market.

Americans pay the highest health-care prices in the world, includ-ing the highest for drugs, medical devices, and other health-care ser-vices and products. PBMs extract vast amounts of money out of the medical system, with almost no public knowledge of their role.

PBMs were formed in the late 1960s, and supposedly PBMs would help process paperwork and by aggregating orders, reduce costs. How-ever, the opposite has happened. Much like GPOs, they've been getting kickbacks from drug companies to put their drugs on the "formularies," or lists of what drugs are approved for payments. They've also been get-ting very fat by hiking prices and taking their cut as middlemen. Between 1987 and 2014, spending on drugs in the United States has increased 1,100%. The PBMs have been a major part of this problem. For example, Express Scripts' profit per prescription has risen 500% since 2003, and its earnings per adjusted claim went from $3.87 in 2012 to $5.16 in 2016.[76]

Drug Wholesalers

The Big Three drug wholesalers in the United States – Ameri-sourceBergen, McKesson, and Cardinal Health – handle more than 90% of the drugs in the United States, much of it due to dozens of acquisitions.[77] Four out of every five drugs sold in the nation pass through the hands of the Big Three.[78]

Power corrupts and absolute power corrupts absolutely. When you have as much power as the wholesalers do, you'll abuse it. Recently, the attorney generals of 45 states made sweeping allegations of price-fixing against McKesson, Cardinal Health, and AmerisourceBergen.[79]

The wholesalers have moved beyond inflating prices, and moved into the realm of criminality. Since 2000, almost 250,000 Americans have died from opioid overdoses.[80] The wholesalers have actively contributed to the deaths. In 2014, the DEA found a small pharmacy serving a town of 38,000 25 miles from Denver that was prescribing 2,000 pills a day. When the pharmacy ran up against limits for reporting suspicious orders, McKesson simply raised the limits, again and again. The DEA found that McKesson was supplying enormous numbers of pills to pharmacies that were in turn supplying criminal drug rings. When pharmacies reached limits, McKesson would simply raise those limits. This activity occurred at all 12 McKesson distribution centers that basically served the entire United States.[81] Due to Congressional lobbying, nothing has come of the DEA's work. McKesson has paid a $150 million fine, which is a rounding error for the company.

The prevalence of monopolies and oligopolies in US healthcare and insurance puts the United States in a different league than all other countries, and not in a good way. You could even say that the monopolies in healthcare and insurance are a vast conspiracy to gouge the consumer. America spends far more than all other developed countries with nothing to show for it in terms of improved life expectancy (see Figure 6.4).

Meat and Poultry

The US hog market has been rapidly concentrating. In 1979, there were 650,000 hog farms in the United States. By 2004, the number was down to 70,000, and today it is closer to 65,000. Today, the industry is much more of a franchising operation like McDonald's than the kind of farm your parents might have been familiar with. The "farmer" puts up the cash, and a company like Smithfield puts up the "brand." It provides

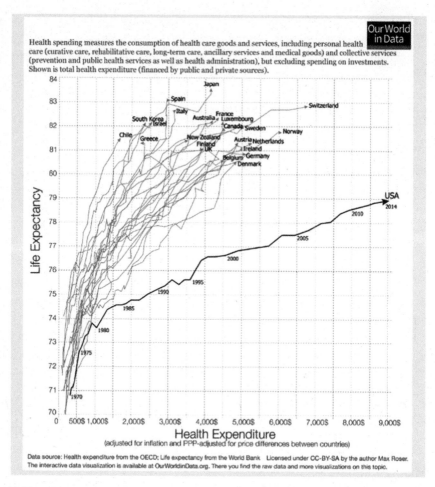

Figure 6.4   Life Expectancy versus Health Expenditure over Time (1970–2014)
Source: Our World in Data.

the "farmer" with the pigs, the feed, the drugs, and detailed instructions on how to assemble this into hogs ready to go on the hook.

Even if a hog farmer or any other farmer manages to escape dependence on such a monopolized system, he or she faces monopolies in almost all other directions (see Figure 6.5). The meat "brokerage" business – which puts meat into the Safeways and Krogers of the United States – is dominated by three big concerns. Cargill and ADM dominate the grain elevators and grain transport, both often with regional monopolies. Monsanto has a monopoly on seeds. Given the

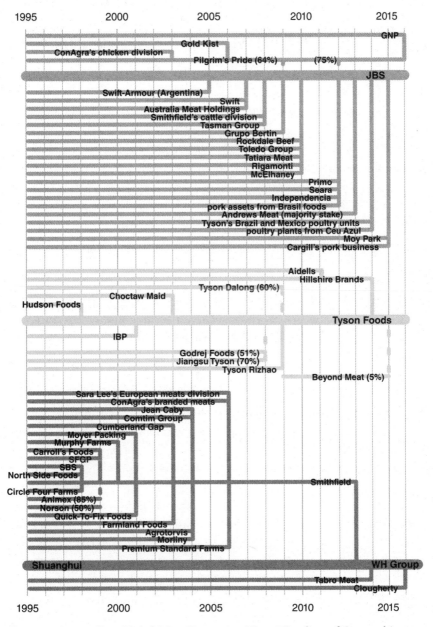

Figure 6.5 Leading Global Meat Processing Firms Timeline of Ownership Changes, 1996–2016

SOURCE: Courtesy of Philip Howard.

various oligopolies a farmer has to deal with, it is no surprise that farm incomes have collapsed and most farmers have gone broke.

Agriculture

The "Big Four" or the "ABCDs" – ADM, Bunge, Cargill, and Louis Dreyfus – control between 75% and 90% of the global grain trade, according to estimates. Figures are imprecise because two of the four companies are privately owned and do not give out market shares.[82] The companies use networks of silos, ports, ships, and farmer relationships to buy in surplus and sell to customers all over the world, ranging from Kellogg's for cereal to governments like Egypt.

Media

National mass media and news outlets are a prime example of an oligopoly, with 90% of US media outlets owned by six corporations: Walt Disney, Time Warner, CBS Corporation, Viacom, NBC Universal, and Rupert Murdoch's News Corporation. Almost all the media companies have a headquarters in New York, which encourages groupthink at worst, and at best is far removed from the daily lives of average Americans. Trust in the mass media peaked in 1976 at 72%, and has steadily decreased since the 1980s, reaching an all-time low of 32% in 2016. Over the past 40 years, media trust has shown a strong inverse correlation with corporate ownership, and industry concentration.

As if the media landscape were not concentrated enough, as we write this, Disney and Comcast are bidding for Fox's media assets, including its movie and TV studios for $52 billion. Why? Well, why not, given antitrust authorities are asleep on the job? Disney already owns Pixar, ABC, ESPN, Marvel, A&E, Lifetime, Touchstone, and many more. The merger will harm not only consumers, but also content creators. Fewer and fewer people will decide what TV shows or movies are made, and what will be produced. The Writers' Guild of America vehemently opposed the merger. In their words, "In the relentless drive to eliminate competition, big business has an insatiable appetite for consolidation. Disney and Fox have spent decades profiting from the oligopolistic control . . . often at the expense of the creators who power their television and film operations."[83]

Title Insurance

Title insurance is an almost completely unnecessary scam perpetrated on the public by an oligopoly with the help of regulators. The four major underwriters – Fidelity, First American, Stewart, and Old Republic – have around 87% market share.[84] They make billions of dollars a year for a product that is outdated, yet required by law.[85] Title companies appeared a century ago, to protect homebuyers from being swindled by fraudsters who didn't truly own the title of the properties they were selling. Today in the world of online title searches, title insurance is completely out of date.

In 2007, the Government Accountability Office warned that the price of title policies was inflated by lack of competition in the title-insurance market, as well as widespread illegal kickbacks paid by title agents to realtors, mortgage brokers, loan officers, and others who sent business their way.[86] The *New York Times* has called the industry a scam.[87] In all but a handful of states, laws bar insurance giants in other fields, such as AIG or State Farm, from offering title insurance and undercutting incumbents' prices.

Every time you go about your daily life, buying cereal, beer, meat, milk, medical care, soft drinks, a mobile phone, and every time you browse the internet, remember that you're sending part of your paycheck to an oligopolist or monopolist. It is a strong form of regressive taxation where the poor send money to the rich.

If you're wondering why income and wealth inequality is so high, it is because the wealthy own almost all the shares in the toll roads of American life. The top 10% of American households now own 84% of all stocks, according to a recent paper by NYU economist Edward N. Wolff. Today, while the average wealth of Americans has surpassed its previous peak in 2007, median wealth was still down by 34%. There is a reason for the disparity. While almost 95% of the very rich reported having significant stock holdings only 27% of the middle class did. The

poor have none and in fact have a negative net worth with significant debts.[88]

The wealthy own the toll roads, while the rest pay to use them.

Key Thoughts from the Chapter

- As Americans go about their daily lives, they have the illusion of choice, but they spend their days paying tolls to a few companies that lack any real competition.
- Dozens of industries are so egregiously concentrated that it begs the question as to what the antitrust authorities are doing with their time.
- If you're wondering why income and wealth inequality is so high, it is because the wealthy own almost all the shares in the toll roads of American life.

Chapter Seven

What Trusts and Nazis Had in Common

Just as we must convince the Germans on the political side of
the unsoundness of making an irrevocable grant of power to
a dictator . . . we must also convince them on the economic
side of the unsoundness of allowing a private enterprise to
acquire dictatorial power over any part of the economy."

—*A Year of Potsdam: German Economy Since Surrender*
United States War Department

Cornelius Vanderbilt was the embodiment of the nineteenth
century American monopolist. He came to represent the idea
of the corporation as a Goliath, yet he started out as a David.

In 1808 the State of New York created a monopoly on ferry
travel for a term of 20 years. Former New Jersey Governor Aaron
Ogden purchased the monopoly rights and entered into partnership
with Thomas Gibbons, a wealthy lawyer. When their partnership collapsed, the two began competing with each other between New York
and New Jersey. The partners ended up suing each other in the New
York court.

Gibbons decided to take his case against the monopoly all the way to the Supreme Court. As history would have it, Gibbons had hired a boatman in his mid-twenties named Cornelius Vanderbilt to pilot his ferries. Vanderbilt captained the boats, defying jail, cutting prices against the big monopolists.

The case *Gibbons v. Ogden* in 1824 became a legal landmark in favor of free trade. The Supreme Court decided that Congress's power to regulate interstate commerce included the power to regulate transportation. The New York waters were free for commerce after the decision, and one company could not have a legal monopoly between states. It was another win in the long American fight against monopolies. Gibbons and Vanderbilt could ply their trade freely.

Within a few years, Vanderbilt was operating his own ferries around the New York region and began branching out into railroads. He was ferociously competitive, and by the late 1840s, almost everyone who traveled between New York and Boston took a Vanderbilt boat or a Vanderbilt train. A few years later, he would come to dominate the New York to Chicago routes as well.

Vanderbilt's consolidation of the railways led to one of the greatest fortunes in American history. He bought the New York & Harlem and Hudson Line and then went after the New York Central Railroad, using any means he could. Vanderbilt often took over companies by manipulating their shares, cornering the market, and engaging in what today would be known as insider trading.

Vanderbilt could be ruthless. In a bitter winter when the Erie Canal was frozen over, he refused to accept Central's passengers or freight, cutting them off from connections. The Central Railroad had no choice but to surrender and sold Vanderbilt the controlling interest. Soon he controlled all rail traffic from New York City to Chicago. His power through the Central, as his company was known, was so vast that in the words of *The Atlantic*, he built "a kingdom within the republic."[1]

Businessmen learned not to cross him. On one occasion, when partners conspired to steal one of his properties, he informed them coldly via the press: "Gentlemen: You have undertaken to cheat me. I won't sue you, for the law is too slow. I'll ruin you."[2]

His biographer, T.J. Stiles, loved his subject but had to admit that Vanderbilt made worse "problems that would never be fully solved: a huge disparity in wealth between rich and poor; the concentration of great power in private hands; the fraud and self-serving deception that thrives in an unregulated environment."[3]

Commodore Vanderbilt said that only one man could dictate to him, and that was John D. Rockefeller.[4] When Vanderbilt died, he was the wealthiest man in America. Rockefeller himself would soon consolidate the oil industry, as Vanderbilt had the railroad industry. At the peak of Rockefeller's power, his company Standard Oil controlled 90% of the refined oil in the United States. In time, Rockefeller would surpass Vanderbilt's wealth.

Today when we hear the term "robber baron," we think of nineteenth century industrialists like Vanderbilt and Rockefeller, who dominated industries. Their names are often on universities such as Stanford, named after the railroad magnate Leland Stanford, or Vanderbilt University, named after the Commodore. Carnegie Mellon was named after Andrew Carnegie, who controlled US Steel.

While they are remembered as big philanthropists, these men had a dark side, as well. Many robber barons bribed elected officials to get what they wanted. Rockefeller and his partners often squeezed small competitors by colluding secretly with other firms and the railroads. He could trade on better terms than smaller merchants by receiving rebates up to 75% of the cost of shipping.[5] When other companies couldn't compete, he would offer to buy them out or run them out of business.

Small farmers, refiners, and businessmen resented the tycoons because they controlled the highways of industrial traffic, the means of production, and all avenues through which the stream of commodities passed from producer to the consumer. The large could squeeze the small.

As Vanderbilt had discovered after acquiring one railway, owning the arteries of commerce meant you could expand your reach ever further. The desire to exploit power at the time was endless. In the words of Matthew Josephson in his classic book *The Robber Barons*:

> So railroads would get the best of coalmine operators, then having conquered them, would exploit the industries which depended upon supplies of coal. Or syndicates owning grain elevators or slaughterhouses would enter into collusion with the railroads to exploit the producers of grain and of cattle;

oil-refiners would exploit those who drilled for petroleum, then would conquer or combine with their erstwhile opponents to exploit the underlying consumers altogether.[6]

As railroads moved west and the United States was stitched together with steel, the power of the robber barons grew. Much like today, owning one industry allows you to squeeze suppliers in another.

Farmers in the west resented the control of the railroads on wheat transportation. They could not reach their customers and had to pay whatever rates the railroad dictated. Farmers organized, and political candidates picked up their cause. What became known as the Progressive movement sprang up and called for regulation of businesses to ensure competition and free enterprise.

Congress responded to the political pressure from voters and enacted a law regulating railroads with the Interstate Commerce Act in 1887. They next turned to monopolies.

In 1890, Congress passed the Sherman Act, a groundbreaking law that has become the basis for antitrust laws around the world. The Sherman Act had two sections. Section 1 outlawed collective action forbidding "every contract, combination in the form of trust or otherwise, or conspiracy," that restrained inter-state or foreign trade. Section 2 barred individuals or companies from trying to monopolize commerce. The language was extremely broad, and there was not a formulaic way of applying its goals. This is still true today and is at the heart of our problems. Today, almost all countries have similar laws. The European Union bars "abuse of a dominant position," while in the United Kingdom antitrust law prohibits acts contrary to the "public interest."

The Sherman Act was praised as great political victory when it passed. Senator John Sherman, the sponsor of the Act, called it "a bill of rights, a charter of liberty." There were many reasons for passing the act. During the debates, some senators focused on restraining prices for farmers. Others disliked the coordination that came from trusts and agreements between producers and the railways, while others resented having one tycoon dominate an industry. What is undeniable is that the aims of the act were not purely economic. Restraining price gouging by large monopolists was one goal, but the political and social goals were of equal if not greater importance.

Avoiding the concentration of power in any sector was the driving force behind the Sherman Act. Senator Sherman saw the industrial tycoons as modern day economic monarchs. In the senate debates in 1890, he declared, "If we will not endure a king as a political power, we should not endure a king over the production, transportation, and sale of any of the necessities of life. If we would not submit to an emperor, we should not submit to an autocrat of trade, with power to prevent competition and to fix the price of any commodity."

The era of antitrust started with high hopes that were immediately disappointed. In fact, due to the reticence of the courts to implement the act, the next decade kicked off the first great merger wave in US history. The period in the 1890s to 1904 saw widespread, monopolistic mergers across all industries, and the US economy was transformed from one of many small companies to larger firms dominating entire industries.

Companies continued to operate as if nothing had changed. They were right. For over a decade after its passage, the Sherman Act was almost never applied against monopolies. Theodore Roosevelt later said in a speech, "When I took the office the antitrust law was practically a dead letter and the interstate commerce law in as poor a condition."[7]

There were several reasons for the lack of antitrust enforcement. Antitrust law was an entirely new legal area, and courts had difficulty interpreting the very broad language of the law. But perhaps the worst failing was that the Justice Department lacked the resources to oppose most mergers.[8] In the end, the first great mania only ended with the slowdown of the economy in 1903 and a stock market crash.

Much like today, the courts were a key problem in the implementation of the spirit of the Sherman Act. Challenges against trusts generally failed in courts because of a very narrow definition of what trade and commerce meant. For example, just five years after the Sherman Act was passed, in *United States v. E. C. Knight Co.*, the courts completely rejected a challenge to a sugar trust that controlled over 98% of sugar refining. Astonishingly, the Court held that manufacturing was not interstate commerce. This was essentially a green light for monopolists to corner markets entirely.[9]

The Sherman Act was a lofty ideal too far removed from the gritty reality of the 1890s. As G.K. Chesterton, the great defender of Christian orthodoxy, once wrote, "The Christian ideal has not been tried and found wanting. It has been found difficult; and left untried."

Astonishingly, while antitrust laws were intended to rein in monopolies, its main early use was against trade unions, which the courts considered to be illegal combinations. In *Loewe v. Lawlor*, the Supreme Court held that labor unions were not excluded from anti-trust regulation, and after that many union activities were viewed as being restraints of trade.[10]

The Sherman Act was broadly a failure in its early years, but there were a few big successes in the fight against trusts.

In 1911, the US Supreme Court broke up the Standard Oil Company and the American Tobacco Company in landmark rulings that brought down two of the most powerful industrial trusts. American Tobacco was broken up into four companies. Standard Oil was broken up into 33 companies. President Theodore Roosevelt called it "one of the most signal triumphs for decency which has been won in our country."[11]

Creating the trusts was easy, but breaking them up was a harder task. How do you unscramble an omelet? This is a thorny question that we will have to answer again today as we break up our modern monopolies.

The American Tobacco Company was founded in 1890 and merged over 200 companies to control the cigarette market. The company initially succeeded because it was much more efficient than its competitors. While other companies were rolling cigarettes by hand, James Buchanan Duke bought a machine that rolled them cheaply, with great precision. It offered cheaper cigarettes and gained happy customers – a capitalist success story. Yet the company truly gained scale by merging with its five major competitors to gain 90% market share. It was known as the "Tobacco Trust." Prices were low, but one company completely dominated the market. Not content to own all the cigarette companies, American Tobacco started vertically integrating, owning every step of the cigarette production, even managing its own tobacco leaf growing.

It was not an easy job to return to the premerger days, as these brands had already been fully integrated into one vast machine. Yet in the end American Tobacco was split off into an oligopoly of American Tobacco Company, R. J. Reynolds, Liggett & Myers, and Lorillard.

Standard Oil was a different beast. It, too, had grown through many mergers, but a large part of its size came from vertical integration. There is a vast chain of production between when oil comes out of the ground and when it is burned as gasoline in cars. Standard Oil controlled every step along the way. It would be easier to break up the various steps from oil exploration and production through refining to marketing and final sale. Each part of the company had a completely different function.

When Rockefeller heard the news, he was out on the golf course. "Buy Standard Oil," he advised his playing partner. It was an excellent stock tip. As we've learned earlier, bigger is not always better. The pieces of Standard Oil were worth far more apart than together. Rockefeller became far richer after Standard Oil was broken up than before.

Most other trusts escaped notice, and the issue of monopolies would not go away. Voters demanded greater action against the increasingly powerful tycoons who dominated American industry.

In 1912 Theodore Roosevelt ran for President as a progressive on a trust-busting platform arguing for the need to control corporate power and end monopolies. While Roosevelt made many political speeches about the dangers of monopoly, as president he brought few antitrust cases. Indeed, his entire Antitrust Division had only five lawyers, and he was facing the richest men ever in American history – Rockefeller, J.P. Morgan, and Carnegie.

Unlimited corporate power dominated the campaign. A month before the election, Democratic candidate Woodrow Wilson addressed supporters in Lincoln, Nebraska, in a speech that has become a classic in its call for economic and political freedom:

> Which do you want? Do you want to live in a town patronized by some great combination of capitalists who pick it out as a suitable place to plant their industry and draw you into

their employment? Or do you want to see your sons and your brothers and your husbands build up business for themselves under the protection of laws which make it impossible for any giant, however big, to crush them and put them out of business, so that they can match their wits here, in the midst of a free country with any captain of industry or merchant of finance . . . anywhere in the world?

Why, gentlemen, America is never going to submit to monopoly. America is never going to choose thralldom instead of freedom.[12]

Notice there is not a word of appeal to lower prices, consumer welfare, or efficiency.

After the election in 1914 Congress passed two laws to give teeth to the Sherman Act. The first was the Clayton Antitrust Act. The second was the creation of the Federal Trade Commission, providing the government with an agency that had the power to investigate violations of antitrust law and issue orders forbidding unfair competition practices.

Even after the Clayton Act and the creation of the FTC, there was little enforcement of antitrust laws. It was only a few years later in the 1920s that the United States experienced one of the largest merger waves in history. This second great merger wave coincided with the stock market boom of the 1920s. It should not be surprising that stock market booms accompany merger waves. Economists have now found that when stock prices go up, CEOs can use their inflated shares to build bigger empires.[13]

In many ways, it resembled today's landscape. Because of antitrust laws, companies didn't try to corner over 90% of any market, lest they be broken up like Standard Oil. Instead, they went for what has been called "merger for oligopoly" rather than outright monopoly. Industries organized themselves into a few leaders per industry that could tacitly collude, rather than one overall monopolist.[14]

Much like the first merger wave, the second ended with the Great Crash of 1929. It was not regulators who put an end to the merger frenzy,

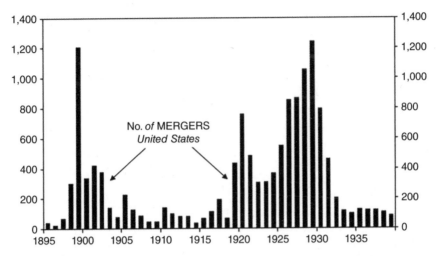

Figure 7.1 The First and Second Merger Waves (1890–1903, 1920–1930)
SOURCE: Courtesy of Taylor Mann.

but the collapse in markets. However, by the time the Great Depression came around, many industries had become oligopolies (Figure 7.1).

If the 1920s were a time of speculation and excess, the 1930s were a time of reform and reversal. After the epic merger wave, politics turned against oligopolies. Much like today, economists turned their attention to monopolies. Arthur Robert Burns's classic *The Decline of Competition* in 1936 looked at the emerging oligopolies. Yet antitrust enforcement was still lax.

When President Franklin D. Roosevelt took office in 1933, the Antitrust Division had 15 lawyers and was not that much bigger than it had been 20 years earlier. This changed decisively in March 1938, when President Roosevelt appointed Yale Law Professor Thurman Arnold to head the Antitrust Division. Arnold vastly expanded antitrust enforcement and began to develop it into a coherent policy.

Arnold vastly increased antitrust enforcement, expanding the antitrust division to 583 lawyers by 1942. The work of his office was monumental, and in his five years in office, he brought almost half of all the antitrust cases that had been brought in the first 53 years of the antitrust laws.[15] More broadly, Roosevelt's administration held hearings on economic concentration. Between 1938 and 1941, it produced 45 volumes on the monopoly problem.

The change in attitude to antitrust continued longer after Roosevelt, showing that the machinery of regulation and the courts move like an oil tanker. Truman, Roosevelt, Eisenhower, Nixon, Ford, and Carter all followed a much tougher line on antitrust.

After FDR, antimonopoly policies remained a cornerstone of American politics for decades, under both Democrats and Republicans. Harry Truman condemned monopolies in his 1950 State of the Union address when he urged a renewal of efforts to curb monopoly, lest the economy "fall under the control of a few dominant economic groups whose powers will be so great that they will be a challenge to democratic institutions." Dwight Eisenhower in his last State of the Union address attributed the strength of the US economy to his administration's "vigorous enforcement of antitrust laws over the last eight years and a continuing effort to . . . enhance our economic liberties."[16]

For decades, the Department of Justice was vigorous in opposing any combinations that created oligopolies. It did not matter whether presidents were Democrats or Republicans, the consensus had become that mergers between large competitors was not good.

The victory against concentration was total.

Carl Duisberg, the CEO of the German company Bayer, traveled to the United States in 1903, visiting chemical plants. He was not impressed with what he saw, but he would walk away with a far greater insight: the power of US trusts.

The factories in the United States were nothing like the German plants. They were poorly equipped, the managers were unprofessional in his view, and the workers appeared to have too many union rights. But even though the chemical plants failed to impress him, he was in awe of John D. Rockefeller's Standard Oil. Duisberg spent the rest of his trip back to Germany thinking about how he could apply the lessons from US trusts.

Six months later, he delivered a 58-page memo to his main competitors: Hoechst, BASF, and Agfa. His great vision was to emulate the

US trusts and completely coordinate production, pricing, and competition.[17] Through this memo he created the vast conglomerate of IG Farben.

Duisberg is one of the central figures in the history of German health care and the chemical industry.[18] After his first chemistry lesson when he was a child, he knew what he wanted to do with the rest of his life. "I want to be a chemist," the fourth-grader told his mother. That is exactly what he spent his life doing. When Duisberg died in March 1935, he was a celebrated figure in Germany and around the world. *The Times of London* summed up Carl Duisberg's achievements in its obituary: "His country loses a man who, all things considered, I believe may be regarded as the greatest industrialist the world has yet had."[19]

When Duisberg died, he had achieved his dream; IG Farben was a fierce corporate titan rivaling America's Standard Oil. According to Diarmuid Jeffreys, who wrote a book titled *Hell's Cartel* about the company, IG Farben was "a mighty corporate colossus, a vast, sprawling octopus . . . with tentacles reaching to every major country." It had immense economic power and was known as a "state within a state."[20] The company employed several Nobel laureates, and invented wonder drugs like aspirin. At its height, the company employed several hundred thousand workers.

Yet a little over a decade after Duisberg's death, his creation would be broken up, and all of IG Farben's top executives would be tried for war crimes at Nuremberg.

The indictment was filed on May 3, 1947, against the IG Farben executives. They were charged with the planning, preparation, initiation, and waging of wars of aggression and invasions of other countries, and committing war crimes and crimes against humanity. IG Farben had manufactured the Zyklon B gas that was used to commit genocide against millions of Jews.[21]

The defendants were cleared of most counts, but the tribunal concluded that 13 defendants could be held responsible for their crimes at Auschwitz.[22] They received prison terms ranging from one and one half years to eight years in prison, including time already served.[23]

IG Farben, though, had already ceased to exist.

On July 5, 1945, the US Army had dissolved it into three main companies: BASF, Bayer, and Hoechst. General Dwight D. Eisenhower ordered the breakup of the monopoly. A few months earlier, a report commissioned by Eisenhower concluded that the company had been crucial to the German war effort. Without its manufacturing capacity and scientific ingenuity, Hitler could never have achieved what he did.[24] It is difficult to understate the importance of concentrated industry to the Nazi rise.

Twenty days after seizing power, the Nazis enlisted 20 of the leading German industrialists in a secret rearmament program. Among them were Krupp von Bohlen of the Krupp armament works and representatives of IG Farben and other industrialists. Adolph Hitler and Hermann Göring explained their program to the industrialists, who helped raise three million Reichsmark for the Nazi party.[25]

Germany never had a mass antimonopoly movement like the United States. Leaders of industry and finance were convinced that "the cartel and trust represented the highest forms of economic organization."[26] Many in academia and government believed that cartels were a "higher" form of economic organization that replaced the brutal ethos of competition with a system of cooperation and cartels.[27]

The German industry's desire to restrict competition extended far beyond Germany's borders. In 1939 German industrialists signed the Düsseldorf Agreement with the Federation of British Industry. "It is essential to replace destructive competition wherever it may be found by constructive cooperation," they declared. Had World War II not started a few weeks later, perhaps the agreement might have succeeded in eliminating international competition from the chemical, coal, and steel industries.

Under the Nazis, trusts, combines, and cartels covered the whole economy. Monopolistic price fixing was the norm in most industries. Cartels set prices, limited production, and agreed to divide markets.[28]

Nazis had their reasons for preferring monopolies and cartels. The economist Arthur Schweitzer wrote about the power structure that existed between the Nazi party, large corporations and the generals in 1936. In his book *Big Business and the Third Reich* he wrote, within a few years of Hitler's accession, "middle-class socialism" had been defeated, collective bargaining had been banned, and unions had been outlawed. Unions were crushed as alternative centers of power. Large companies were favored over small businesses because, as Schweizer noted, "it is easier for the authorities to deal with a number of large companies than with innumerable small ones."[29] Consequently, the Nazi regime favored the process of monopolistic concentration, reinforcing the power of industrial magnates and weakening the position of the middle and working classes.[30]

The Nazis wanted almost all industries to become cartels. In 1936 they passed a cartel law to force industries to form cartels where none existed.[31] The consolidation of cartels under the Nazis was part of the general policy of reducing the number of private business entities with which the government must deal.[32]

The United States might not have focused on IG Farben if they had not done a secret deal with Standard Oil to carve up the world. In 1929, the "marriage," as IG Farben called it, was achieved. The agreement declared that Standard Oil would stay out of the chemical business, including synthetic rubber.[33] In exchange Farben would steer clear of the oil industry, except in its home market of Germany.[34]

It was only after the bombing of Pearl Harbor when the United States woke up and found itself hostage to large industrial trusts. When the United States was cut off from the world's largest supply of natural rubber, the country had to rely on its own resources. America did eventually manage to produce synthetic rubber, but only with great cost and delay.[35]

Given the rubber shortage in the United States, the Department of Justice began to piece together the oil giant's relations with IG Farben. Soon every facet of Standard Oil's partnership with the Germans was revealed. The result was that Standard Oil and six subsidiaries and many executives were indicted and convicted on charges of criminally conspiring with IG Farben to restrict trade in synthetic oil and rubber throughout the world.[36]

The Standard Oil case was the launching pad for planning what to do with monopolies and international cartels after the war. Breaking up global cartels became a central war aim for the United States.[37] This forgotten history is told in Wyatt Wells' book *Antitrust and the Formation of the Postwar World*, but it has been abandoned by most historians and Americans.

In a September 1944 letter, addressed to Secretary of State Cordell Hull but intended for public consumption, the president declared, "Unfortunately, a number of foreign countries, particularly in continental Europe, do not possess . . . a tradition against cartels. On the contrary, cartels have received encouragement from some of these governments. Especially is this true with respect to Germany. Moreover, cartels were utilized by the Nazis as government instrumentalities to achieve political ends . . ." The cartels, he judged, would have to be curbed.[38]

While the Allies planned for a postwar world, the Justice Department focused on German cartels. Wendell Berge, head of US antitrust, wrote a powerful book *Cartels: A Challenge to a Free World* in 1944 decrying the influence of IG Farben and other Germany industrial combinations. Berge wrote, "It seems abundantly clear that the United States can never have a foreign policy based upon principles of democracy, international good-will and free enterprise so long as international trade is dominated by private industrial governments."[39]

Lasting peace, however, required more than the elimination of international cartels, which represented only one aspect of German industry. The real problem was the concentrated power of German business, which also operated through domestic cartels and large firms like IG Farben that dominated entire sectors of the economy. The US Army concluded that large monopolies and cartels were key to Hitler's military rearmament. It is unlikely Hitler's war machine would have rearmed so quickly, if economic and political power were not so centralized. A lasting peace required a policy of "decartelization and deconcentration."

The Allied powers gathered after the war at Potsdam to agree on the reconstruction of Germany and the strategy toward Japan, which remained at war. They gathered to decide how to administer the defeated Nazi Germany, which had agreed to unconditional surrender nine weeks earlier. Even though most of the issues were of a military nature, the final treaty itself included a strong reference to Germany cartels and monopolies.

The Article 12 of the Potsdam Treaty of August 2, 1945, stated: "At the earliest practicable date, the German economy shall be decentralized for the purpose of eliminating the present excessive concentration of economic powers as exemplified in particular by cartels, syndicates, trusts, and other monopolistic arrangements."[40]

In April 1945 General Eisenhower had already issued an order to his soldiers, "You will prohibit all cartels or other private business arrangements and cartel-like organizations," continuing, "It is the policy of your government to effect a dispersion of the ownership and control of German industry."[41] When he later became president, he continued to place great importance on antitrust.

After the German surrender in 1945, the United States had three principles for its occupation of Germany: denazify, demilitarize, decartelize. United States policymakers looked for an economic cause that would explain why something so exceptionally horrible as the Third Reich could occur. Cartels appeared to be the answer. Germany was more extensively cartelized than any other country, and Americans thought it must have provided a unique contribution to the Third Reich.[42]

The United States even made economic aid conditional on reducing barriers to competition in industry. A $100 million loan to the European Coal and Steel Community was to be used "in a manner consistent with the operations of a common market free from national barriers and private obstruction to competition."[43]

The US Army fully intended to instill antitrust as a cornerstone for German reconstruction. Indeed, in 1946, the US Army wrote a report on the progress of the German economy and post-war reconstruction a year after Potsdam. In the long history of antitrust, there is probably not a clearer declaration of the philosophy or rationale for opposing the concentration of economic and political power. The entire passage is worth quoting in full:

> The Decartelization Branch . . . is making every effort to decentralize and decartelize all excessive concentrations of economic power in Germany. *In carrying out this program it will strive to convince the German people that economic democracy is a necessary basis for political democracy.* [Emphasis added]

> In some respects the reorganization of the Germany economy along democratic lines is more important than mere mechanical decentralization. The German people must be taught that

a democratic economy is the most favorable medium for the full development of an individual, and that in such a medium the material success of the individual will depend primarily on his own ability to satisfy the economic requirements of others. It is in such a system that an individual will exercise an alert and effective control over his government and will compel its officials to act for the general welfare rather than in the interest of some special class. Just as we must convince the Germans on the political side of the unsoundness of making an irrevocable grant of power to a dictator or an official authoritarian group, we must also convince them on the economic side of the unsoundness of allowing a private enterprise to acquire dictatorial power over any part of the economy.

The Branch will draw heavily on the experience acquired in the development of economic democracy in the United States and will endeavor to convince the German people that the development of free markets, the prevention of discrimination among businessmen and industrialists, the elimination of economic toll bridges, and the protection of the consumer, are cornerstones to the reconstitution of a new democratic German economy.[44]

The US War Department did not mention consumer welfare or efficiency. The political, rather than purely economic aims, of the United States could not be clearer.

The Americans helped pass the German Decartelizing law of 1947 to avoid the concentration of economic power. They believed that competition was the most appropriate instrument to provide a check to power and prevent the concentration of political and economic power in a rebuilt Germany.[45]

Not only did the United States influence Germany, American pressure led government after government to restrict cartels. Over the next two decades over 20 industrialized countries had enacted measures directed against cartels.

It would be unfair to attribute the entire emphasis on antitrust to Americans in Europe. The European concern with industrial concentration has its own roots in German intellectual thought, particularly ordoliberalism.

European ordoliberalism is an offshoot of classical liberalism that sprouted during the Nazi period, when dissidents gathered around Walter Eucken, an economist in Freiburg. They reacted against the planned economies of Nazi Germany and the Soviet Union. The Austrian economist Friedrich Hayek was a believer in free markets and railed against concentrations of power. He believed that inevitably once economic power was consolidated, the monopolies and cartels would become "governmental instrumentalities to achieve political ends."[46]

Ordoliberalism argued that capitalism requires a strong government to create a framework of rules that provide the order (ordo in Latin) that free markets need to function properly.

The Ordoliberals thought state intervention through antitrust was an essential ingredient to make markets function. Government had to maintain a level playing field to allow competition to flourish. To Ordoliberals any competitor disappearance can harm consumers because it reduces consumer choices and strengthens the dominant firm. Competition, in their view, was the best way to prevent excessive private or public concentrations of power. Competition was the best guarantee of political liberty, as well as providing a superior economic mechanism.

They counted among their members Ludwig Erhard, West Germany's first economics minister and second chancellor. Through his high position Ordoliberalism strongly influenced postwar economic policy. German competition policy was driven by a determination to prevent concentrations of power, whether it was political or economic, and prevent any return to dictatorship.[47] Germany, in turn, passed its antitrust vigor on to the European Union when it was created.[48]

The US military rebuilding Europe and Ordoliberal intellectuals agreed on one thing: economic freedom goes hand in hand with political freedom, and it is the government's role to avoid concentrations of economic power.[49]

Like any revolution, the movement against monopolies and oligopolies went too far at times. The two landmark cases that became rallying cries against antitrust regulation were the Brown Shoe case and Von's. Both stood out as poor decisions that then justified the counterrevolution that was to come.

In 1962 the US Supreme Court prohibited the merger between Brown, a shoe manufacturer, and G.R. Kinney Co, a retailer. The companies were minnows and had only 2.3% of the total shoe retail outlets. The entire industry was not consolidated, and with over 800 shoe manufacturers, the industry was as close to a model of textbook perfect competition as you could find.[50]

Four years later, the US Supreme Court also prohibited the merger between two Los Angeles grocery stores. Von's Grocery and Shopping Bag were the third- and sixth-largest, respectively, supermarket chains in the Los Angeles area and had a combined market share of less than 10%. The court disliked the move towards consolidation, even though there were thousands of grocery stores in Los Angeles. In Justice Stewart's dissent, he concluded that there were no substantial entry barriers into grocery retailing. He wrote: "The sole consistency that I can find is that in litigation under Section 7, the Government always wins."[51]

Given almost no mergers within the same industry were possible, the CEOs of the 1960s launched the third merger wave that built conglomerates with completely unrelated, far-flung business. Companies like ITT, Tenneco, and Gulf & Western bought completely disparate businesses. Gulf & Western, for example, had such a grab bag of companies that it owned Simon & Schuster, which published books; Paramount, which made movies; APS, which made car parts; and Consolidated Cigars. There was no reason a book publisher should have any connection to an auto parts maker, but the idea was that the unrelated divisions would counterbalance each other's up-and-down business cycles.

The conglomerates used their overvalued stock to buy small firms, and each acquisition made them bigger and more bloated. As conglomerates grew, Wall Street bid conglomerate stocks even higher, allowing for still more deals. Eventually, when markets declined, it became clear that putting a Hollywood studio with a cigar maker and an auto parts company was a really stupid idea.

Bigger was not better, yet CEOs longed for the days when they could buy their competitors. Yet they would not have to wait long.

The economist John Maynard Keynes once said, "Practical men who believe themselves to be quite exempt from any intellectual influence, are usually the slaves of some defunct economist." He should have included defunct law professors.

The state we find ourselves in today can be traced back to the economists of the Chicago School. We would not have highly concentrated industries if it were not for Robert Bork and the Chicago School.

Like all revolutions, an organized group of ideologues developed the ideas and spread them zealously. The Chicago School, led by Milton Friedman and George Stigler, was the vanguard of attack against antitrust laws. The great irony is that they decried monopolies and concentration of power, but in practice they created all the conditions necessary for them.

Friedman and Stigler started out as proponents of antitrust, but they came to dislike any form of state regulation. According to Friedman, "instead of antitrust laws promoting competition, it tended to do exactly the opposite . . . And so I have come to the conclusion that antitrust does far more harm than good and that we would be better off if we didn't have it at all, if we could get rid of it."[52] Indeed, the Chicago school spent decades trying to get rid of it.

Their antipathy to the state and belief in perfect markets was so total, that they advocated that the state should not regulate commerce under almost any circumstances. They assumed a perfect world where there were no barriers to entry. If no competitors existed, they assumed them into existence. All markets were theoretically "contestable" by yet-to-be-identified firms that did not exist. Even if a firm had 100% market share, it was not a problem, because new entrants would emerge in some distant future to change things. With the stroke of a pen and economic fairy tales, they dismissed decades of experience and practical judgment.

For Friedman and Stigler, monopolies were like dragons. They are dangerous and horrible creatures, but not real, and therefore not a concern. Anything that looks like a monopoly merely dominates industries because of greater "efficiency." Even if it appears to be a monopoly, you shouldn't be worried about it because it won't persist due to competition. Also, keeping a monopoly is costly and difficult, so therefore impossible.

For the Chicago School, if it looks like a monopoly, walks like a monopoly and quacks like a monopoly, it is probably just your imagination.

Not only did the Chicago School not believe in monopolies, they didn't believe in practically anything. Collusion between companies? It couldn't happen. There were too many incentives to cheat and avoid cooperation. Even if it did happen, it wouldn't last. Cartels were highly unstable anyway and would break apart. They could only work with very few players. And even if they did last, new firms would want to enter the market and compete, so it would be best to leave things alone. You say it is too hard for new firms to enter the market? Not so, barriers to entry are a myth. New competitors don't exist today? The market will conjure them into existence. Anything they disagreed with was eliminated at the level of theory by thought experiments or bold statements.

In case you think this is a caricatured view, we're simply turning their key views into plain English. Try reading "The Chicago School of Antitrust Analysis," written by fellow Chicago School lawyer and economist Richard Posner.[53] He was a highly articulate professor who eventually became a judge and was able to help put his views into practice.

After the global financial crisis of 2007–2008, Posner wrote *A Crisis of Capitalism*, in which he revealed that there might be flaws in his rational choice, laissez faire theories of capitalism. The damage of his views, though, was already done.

Economics is perhaps the only profession where facts don't matter and theory predominates. In the sciences there is a scientific method and experiments. In economics, men like Friedman, Bork, or Posner can make assertions based on pure theory.

Monopolies are not as rare as dragons, so Friedman and Stigler needed to explain them away. They gave lectures and engaged in a rewriting of history, attempting to deny any distasteful policies that had led to the rise of Standard Oil. At the same time, historians began to rehabilitate the older robber barons. Business historian Allan Nevins in his *John D. Rockefeller: The Heroic Age of American Enterprise* argued that while Rockefeller may have engaged in some illegal business practices, this should not undermine his creation of an organized industry.

This line of thinking began to infect other economists. At a speech to an antitrust conference in the early 1960s, a little-known economist named Alan Greenspan bemoaned the loss of monopolies. Echoing Schumpeter, he argued, "No one will ever know what new products, processes, machines, and cost-saving mergers failed to come into existence, killed by the Sherman Act before they were born. No one can ever compute the price that all of us have paid for that Act which, by inducing less effective use of capital, has kept our standard of living lower than would otherwise have been possible."[54] Never mind that when he said that the US economy was booming, productivity was high, investment was high, and wages were rising for the middle class.

You may remember Greenspan as the man who became chairman of the Federal Reserve and brought us "too big to fail" and the financial crisis. For him, big was beautiful, and markets always worked perfectly. After the crisis, he, too, wrote a book saying there may have been flaws in his views on the perfect functioning of markets. We'll never know how much damage he caused.

Yet if there is one man who is responsible for the revolution in antitrust thinking, it is Robert Bork. Most American baby boomers remember him for his highly charged Supreme Court nomination hearings in 1987. Other readers may remember him as the only man willing to fire Special Prosecutor Archibald Cox at President Richard Nixon's orders in the Saturday Night Massacre.

In the 1960s, Robert Bork published a series of highly influential articles that were hand grenades. His writing was brilliant, original, and entirely wrong. He attacked the state of antitrust policy in the United States. Most notably, he opened his article "The Goals of Antitrust Policy" with a phrase that became a classic: "The life of the antitrust law . . . is . . . neither logic nor experience but bad economics and worse jurisprudence."[55] To correct the misguided approach to antitrust laws, Bork argued that the one and only thing that should matter in antitrust is "consumer welfare." And the welfare of the consumer is really only measured by low prices. Everything else was demagoguery.

Under Bork, gone was any interest in keeping markets open to all new entrants, dispersing economic and political power, preventing collusion, and protecting small suppliers from predatory pricing. The only thing that mattered was price.

Bork argued that a very high market share by a particular company was probably due to economies of scale and greater efficiencies by large firms. In his view, antitrust policy only served to protect small firms from competition, keeping industries fragmented at the expense of cost efficiencies.[56]

For decades lawmakers protected Americans as businessmen, entrepreneurs, and workers, but Bork led an intellectual revolution that sacrificed citizens at the altar of efficiency and cheap goods. *The Antitrust Paradox* reduced people to mere consumers.

Bork's views were extraordinarily influential among economists and lawyers, and when President Ronald Reagan came to office, he appointed men to the Department of Justice who put the Chicago School's ideas into practice. Professor William F. Baxter headed the Antitrust Division, and he immediately changed all the Merger Guidelines. Former Assistant Attorney General for Antitrust J. Paul McGrath stated that the primary goal of the Division was "to reinforce the notion that the sole basis of antitrust enforcement should be that decisions should be based on economic efficiency notions"[57] Attorney General William French Smith declared that "bigness is not necessarily badness."[58] If former Commerce Secretary Baldridge had had his way, the Administration would have sought complete repeal of the anti-merger law.[59]

The change in antitrust regulation was nothing short of a revolution by unelected bureaucrats. The Department of Justice overrode the express will of Congress and changed the nature of antitrust without a new law, public debate, or vote. The inmates took over the asylum. The burden of proof in antitrust cases completely shifted, and the bar was set impossibly high to stop any merger.

The Reagan Department of Justice radically changed how we deal with monopolies. By only looking at the price of goods, to the exclusion of all other considerations, the government created a system that any company could game. As long as you promised a merger would keep prices low, you had a blank check to merge. No matter what your market share was, you could claim that markets were "contestable" and new entrants could compete. It took decisions about whether mergers should be allowed or not out of the regulators' hands and put it into economists. The entire debate on antitrust has been on Bork's terms ever since.

It is supremely ironic that Bork conjured "consumer welfare" from thin air. Outside of the area of antitrust, Bork is best remembered for the doctrine of original intent. Basically, this means that judges need to understand what the framers of the Constitution intended before deciding cases. Yet when we look at Bork's antitrust views, they are *contrary* to the original intent of Congress. They are ahistorical, and his ideological blindness is astounding. According to Bork, Congress only enacted the Clayton, Federal Trade Commission, and Sherman Acts in order to achieve lower prices and "consumer welfare." Any mergers that promised efficiency and lower prices should be allowed, regardless of the effects on consumers, producers, or competitors.

Many historians have studied the debates of the Sherman Act, Clayton Act, and the creation of the FTC. None – *absolutely none* – have found the words "consumer welfare" in the acts. Bork's views are so at odds with original intent, it is staggering that we now have to contend with decades of antitrust law built on Bork's views. Every single Merger Guideline since has only made it easier for firms to completely dominate their industry and gain greater market share through acquisitions.

The Antitrust Revolution under Reagan ushered in one of the biggest merger waves in US history. The 1980s unleashed all the pent-up desire to buy competitors from the previous decades. The stock market boomed as it had not since the 1920s, and not even the 1987 Crash could contain the enthusiasm for deals.

The Reagan presidency let loose the animal spirits in markets. Diana Vreeland, the stylish editor of *Harpers Bazaar* and friend of Nancy Reagan, said of the times, "Everything is power and money and how to use them both . . . We mustn't be afraid of snobbism and luxury."[60] Right around the time of the Crash, the film *Wall Street* captured the feeling of the era. In a memorable scene, Gordon Gekko wants to buy a company and rises to speak to the shareholders:

> The point is, ladies and gentleman, that greed – for lack of a better word – is good.

> Greed is right. Greed works. Greed clarifies, cuts through, and captures the essence of the evolutionary spirit.

> Greed, in all of its forms – greed for life, for money, for love, knowledge – has marked the upward surge of mankind.

> And greed – you mark my words – will not only save Teldar Paper, but that other malfunctioning corporation called the USA.

The bond market boomed, and Wall Street provided financing to corporate raiders who bought companies. Speculating on deals promised vast riches, and merger arbitrage became one of the most profitable trading strategies on Wall Street. It spawned a cottage industry of insider trading on merger tips. Men like Ivan Boesky were kings of Wall Street, until the SEC arrested him and others in insider trading rings.

Regulators no longer cared about mergers, and the only thing that brought the merger wave to an end was the recession of 1990–1991 and the stock market decline. Authorities did not lift a finger against almost any mergers (Figure 7.2).

Since Reagan, no president has enforced the spirit or the letter of the Sherman and Clayton Acts. It doesn't matter what party has controlled Congress or the presidency, there has been no difference in policy toward industrial concentration. In fact, the budgets for antitrust enforcement have steadily shrunk with each passing president. Both parties may appeal to voters on social issues, but when it comes to corporations, the parties are completely interchangeable. (If we dislike duopolies in markets, we should dislike the duopoly between Republicans and Democrats. The evidence of tacit collusion on the issue of antitrust is depressing.)

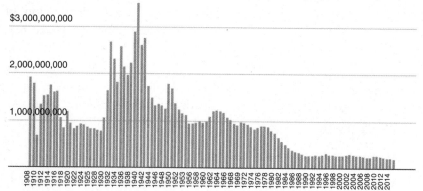

Declining Antitrust Enforcement

The chart shows how much money the Justice Department and the Federal Trade Commission have spent on antitrust enforcement, adjusted for inflation, GDP, and productivity. Figures are in 2009 dollars.

Figure 7.2   Antitrust Enforcement Budget
SOURCE: The Conversation, Ramsi Woodcock, Professor of Legal Studies, Georgia State University.

While merger waves were rare historically, we've seen a merger wave in *every single decade* since Reagan gutted antitrust. Like a ratchet effect, companies only get bigger and more bloated. The 1990s launched an even greater merger wave than the 1980s. While Reagan may have gutted the Sherman and Clayton acts, President Bill Clinton promoted mergers with even greater fervor. Under Clinton, the defense companies went from over 100 down to 5 major defense contractors, many with no competitors in their respective weapons systems (Figure 7.3).[61]

On social issues, George W. Bush and Barack Obama may have differed, and their rhetoric may have differed when it came to corporations, but there was absolutely no difference in policy when it came to monopolies and oligopolies. For example, the Bush administration allowed Whirlpool to acquire Maytag even though they controlled 75% of the market for many home appliances. The mobile phone market consolidated from six to four companies. The two biggest now control 70% of the entire US market.

Obama talked tough on big business and Wall Street, but he raised as much money from them as possible and was arguably even more pro-merger than Bush. His Department of Justice approved all the airline mergers, creating an oligopoly of four airlines while doing nothing to challenge the existence of monopoly fortress hubs. He allowed Google's major acquisitions that vertically integrated parts of the ad industry.

The situation became extreme under Obama. His head of antitrust enforcement said at a Congressional hearing, "There was mention of a merger wave. We kind of look at it as a tsunami." Yet despite the tsunami, the Antitrust Insitute published a report saying, "merger control in moderately concentrated sectors appears to have virtually ceased."[62] (see Figure 7.4).

The evidence confirms the death of antitrust. When surveying merger challenges, Grullon found that enforcement of Section 2 of the Sherman Act fell from an average of 15.7 cases per year from 1970–1999 to less than 3 over the period 2000–2014. *Incredibly, no cases were filed in 2014.*[63] The recent failure to enforce antitrust is horrifying, considering how industries have become more concentrated every year.

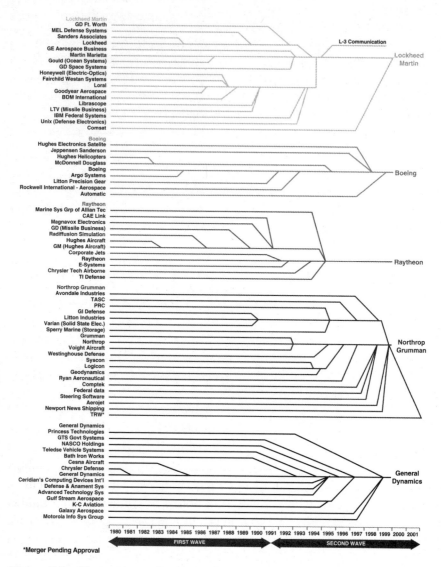

Figure 7.3 Twenty Years of Industry Consolidation
SOURCE: Final Report on the Future of the United States Aerospace Industry.

Every president has been more lax than his predecessor, and the
Department of Justice now essentially works to serve the interests of
companies. The premier economists in the field move back and forth

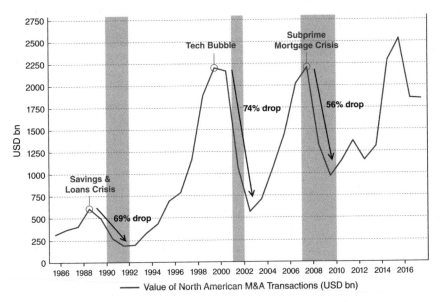

Figure 7.4   Three Mega Merger Waves in the Past Three Decades
SOURCE: Variant Perception.

from consulting firms to the top positions at the Justice Department and the Federal Trade Commission.

To give you a sense of how profitable it is to argue that mergers are good for society, consider the case of Dennis Carlton, an economist at the University of Chicago's Booth School of Business. He charges at least $1,350 an hour. In his long career, he has made over $100 million, while he has moved in and out of government.[64] He and dozens of other economists are paid millions of dollars to produce papers arguing that mergers have no harmful effects. Essentially, it is a form of highly paid intellectual prostitution. They have backed merger after merger where prices have increased and workers have been squeezed.

Merger enforcement is dead. At this stage the FTC is a highly paid employment agency for economists and lawyers as they move in and out of government. Professor Gustavo Grullon found that the proportion of merger deals that are completed is close to 90%.[65] (See Figure 7.5) The only reason deals do not go through, is generally poor market conditions, such as the financial crisis, or because companies get cold feet, not because of antitrust.

This figure depicts the proportion of completed M&A deals as a fraction of total deals for the period 1979–2014. The sample consists of all transactions on the Securities Data Corporation's (SDC) Mergers and Acquisition database that meet all of the following conditions: (i) percent of ownership by acquirer prior to event is less than 50%; (ii) percent of ownership by acquirer after event is more than 50%; (iii) both acquirer and target are identified as public firms (since we are interested in total market reaction, to both public and target firms); (iv) acquirer and target firm have different identifiers; (v) the transaction is completed: (vi) return data around the announcement date is available on CRSP; and (vii) offer price is available on SDC.

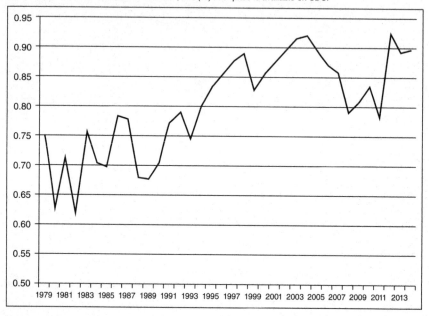

Figure 7.5   Proportion of Completed Mergers and Acquisitions
Source: Gustavo Grullon, Yelena Larkin, and Roni Michaely, "Are U.S. Industries Becoming More Concentrated?" (August 31, 2017). Available at SSRN: https://ssrn.com/abstract=2612047.

The process of merger reviews is a scene where lawyers and economists argue with future colleagues in a revolving door of money and influence peddling.

The Department of Justice has waved through many mergers in industries with as few as four and even three major competitors, creating highly concentrated oligopolies and even duopolies. According to Professor John Kwoka, "There has been a documented narrowing of focus among merger enforcement agencies. Data show that for industries where there are 5 or more firms remaining after a merger, challenges at that level have virtually disappeared, which gives rise to broad increases in concentration."[66] His comprehensive studies have shown that, even after review by the agencies, mergers have resulted in price increases.

Presidents could use the Department of Justice to block mergers, but so far there is little will to do so. On the rare occasions where the government has moved to block a merger, it has won. The Federal Communications Commission prevented Comcast from buying Time Warner Cable in 2015 and AT&T from acquiring T-Mobile in 2011. These were the only notable mergers Obama's Department of Justice blocked.

Enforcement is extremely rare and selective. A recent study found that firms connected to politicians that oversee antitrust regulators are more likely to receive favorable merger reviews.[67] Today, except in extreme circumstances, such as outright monopoly, courts are unlikely to block mergers because of an increase in market concentration.[68] The Supreme Court has now tilted so far the other way that it would prefer to allow too much concentration rather than too little. They made this clear in the *Verizon Communications Inc. v. Law Offices of Curtis V. Trinko LLP* decision. The Court stated its preference for minimizing incorrect mergers challenges rather than preventing excessive concentration. Not only have the lunatics taken over the Department of Justice, but they have completely taken over the courts.

Professor John Kwoka reviewed decades of merger cases and concluded that "recent merger control has not been sufficiently aggressive in challenging mergers." The overall effect has been "approval of significantly more mergers that prove to be anticompetitive."

The damage has already been done.

Max Planck once said, "Science progresses one funeral at a time." Any reform of antitrust laws will likely have to come when those influenced by Bork die away. Law does not proceed in a straight line toward greater fairness and justice. In 1962 Thomas Kuhn wrote *The Structure of Scientific Revolutions*. It has become one of the most cited books of all time. He rejected the idea that scientific progress was "the addition of new truths to the stock of old truths" and the correction of past errors. Kuhn saw science as shifting radically from one paradigm to another, going from normal to revolutionary phases.

Antitrust law has experienced its own revolutions with each passing generation. It is time to go back to the lessons the United States brought to Germany after World War II.

Key Thoughts from the Chapter

- Avoiding the concentration of power in any sector was the driving force behind the Sherman Act.
- After FDR, anti-monopoly policies remained a cornerstone of American politics for decades, under both Democrats and Republicans.
- The state we find ourselves in today can be traced back to the economists of the Chicago School.
- Since Reagan, no president has enforced the spirit or the letter of the Sherman and Clayton Acts.
- If we dislike duopolies in markets, we should dislike the duopoly between Republicans and Democrats. The evidence of tacit collusion on the issue of antitrust is depressing.

Chapter Eight

Regulation and Chemotherapy

I do not know whether the elderly woman died from cancer or its cure.

       —*Dr. Siddhartha Mukherjee, The Emperor of All Maladies*

Jeff Dirlam had gone to a local optometrist on a routine visit to get contact lenses, yet during the exam the doctor recognized strange copper-colored rings around his irises. He advised Jeff to see a doctor immediately. He was diagnosed with Wilson's disease at first, but a second opinion meant that he would stumble around in darkness searching for clues for the next two years.

Wilson's disease is an extremely rare disease that is a genetically inherited malfunction of the liver. It causes the liver to store excess amounts of copper until it becomes saturated and eventually, the accumulated copper starts to destroy the liver and also enters the eyes and the brain. Only 1 in 30,000 people worldwide has it. Symptoms include neurological damage, vomiting, weakness, fluid build-up in the abdomen, and fatal liver failure and death.

The second opinion had discarded Wilson's disease and Jeff went from doctor to doctor. While they flailed about trying to find the cause of the problems, Jeff's physical situation began to deteriorate rapidly. He started to drool and slur his speech, and his colleagues at work began mocking him. He had trouble swallowing and problems with walking. He lost his job due to absences.

Jeff moved back in with his father. His father took him from doctor to doctor. In passing, he mentioned Wilson's disease to a doctor. Finally, the original, correct diagnosis of Wilson's disease was established.

It was too late. Jeff had severe neurological symptoms for the nine months that he lived after the final diagnosis was made. He could no longer eat or swallow, walk, talk, or use his arms. In the last three months of his life, his mouth was frozen open the size of a baseball 24 hours per day, even when he slept.

He died on August 30, 2002, at the age of 25.[1]

If caught early and treated, Wilson's disease is not a problem. For years, the answer was pills of Syprine or Cuprimine. These cost around $1 a pill in most countries. The pills were always affordable for a good reason: they were not expensive to produce.

Merck, which had originally owned Cuprimine and Syprine, had kept the prices low. But in 2006, they sold the drugs to a small company called Aton, which began raising the prices. Then, in 2010, Aton sold the drugs to Valeant Pharmaceuticals. That is when prices soared.

Valeant raised the list price to around $300,000 for a year's supply in the United States, or $25,000 a month. There was no generic version of either drug, due to a backlog of drug approvals at the FDA.[2] Most patients cannot afford the drugs, and they will die like Jeff Dirlam if they do not get the drugs.

The playbook was the same whenever Valeant acquired a company. It fired almost all of the scientists, cut research and development, and started hiking prices. Valeant made over 34 acquisitions after CEO Michael Pearson took over.[3] Valeant raised prices on almost all of its drugs. In 2015, for example, Valeant raised the price of Glumetza, its diabetes drug, from $572 to $5,148. It hiked the price of Zegerid, a treatment for acid reflux and other stomach problems from $421 to $3,034.[4]

There were no patients that Valeant would not gouge. Valeant raised the price of a lead poisoning treatment by more than 2,700% in a single year.[5] The World Health Organization has included this drug on its list of essential medicines.[6] The original cost was $950 when Valeant acquired the drug as part of its purchase of Medicis in 2013.[7] After the price hikes, the US poison control centers now pay about $5,000 per gram for the drug, compared to $15 per gram paid by Canadians, a 33,300% difference.[8] The ingredients are not expensive. Formulations can be purchased at ridiculously low prices for laboratory use. If you order the ingredients from a lab catalogue, the cost is roughly $0.33 per gram.

Rival companies can't compete and offer cheaper alternatives due to regulation and the speed of bureaucracy. The Food and Drug Administration's policy makes it close to impossible to get around the high prices.[9] Compounding pharmacies are limited in what they can provide because by law, they can't make drugs that are essentially copies of commercially available drugs.[10]

"This is a drug that has long been a standard of care, and until recently it was widely accessible at an affordable price," said Dr. Michael Kosnett, an associate clinical professor in the division of clinical pharmacology and toxicology at the University of Colorado's School of Medicine. "There's no justification for the astronomical price increases by Valeant, which limit availability of the drug to children with life-threatening lead poisoning."[11]

While patients saw their bills and insurance co-pays go through the roof, Valeant's then–CEO Michael Pearson made $143.1 million in 2015.[12] He was eventually fired amid accusations of billing fraud, but most drug prices never came down.

It would be tempting to blame Valeant as a rogue player in the pharma industry, but a survey of 3,000 brand-name prescription drugs found that prices more than doubled for 60 and quadrupled for 20 since December 2014.[13] The average price increase for products made by specialty pharmaceutical companies was 16% in 2012, 29% in 2013, 22% in 2014, and 19% in 2015.[14]

Regular price increases by the largest drug companies have received less press coverage than Valeant's overpricing, but still prices are soaring. Sales for the top 10 drugs went up 44% to $54 billion in 2014, from 2011, even though prescriptions for the medications *fell* by 22%, according to IMS Health data.[15] Spending on drugs is increasing much faster than inflation, doctor visits, or the rates of hospitalization.

In the words of Scott Knoer, chief pharmacy officer at Cleveland Clinic, "Drug companies raise prices far exceeding inflation because they can," he said. "In the absence of regulation and without consumer awareness—since consumers don't generally see the price due to insurance—the sky is the limit."[16]

Blade Runner is now considered a classic of science fiction, but it bombed when it first came out. The film is now regarded as a masterpiece, with its striking billboard and bright neon advertisements dominating the skyline of Los Angeles in 2019. Ridely Scott, the director, had worked in advertising and knew the power of brands.

In the original version of *Blade Runner*, Harrison Ford navigates a dark, rainy future as giant advertisements glimmer in the background. Scott was tapping into a deep fear that corporations will control our lives. This theme has run through science fiction for generations. *Terminator* had Cyberdyne Systems, *Robocop* had Omni Consumer Products, and *Blade Runner* had the Tyrel corporation. As Ford's character goes about his grisly job of killing replicants in the movie, you can see ads for RCA, Bell Telephone, Coca-Cola, Atari, TsingTao, and Koss Corp. among others.

Many of the companies that appeared in the movie disappeared not long after it came out. Many either went bankrupt or were wiped out by competition after being featured in the film. Appearing in *Blade Runner* turned out to be a harbinger of oblivion. Critics even began to refer to "The Commercial Curse of *Blade Runner*."[17]

The companies Scott depicted were completely dominant, and some were even monopolies. Atari had an 80% share of the home videogame market in 1982. Within a year of the film, the company was dumping its unsold games into a New Mexico landfill after a massive videogame crash, and the company was split up and eventually went bankrupt. Headphone maker Koss Corp. filed for Chapter 11 reorganization in 1984. Food-processor pioneer Cuisinart filed for bankruptcy soon after. RCA Corp. disappeared. Bell Telephone was the big phone monopoly, and the government finally broke it up.

Not all brands have disappeared. Harrison Ford's character sipped Johnnie Walker in the 1982 version, and the brand has aged well like a good whiskey. Coca-Cola survived. TsingTao beer is still the most popular beer in China.

In the recent sequel *Blade Runner 2049* many corporations paid for ad placements: Johnnie Walker whisky, Sony, Peugeot, and Coca-Cola.[18] Time will tell which brands will survive.

What is certain is that there is no *Blade Runner* curse. The film shows that even though corporations make wonderful movie villains, they are often completely impotent when it comes to simply surviving. For example, only 67 of the firms in the Fortune 500 in 1955 were still in it by 2011.[19] Fewer than 10% of the 400 wealthiest Americans who appeared on the Forbes list in 1982, when *Blade Runner* was released, were still on the list in 2012.[20]

Capitalism is at its core dynamic, fluid, and daring. Young companies are always coming up with new, innovative products and challenging older brands. Atari's loss was Nintendo and Sega's gain. Koss's loss was Sony's gain. Innovation and the desire for riches drive start-ups. Historically, brands have risen and fallen with changing tastes and technology.

One thing that can make a monopoly permanent is government, because only government can prevent the sort of innovation and competition that undermines every corporate giant. As the Austrian economist Friedrich Hayek recognized, "Private monopoly is scarcely ever complete and even more rarely of long duration or able to disregard potential competition. But a state monopoly is always a state-protected monopoly—protected against both potential competition and effective criticism."[21]

When people think of monopolies, they think of Comcast owning the local cable system, Microsoft having over 90% market share in computer operating systems, Google having close to 90% market share in search. But monopolies in markets often come from patents and intellectual property. In the case of pharmaceuticals, they often cover an individual drug.

Patents give drug makers a period of time with no competition where they can be rewarded for their innovations. This encourages drug companies to invest in costly research and development that might take years to pay off. The logic behind patents is sound, and drug companies devote billions of dollars to find extraordinary cures that extend our lives.

Patents have a long history, and the countries that instituted patents were generally the most prosperous and advanced. The city-state of Venice, near the height of its riches, enacted the first patent law in 1474. The law gave a protection of 10 years to "any person in this city who makes any new and ingenious contrivance, not made heretofore in our dominion . . ."[22] Wherever Venetian traders went around Europe, they asked for similar terms to protect their innovations.

In England, letters patent had existed since the thirteenth century in which the monarch could grant economic privileges much like a monopoly on an invention or trade. England was far behind the continent in many technologies and industries, and patents encouraged artisans to move to England and bring new technologies with them.

Under Queen Elizabeth in the sixteenth century, grants of patent became so widespread that they began to cover almost any area the monarch chose. Grants of patent covered entire existing industries for such basics as: salt, iron, cards, drinking glasses, and so on. David Hume in his history of England says "These monopolists were so exorbitant in their demands that in some places they raised the price of salt from sixteen pence a bushel to fourteen or fifteen shillings."[23] As the practice grew more egregious, Englishmen protested and called upon Parliament for redress.

England passed a Statue of Monopolies in 1624, ending all monopolies, but allowed an exemption for patents to protect inventors' rights in their work for a limited period of 14 years. When the United States became an independent republic, Article I, Section 8 of the US Constitution empowered Congress to "promote the progress of science and useful arts, by securing for limited times to authors and inventors the exclusive right to their respective writings and discoveries," and Congress enacted the Patents Act in 1790. It provided a 10-year period for exploiting new inventions. Revolutionary France passed a patent law the next year.

Patents have a dark side – as the English discovered when patents were granted for the salt industry – and are often used as a tool to gouge customers. In the case of drug companies, patents allow them to rip off patients. The longer the drug lacks competition, the longer companies can charge extortionate prices.

The move to exploit intellectual property law in ways that are harmful to society started in the early1980s. It is not a coincidence that inequality started rising when effective monopoly grants were extended.

Until the 1970s, intellectual property was an unremarkable area of law. From 1900 to 1982, the number of patents increased by around 138%. After 1982, the number of patents extended increased by an astounding 416% by 2014.[24] Not only did the number of patents explode, the areas that patents cover has expanded in ways the Founding Fathers never intended. Over the past few decades, copyright protection has been extended to unpublished works, the requirement to register one's copyright has been dropped, and copyright terms have grown from 28 years to the life of the author plus 70 years.[25]

Almost half of the increase in patents is tied to low quality patents and software, which are likely not even enforceable under current law. Nevertheless, they stifle innovation and impose enormous costs on society.[26] See Figure 8.1.

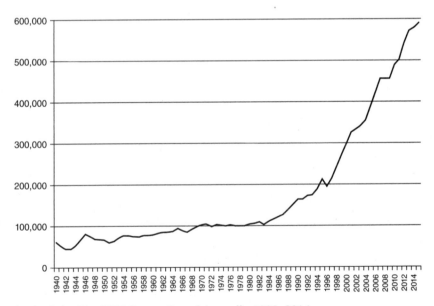

Figure 8.1   Total US Patents Issued Annually, 1900–2014

We can thank Walt Disney in part for the dire state of US patent laws. Even though Mickey Mouse is now almost 90 years old and should have long ago entered the public domain, every time Mickey's copyright is about to expire, Disney spends millions lobbying Congress for extensions. Over the years, the lifetime of a copyright has become longer and longer. The latest judgment occurred in 1998, when Congress passed the Copyright Term Extension Act, which increased ownership from 75 to 95 years. The Act became known as the Mickey Mouse Protection Act.

The supreme irony is that while Disney gets perpetual extensions in copyright legislation, more than 50 of its own films come from tales and stories in the public domain: *Alice in Wonderland*, *Aladdin*, *Frozen*, and *The Lion King*. If only Hans Christian Andersen could have lobbied Congress, he could also endlessly extend his copyright.[27]

Endless extensions of patents and copyrights impose a burden on society. In the words of Brink Lindsey and Steven M. Teles, who have written extensively on the effects of copyright law, "The current state of intellectual property law may be bad for economic growth overall, but it is highly effective at showering riches on a favored few." They note that "in the entertainment, software, and pharmaceutical industries, the monopoly power created by copyright and patent protections encourages industry concentration and inflates corporate profits. As a result, income and wealth are even more highly concentrated at the top than would otherwise be the case."

The cost to society from patents and copyrights abuse is impossible to understate.

The United States spends over $3 trillion annually on health care, and 10% is spent on drugs. The average American spends more than $1,000 a year on prescription medications, 40% more than the next highest country, Canada, and double what Germany spends.[28]

The broadest study done on the reasons for the increase in costs appeared in the Journal of the American Medical Association. "The most important factor that allows manufacturers to set high drug prices is market exclusivity, protected by monopoly rights awarded upon Food and Drug Administration approval and by patents."[29] Generic drugs are the main reason why drug prices have fallen, but access to them is generally delayed by numerous business and legal strategies.

The drug industry at one time was called the patent medicine industry, which is a much more accurate description of its true business. Much like Disney, when patents are about to expire, the pharmaceutical industry seeks endless extensions through "reformulation" of their drugs or minor modifications to the methods of delivery.[30] Reformulations involve changing the drug just enough to obtain additional patent protection, while keeping enough characteristics the same so that previous clinical testing results can be relied on to obtain FDA approval. There is no new innovation, no new discoveries, nor any greater benefit to patients, yet companies can continue to charge high prices.[31]

For example, the Orphan Drug Act of 1983 regulated the approval of drugs for rare diseases and gave drug companies even greater exclusivity. In theory, this would encourage drug companies to find cures for diseases that might not have a big market. The problem is that Orphan Drugs are not in fact rare. They make up 20% of all global prescription drug sales. Incredibly, 44% of new drugs approved in 2014 had orphan status, and due to pricing they are almost all the most expensive drugs.[32] Now pharmaceutical companies are taking advantage of these incentives to gouge patients, insurers, and the government.

Patents are a major hurdle to competition, but regulations and bureaucracy are an even greater barrier to entry for challengers who might want to bring new medicines to market. All new drugs are approved by the Food and Drug Administration to make sure that they work and are not harmful. This is an essential job. Generic drugs, though, are not new or unknown. They are identical to a brand-name drug that is off patent in dosage form, safety, strength, route of administration, quality, performance characteristics, and intended use. Yet the current FDA approval process for generics is extremely onerous.

Drug makers can charge what the market will bear because the magic of competition is missing. On average, a generic takes between three and four years to be approved. Given how long this process takes, it is no surprise the FDA's backlog of generic drugs stands at an all-time high. In 2014, nearly 1,600 applications for generic drugs were submitted to the FDA. By the end of the year, not a single drug was approved due to a backlog of over 4,700 generics from previous years. Fast-forward to July of 2016, and 4,036 generic drugs awaited FDA approval, yet very few were even processed.[33]

One bill that that has been submitted to Congress is the bipartisan Creating and Restoring Equal Access to Equivalent Samples Act (CREATES). The bill would remove roadblocks to the approval of lower-cost generic drugs.[34] However, it has almost no chance of passing due to pharmaceutical industry lobbying and has failed every time it has been introduced.[35] Both parties in Congress and the president have called for cheaper prescription drugs, but have done nothing about it. The reason is that the pharmaceutical industry spends hundreds of millions of dollars a year in lobbying to protect the status quo.[36]

There are simple solutions, but the drug industry will lobby to keep regulations. One immediate solution would be to allow drugs approved by European or Canadian regulators to be automatically approved for use in the United States. For new medicines, that may not a good idea, because it might lead pharmaceutical companies to shop for the easiest regulator to get around. But for old medicines such a system would make sense.[37]

When TEVA Pharmaceuticals announced it would bring out generic drugs for Syprine and Cuprimine, sufferers of Wilson disease were excited by the announcement. Little did they realize that in practice, the introduction of a generic merely means markets go from a monopoly to a duopoly. A bottle of 100 pills would cost $18,375.

Patients suffering from Wilson's disease were disappointed. "I had personally hoped for more of a discount," Mary Graper at the Wilson Disease Association said.[38]

TEVA is only one of many companies that gouge patients, but most companies have exorbitant pricing for generics. They do it because they can.

Emil Freireich is a legendary figure in cancer research who helped find the cure for childhood leukemia in the early 1960s. He's 88 and still working. Freireich says. "I'm too motivated to lounge around the house like a dried-up old geezer."

On his first day at the National Cancer Institute in 1955, Freireich was assigned a hopeless job that others had turned down. He was to care for children in the leukemia ward. At the time, leukemia was a horrendous disease. It was a life sentence; most children lived only eight weeks after diagnosis, and 99% were dead within a year.

"Children bled to death. The leukemia ward looked like a slaughterhouse. Blood covered the pillowcases, the floor, the walls . . . it was horrific."[39] Freireich thought that his patients' bleeding was caused by insufficient platelets that help the body form blood clots.

Once he had solved the bleeding problem, he turned toward finding a way to eliminate the cancer. First he administered two highly toxic drugs, then three. With each addition, children became seriously ill, and some were brought to the brink of death. The question was: How much harm could he inflict on the cancer without killing the children?

The world experts on blood cancers thought the humane approach was not to use any drugs at all. Freireich wanted to use four drugs, all at once. When the experimental regimen was approved, some of the junior doctors assisting on the ward refused to take part. They thought Freireich was insane. Nevertheless, Freireich pushed on as children continued to die. He tweaked protocols and continued to learn and make adjustments.[40]

Killing a cancer cell in a test tube is not particularly hard. There are an endless number of chemicals that can kill a cancer quickly and completely. The hard part is finding a selective poison that eliminates all cancer without killing the patient. This critical distinction is known as selective toxicity where the host takes on just enough poison to ensure that the host survives while the parasite dies. Selective toxicity is the basis of cancer chemotherapy, and the effectiveness of drugs for the treatment.

He noted the importance of using the right amount of toxicity. From an early patient, they discovered that "The doses we gave her were too high, and she almost died of toxicity . . . By not recognizing when to stop, the first patient got two extra days of chemotherapy and that was the thing that almost killed her."[41]

Freirich's findings became the basis for curing children's leukemia. Today, the cure rate is more than 90%, and it is estimated that Freireich's team has saved the lives of at least 100,000 children with childhood leukemia in the United States.[42]

The idea of selective toxicity has applications beyond fighting cancer. Big businesses regard startups like a horrible cancer attacking them, and they are willing to put up with anything painful that will kill startups.

This brings us to the very ugly truth about regulation: while big businesses often complain about regulation, the truth is that even though it is painful and annoying, they don't mind it and even favor it. Regulations that are burdensome enough to kill small companies but are not strong enough to kill large ones are, in fact, ideal.

Chemotherapy has the capacity to kill nearly every cell – tumor or normal. Chemotherapy kills through various mechanisms, but the most common way is to damage DNA, the genetic blueprint of the cell. The damaged cells do not die right away – only when they try to replicate with the damaged DNA do the cells die. Sometimes replicating with damaged DNA triggers cell suicide, called apoptosis. This is a highly regulated form of cell death. The other ways of cell death are variants of necrosis – cells undergo a catastrophic event triggered by the poison and can never recover. Usually this happens when the cell tries to divide and grow.

Normal tissues of the body can repair themselves more efficiently than tumors, whereas cancers grow uncontrollably. Their genetic programs have changed whereby the limited energetic resources of the cells are diverted to growth and not to basic housekeeping. One such important pathway is DNA repair. Our cells are bombarded with damage on a daily basis (from normal exposures to ultraviolet radiation and dietary carcinogens), and it is critical to be able to repair any damage. After chemotherapy, the tumor and surrounding normal tissues experience a tremendous amount of DNA damage.

Normal tissues can repair themselves because they have the resources and DNA blueprint to repair damage, even if it means slowing growth. Cancers, on the other hand, grow at the expense of any DNA repair. When they try to grow with damaged DNA, they then undergo cell death, through apoptosis or necrosis. Hence, the basis of selectivity of chemotherapy.

Bigger companies favor regulation because they are akin to the normal tissues where they are large enough to divert enough energy to repair and maintenance. Big companies are not in the exponential phases of growth like many startups are. (Interestingly, most cancers in normal tissues come from tissues that grow rapidly: intestines, skin, hair, bone marrow.) These smaller companies need to grow and do not have the resources to repair themselves from this excessive "DNA damage" from regulations and therefore are more susceptible.

Large companies welcome oppressive regulation, because they have teams of lawyers, compliance personnel, and lobbyists to take it on. Startups, on the other hand, don't have the budgets to hire an army of lawyers and compliance officers. These fixed costs are a bigger drag on the profitability of small firms than large firms. Excessive regulation selectively kills off the small startups attacking big corporations. It is a formidable barrier to entry for any industry.

Bruce Greenwald, a professor at Columbia Business School, has noted that one of the big impediments to competition comes from regulation. "In addition, there are also advantages emanating from governmental interventions, such as licenses, tariffs and quotas, authorized monopolies, patents, direct subsidies, and various kinds of regulation."[43]

Greenwald, in a way, was echoing Milton Friedman who argued that competition would generally kill monopolies, and in the cases where monopolies persist, it is because of the law. "In practice, monopoly frequently, if not generally, arises from government support," according to Milton Friedman.[44]

Today, small businesses are feeling the scorching heat from the chemotherapy of regulation. In 2016 a survey by the National Federation of Independent Business found that "unreasonable government regulations" are now the number 2 concern of small business, up from number 5 just four years ago. Only healthcare costs were a bigger worry.[45]

Dustin Chambers, Patrick A. McLaughlin, and Tyler Richards of George Mason University have found that a 10% increase in the regulatory restrictions on a particular industry is associated with a decrease of about 0.5% of the total number of small firms within that industry. Large firms are unaffected by changes to regulation.[46] The problem isn't a one-off increase in regulation, but the cumulative impact. These results are amplified after several years of regulatory growth. Regulations impact small businesses disproportionately, and at an increasing rate. The poor are the biggest losers, as small businesses are more common in low-income areas.

Regulations in the United States have exploded. The most comprehensive source of data on new regulations is the Federal Rules Database maintained by the Government Accountability Office

(GAO). Over the past 60 years, the population has grown by 98% while federal regulations increased by 850%.[47] In the past 22 years, federal agencies have published more than 88,000 final rules.[48] By 2016, regulations have expanded to 104.6 million words. The King James Bible comes in around 783,137 words.[49]

Congress passes laws, but much of the growth in regulations comes from departments. For every one law Congress passes, the federal government issues 16 new regulations. Between fiscal year 2005 and fiscal year 2014, federal agencies published 36,457 final rules. Meanwhile, formal appeals to the Small Business Administration's office for assistance in dealing with federal regulators rose 65% between 2012 and 2014. If you add in regulations from the more than 90,000 state and local governments, each layer of government makes it harder to operate a business.

You can't measure the burden of regulation solely by the number of pages. Not all pages in the Federal Register are devoted to rulemaking. To solve this problem, researchers at George Mason University put together a database called RegData. It analyzes the text of the Register and finds commands like "shall," "must," "may not," and "required" to estimate the extent of regulation in specific industries. The database confirms the growing weight of regulations.

Excessive regulation has the ability to choke off growth, create barriers to entry, and kill potential competitors. James Bailey and Diana Thomas of Creighton University analyzed the RegData database and data on firm births and employment from the Statistics of US Businesses (see Figure 8.2). They found that "the more-regulated industries experienced fewer new firm births and slower employment growth in the period 1998 to 2011. Large firms may even successfully lobby government officials to increase regulations to raise their smaller rivals' costs."[50] They also found that regulations inhibit employment growth in small firms more than in large firms.

The correlation between regulation and higher profits holds across countries. The economist Fabio Schiantarelli looked at OECD countries, and found that high barriers to entry contributed to higher markups. It also explains the loss of dynamism in the economy with fewer startups.[51] This is exactly what has been happening in the United States, as industries have concentrated.

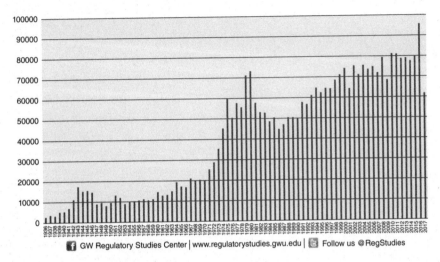

Figure 8.2   Pages in the Federal Register (1936–2015)
Source: GW Regulatory Studies Center.

If you doubt that regulations can effectively kill any new entrants, consider what has happened to the banking industry. According to the Federal Reserve between 2009 and 2013, only seven new banks were formed.[52]

The main reason for almost no new competition is extensive new regulations. A study by the Manhattan Institute concluded that the Dodd–Frank Act has created a protected class of financial firms with assets above $50 billion. The Act did nothing to break up America's largest banks or end the status of banks that are too big to fail. What it has done is to discourage new competition.[53]

Just as Freireich discovered, Dodd Frank is selectively toxic; choking off smaller banks. That's why carefully selecting drugs and calibrating the dose is essential in cancer treatment, but it is not even considered when it comes to regulation.

For the past 15 years, compared to big banks, community banks and credit unions have had lower loss rates across nearly every category of individual and commercial loan. While credit unions and small and mid-sized banks account for only 24 percent of all banking assets, they supply 60% of lending for small businesses.[54]

The disappearance of small banks has hit their customers hard. Even industries with almost no economies of scale have concentrated. As small banks close or are acquired, small businesses that depend on their lending are also disappearing. According to the Federal Reserve Bank of Atlanta, in 2005 the top 10 home construction firms had only 25% market share. However, after the recession, when lending to small builders dried up, the market share of big builders rose in regions where small banks shut down.

The Dodd–Frank Act has been called the 2010 Full Employment Act for Lawyers, Accountants, and Consultants.[55] For large banks that already had armies of compliance workers, the act was burdensome, but not lethal. For small banks, the Act was an insurmountable barrier to entry.

Jamie Dimon, the CEO of JP Morgan, has said that Dodd–Frank creates a "moat" around the big banks.[56] In 2015 at an investor conference, Lloyd Blankfein, then CEO of Goldman Sachs, explained how higher regulatory costs are killing competition. "More intense regulatory and technology requirements have raised the barriers to entry higher than at any other time in modern history," said Mr. Blankfein. "This is an expensive business to be in, if you don't have the market share in scale."[57]

Big banks have never had it so good. The CEOs of the big banks are laughing. "You guys thought I was kidding when a few years ago I said you can have a golden age of banking," Jamie Dimon, chief executive of JPMorgan Chase, said in June 2018. "I mean, you're going to have a golden age of banking. You have a golden age of banking."[58]

It should be no surprise that a Goldman Sachs lobbyist was quoted by Politico saying in April 2010: "We are not against regulation. We're for regulation. We partner with regulators."[59]

A decade after rating toxic subprime loans as AAA and helping cause the worst financial crisis since the Great Depression, Moody's and Standard & Poor's still completely dominate the ratings market.

The two ratings agencies control 80% of the bond ratings market in the United States and 93% of the market in Europe. They aren't on top because they're the best. During the financial crisis, they hid subprime junk within AAA-rated bonds, yet it did not matter. They did not go out of business, and there have been no new entrants since the financial crisis, despite the dire need for new ratings agencies.

Regulation is the barrier to entry. In 1975 the Securities and Exchange Commission created a protected class of ratings agencies known as the Nationally Recognized Statistical Rating Organization (NRSRO). The US government created a duopoly with the stroke of a pen. Ever since, the two big ratings agencies have had a legal and bureaucratic fence surrounding their business. This fence was made even higher because regulators use their ratings as a primary source for measuring risk.

Bond issuers are forced to pay for ratings if they want to have a rating on their bonds. Likewise, issuers need the ratings, because most investment firms need an NRSRO rating on their holdings. Any municipal bond that is issued in the US needs to be rated by the two players by law. That means that struggling counties often end up paying very high fees to this cozy duopoly for ratings. This often has meant firing teachers and closing schools in order to send money to Moody's and S&P.[60]

A government granted barrier to entry creates a fabulous business. Writing a ratings report requires almost no investment or capital, yet anyone issuing bonds has to pay the ratings agencies. It is the perfect toll road that exists only because of regulation. They have enormous pricing power and are able to increase fees at a faster rate than inflation. Moody's has averaged a stratospheric 77% return on invested capital (ROIC) over the past three years, while S&P has had an even higher return of 84%, versus 11% ROIC for a company like Walmart or 12% for Tiffany. Even a monopolist like Google has only a 24% return on invested capital.

"It's easier to raise a militia with armed assault rifles in Michigan than it is to become an NRSRO (Nationally Recognized Statistical Rating Organization)," said Glenn Reynolds, CEO of credit research firm CreditSights.

Moody's and S&P defend the regulatory obstructions to competition by saying they ensure the quality of rating agencies. They have also spent millions of dollars over the past decade lobbying to keep the regulatory moat around their business. It is difficult to see how they can justify their existence. Once the SEC grants the NRSRO designation, it does not maintain any form of ongoing oversight or quality control. The rating title is merely a government granted license to print money.

Other companies that rate debt have done a better job on many occasions, yet they find it next to impossible to compete. A new ratings agency has to rate products for at least three years before it can apply. Even then, the vetting process takes much longer. Egan-Jones, the latest NRSRO, was admitted in 2007, nine years after applying.

The government should have no role dictating who is a reliable ratings agency or not, and regulation governing ratings agencies is completely unnecessary. Lawrence White, a professor at New York University's Stern School of Business, has noted that over 80% of investors in bonds are large institutions like investment banks or mutual funds which have extensive research capabilities of their own. They have a reputation for knowing who can be trusted and who cannot. "This makes more competition an unmitigated good," he says.[61]

Even though many critics have called for ending the NRSRO rating, the regulatory stamp of approval still protects the business of S&P and Moody's. Even a decade after the financial crisis, bond issuers are still obligated to pay the two for ratings.

The obvious solution is to get the government out of regulating ratings, and encourage competition among many ratings agencies. The response so far has been to create more regulation, which further entrenches the S&P and Moody's duopoly. When Dodd-Frank was passed, it put in place various measures to improve internal controls and rating accuracy. The Act further entrenches the dominance of the ratings agencies with rule writing by the SEC instead of healthy competition in the marketplace.[62]

Many people have heard of the Pentagon famously spending $435 apiece for hammers, due to the government's odd accounting practices.[63] Today, though, the Pentagon is being gouged far more than that.

TransDigm is the Valeant of the aerospace business. It follows the same playbook and has acquired over 30 businesses in the past 10 years.[64] Every time it buys a company, it raises prices. For example, it bought a company that makes motor rotors from GE in 2013 and immediately raised the rotor's price from $654 to $5,474. When it bought Harco, the price of cable assemblies jumped from $1,737 to $7,863.

Like Valeant, after TransDigm acquires a company, it fires staff, cuts spending on research and development, and hikes prices to whatever the market will bear. Morale inside the company plummets, with almost all job reviews being negative on Glassdoor, a job site. In an online review, employees warn others about the toxic culture. "Since we were acquired, Stress is high, Moral is low. 25% of the work force terminated and probably more to come. If your company is unfortunate to get acquired by TransDigm it will be sucked dry. No one is safe."[65]

TransDigm is wildly profitable. Its operating margins are 40%, which is extraordinarily high for a business that makes relatively cheap parts. By comparison, even an iconic company with pricing power like Microsoft has 25% operating margins and Apple has 27% margins.

You're probably wondering: How does TransDigm get away with no competition and such high margins? Again, the answer is regulation.

TransDigm supplies plane makers such as Boeing or Airbus with parts that go directly onto new planes.[66] Aerospace manufacturing is a very regulated industry. The Federal Aviation Administration has to approve every single part on an airplane. Due to the time and cost required for FAA approval, an airplane manufacturer will generally choose only one supplier for any given part. Based on their latest quarterly reports, roughly 90% of the company's products are sole-sourced, and have a legal monopoly status. Because the parts are required for aircraft to fly, TransDigm has complete pricing power and can get away with price gouging.

The FAA, like the FDA, has an incentive to make the approval process extremely onerous, because the career risk is high if a plane crashes or a drug kills people. While safety is a laudable goal, regulations are a formidable barrier to entry for any companies that might want to offer cheaper drugs or airplane panels.

TransDigm is very aware of regulation and goes to great lengths to get around it when it sells parts to the Department of Defense. Short sellers have accused TransDigm of illegal activity, noting that 12 of its subsidiaries failed to report their common ownership on federal forms under penalty of perjury to get around federal procurement cost controls.[67] The company would host quarterly meetings where they taught dozens of techniques to deny procurement officers' requests for information.[68]

As TransDigm's tactics came to light, Representative Ro Khanna, a US representative for California's 17th congressional district, requested an investigation into the company. In a letter sent to US Department of Defense's Acting Inspector General Glenn Fine, Khanna said TransDigm could be involved in "potential waste, fraud, and abuse in the defense industrial base."

Much like Valeant, the CEO of TransDigm was one of America's best-paid executives. In the past five years alone, he took home $278 million. At Boeing, a company 30 times the size, CEO pay was less than half that.[69]

TransDigm, like Valeant, lives and dies by regulation. It should be no wonder that Nick Howley, the CEO, and his wife have given more than $126,000 to political candidates since 2008. Half of that amount, $63,000, was given to seven current members of Congress who have been involved with crafting the defense budget. Unsurprisingly, they sit on appropriations, budget, or armed services committees.[70]

How do Valeant, Moody's, TransDigm, and so many other companies keep the laws working in their favor, preventing any competition? The answer is simple: they spend a lot of money on lobbying.

Lobbying is a critical part of business strategy for most monopolies and oligopolies in the United States. They know that helpful laws and regulations can kill startups, shield them from competition, and fatten their bottom line.

A comprehensive study of six thousand publicly traded firms' reported lobbying from 1999 to 2006 showed that corporate lobbying is directly related to firm size. They found that "Lobbying firms are larger, have fewer investment opportunities, and are in more concentrated industries."[71]

Lobbying and political campaign spending can result in favorable regulatory changes, and several studies find the returns to these investments are spectacular. For example, one study finds that for each dollar spent lobbying for a tax break, firms received returns in excess of $220.[72] That is a return of 22,000%.

With returns like these, it is no wonder that spending on lobbying has exploded. Over the past 15 years, political campaign spending by companies has increased by a factor of 30, while the Regdata index of regulation has increased by nearly 50% for public firms.

To give you a sense of the scale of lobbying, in 2017, drug makers paid for 882 lobbyists and spent more than $171.5 million, in an effort to oppose lower prescription drug prices.[73] The lobbying arm of the drug sector, the Pharmaceutical Research and Manufacturers of America, spent about $10 million in the first quarter of the year on lobbying, including its attempt to slow the approval of generic drugs.[74]

Lobbying's astronomical returns are reflected in the stock market. Over 10 years ago, the consulting firm Strategas created an index to see whether lobbying would provide superior stock market returns. They found that investing in a portfolio of companies that spend the most on lobbying and influencing regulators would consistently beat the market. Companies that lobby can distort the rules of the game in their favor. Currying favor with legislators and regulators pays off spectacularly. Over the past 10 years, the Strategas Lobbying Portfolio beat the Standard & Poor's 500 by five percentage points *every year*.

"Washington, DC, is a factor not accounted for by investors, but should be because an increasing portion of earnings is decided in the capitol," according to Daniel Clifton, the head of policy research for Strategas (Figure 8.3).[75]

It is a very cozy relationship that benefits Washington, DC, as well. Six of the top 10 wealthiest counties in America based on median income are in and around the Washington, DC area.[76]

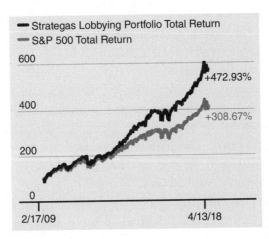

Figure 8.3 Companies That Lobby Extensively Have Higher Returns
SOURCE: Barron's.

James Bessen of the Boston University School of Law has used RegData to see if regulation was tied to higher profit margins. He found that since 2000, political activity and regulation account for most of the rise in valuations and profits. In the past, the returns came from investments in machinery and research and development, especially during the 1990s.[77] That spending improved company products, created new technology, and drove the real economy. Today most of the rise in profitability is from rent seeking and influence peddling.

The correlation between lobbying, regulation, and profits is concentrated in a small number of politically influential industries. Bessen's research found that most of the effect is accounted for by a handful of industries: pharmaceuticals/ chemicals, petroleum refining, transportation equipment/defense, utilities, and communications. When political power is concentrated in a small group of companies, these can distort the distribution of wealth for the whole economy.[78]

Not all industries are highly regulated, and that explains why some industries are concentrated and others aren't. There is a reason why the beer market in the United States is a duopoly and the restaurant industry is highly fragmented. AB InBev and Molson Coors control 90% of the beer market, but it is inconceivable for McDonald's and Burger King to control the restaurant industry. The reason is that the alcohol industry is one of the most highly regulated industries in the United States. Despite an explosion of new craft breweries, it is still difficult to get distribution of alcohol across all states and counties, given the complex patchwork of state and county regulations. Large alcohol companies benefit from extensive barriers to distribution that severely limit the growth of smaller players.

Lobbying creates a perverse feedback loop. The more distorted the economy becomes, the greater the incentive companies have to reinvest those profits in lobbying. As Brink Lindsey and Steven Teles describe in their book, *The Captured Economy: How the Powerful Enrich Themselves, Slow Down Growth, and Increase Inequality*, "Stunted competition is especially problematic, as wealth derived from distorted markets is recycled into influence over government. Incumbents can choose to invest in protecting themselves from competition rather than inventing new products and production methods or improving existing ones."[79]

The greater the incentive to lobby, the more dysfunctional the political system becomes and the more disillusioned voters come to be. It should be no surprise that a Marketplace and Edison Research poll that found that 70.9 percent of Americans think "the economic system in the U.S. is rigged in favor of certain groups."[80] Given the explosion of spending on lobbying and the vast rewards for doing so, most Americans are entirely right.

It is worth remembering that when Adam Smith wrote of "the invisible hand" in *The Wealth of Nations*, he was not simply praising the free market, but condemning the government acting on the behalf of large merchants who were furthering their own interests.

Until lobbying is reformed, there is little hope for reducing barriers to entry for smaller firms to fight it out in the marketplace. There is little chance the invisible hand can work.

In the final days of the 2016 election, Donald Trump ran an advertisement showing the face of Goldman Sachs CEO Lloyd Blankfein. The voiceover did not mention him by name, but the narration described "a global power structure that is responsible for the economic decisions that have robbed our working class, stripped our country of its wealth, and put that money into the pockets of a handful of large corporations and political entities."[81]

Even when Trump campaigned against Hillary Clinton's ties to Goldman Sachs, he kept the revolving door swinging for Goldman, giving many ex-bankers control over American financial policy. Gary Cohn became the second Goldman Sachs executive to head the National Economic Council. Former Goldman Sachs investment banker Stephen Bannon was appointed as Trump's chief strategist, and Goldman Sachs partner Steven Mnuchin was nominated for Treasury Secretary. Trump economic adviser Anthony Scaramucci worked for Goldman Sachs as a vice president of wealth management.[82]

Goldman Sachs has by far been the biggest winner of the revolving door in Washington. During the financial crisis and the bailouts, Goldman Sachs had at least four dozen former employees, lobbyists, or advisers operating in the highest reaches of power both in Washington and around the world. This did not include any lower-level posts, which were also filled with Goldman Sachs employees.[83]

Henry Paulson joined Goldman Sachs in 1974 and later became its chairman and CEO in 1999. When the 2007–2008 financial crisis happened, Paulson decided which banks would be rescued and which would not. Naturally Goldman Sachs survived. Critically, he approved an $85 billion bailout to insurance giant AIG. AIG in response paid Goldman the $13 billion it owed them from credit default swaps.[84] The revolving door paid off spectacularly for Goldman Sachs See Figure 8.4.

Even after the crisis, when Timothy Geithner became Treasury Secretary under President Obama, he spoke daily with the CEO of Goldman Sachs, according to logs obtained under the Freedom of Information Act. According to his official calendar, he met more often with Lloyd Blankfein than with Congressional leaders, including the Speaker of the House and the Senate Majority Leader.[85]

It should be no wonder that Goldman gets what it wants and rarely faces any scrutiny. Carmen Segarra is a former New York Federal Reserve examiner who was placed at Goldman Sachs to oversee their behavior. In her time there, she captured 40 hours of audio recording

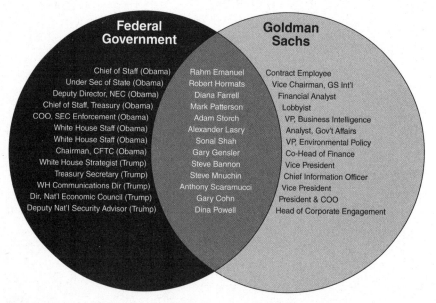

Figure 8.4   Revolving Door between Goldman Sachs and the Federal Government
SOURCE: https://steemit.com/corporatism/@geke/gekevenn-goldman-sachs-updated.

during her tenure as an examiner, showing other Fed employees acting inappropriately by purposely not reporting on bad practices that they witnessed, in order to protect the bank.

How is it that Goldman Sachs could go from the devil incarnate during the campaign trail to a core part of the government?

Economists and political scientists use the term "regulatory capture" to describe the process by which companies take over the government institutions that are meant to regulate them. Over two centuries ago, Adam Smith recognized the problem in *The Wealth of Nations*, "Civil government, so far as it is instituted for the security of property, is in reality instituted for the defense of the rich against the poor, or of those who have some property against those who have none at all." He noted that, "To widen the market and to narrow the competition, is always the interest of the dealers."

In 1892, Richard Olney, a corporate attorney and soon-to-be attorney general, advised Charles E. Perkins, a railroad president, against opposing the Interstate Commerce Act:

> The Commission, as its functions have now been limited by the courts, is, or can be made, of great use to the railroads. It satisfies the popular clamor for a government supervision of railroads, at the same time that that supervision is almost entirely nominal. Further, the older such a Commission gets to be, the more inclined it will be found to take the business and railroad view of things. It thus becomes a sort of barrier between the railroad corporations and the people and a sort of protection against hasty and crude legislation hostile to railroad interests . . . The part of wisdom is not to destroy the Commission, but to utilize it.[86]

Olney's remarks were prescient, and they captured the fate of almost all regulatory bodies that have been set up since.

According to a Public Citizen report, Obama appointed 56 so-called "reverse revolvers," or people who come directly from the industry that they will oversee. Bill Clinton appointed 64 reverse revolvers and George W. Bush appointed 91.[87] When Trump pledged to drain the swamp, many Americans voted, hoping for a change to the revolving door in Washington. Instead they got more of the same. Over half of

Trump's nominations of federal regulators named the very CEOs, lobbyists, and lawyers whom the positions are supposed to regulate.[88]

Goldman Sachs is the tip of the iceberg when it comes to regulatory capture. When the financial crisis struck, Americans were appalled that no one was prosecuted from Wall Street. There was a good reason for that: most of the top jobs at the regulators are headed by former Wall Street bankers.

Many of the biggest Wall Street banks, including Goldman Sachs, JPMorgan, and Citigroup, have provided "golden parachutes" to executives moving to government. The golden parachute is an unspoken quid pro quo that encourages corruption in Washington. For example, Treasury Secretary Jack Lew received an exit bonus of more than $1 million from Citigroup shortly before joining the Obama administration. The package said explicitly that the payout was contingent on his securing a high-level position within a government regulatory body. When Antonio Weiss, a former investment banker from Lazard, was appointed to the Treasury, his financial disclosures showed he would be paid $21 million when he left Lazard for a full-time job in government.[89]

It does not matter where you look, whether it is in pharmaceuticals, genetically modified crops, financial services, or telecommunications, the government has been captured by the companies it is meant to regulate.

Bayer and Monsanto are two of the biggest spenders when it comes to lobbying in Washington. In 2017, Bayer spent $10.5 million while Monsanto spent about $6.5 million.[90] See Figure 8.5.

All government agencies suffer from regulatory capture. Even the granting of monopolies has a revolving door with industry; consider the case of the US Patent and Trademark Office (USPTO), which confers monopolies on those who receive patents. Research by Haris Tabakovic of the Brattle Group and Thomas Wollmann of the University of Chicago shows that patent examiners who moved to private industry behaved very differently from those who didn't. These examiners granted more patents than their peers, particularly to the companies that eventually hired them.[91]

Government is not a passive bystander in the increase in inequality. It is an active participant, granting favors to the wealthy and powerful,

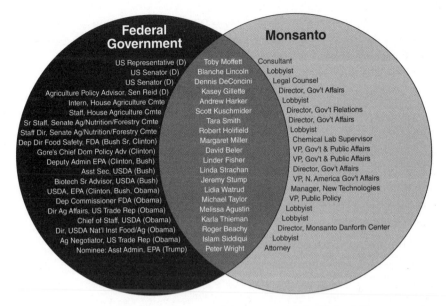

Figure 8.5 Revolving Door between Monsanto and the Federal Government
SOURCE: https://steemit.com/corporatism/@geke/gekevenn-monsanto-updated.

looking after the interests of the well connected. It has distorted society towards inequality. Rather than encourage competition and innovation, it has stifled growth. The increase in inequality comes not from Adam Smith's invisible hand, but from the hands of government.

It is worth remembering the words of Theodore Roosevelt, who opposed monopolies and trusts: "There can be no effective control of corporations while their political activity remains. To put an end to it will be neither a short nor an easy task, but it can be done . . ."[92] While he said these words over 100 years ago, not much has changed.

Key Thoughts from the Chapter

- Monopolies in markets often come from patents and intellectual property.
- Excessive regulation selectively kills off the small startups attacking big corporations. It is a formidable barrier to entry for any industry.

- One thing that can make a monopoly permanent is government, because only government can prevent the sort of innovation and competition that undermines every corporate giant.
- The correlation between lobbying, regulation, and profits is concentrated in a small number of politically influential industries.
- Government is not a passive bystander in the increase in inequality. It is an active participant, granting favors to the wealthy and powerful, looking after the interests of the well connected.

Chapter Nine

Morganizing America

If we will not endure a king as a political power, we should not endure a king over the production, transportation, and sale of any of the necessities of life.

—John Sherman

John Pierpont "JP" Morgan was America's banker. He famously financed superstar scientists of his day like Nikola Tesla and Thomas Edison, and arranged the merger that formed General Electric. Morgan's house was the first in New York City to be wired for electricity, and he spent vast amounts of money amassing a huge private art collection. He inspired confidence and fear; he would stare with his piercing eyes, and one man said that a meeting with Morgan made him feel "as if a gale had blown through the house." When Morgan died, the New York Stock Exchange closed until noon in his honor; it had previously only been closed to honor the passing of kings and presidents.[1]

He was the "boss of bosses" during the Gilded Age, and he single-handedly saved the nation from economic collapse during the Panic of 1907. The Panic arose when the New York Stock Exchange fell 50% and bank runs ensued across the country. Morgan devised a plan to shore up the banking system with his personal money, and cash from wealthy friends and institutions. He provided liquidity to the country when America's own treasury failed. This outraged the nation – how could one man have gained such immense power and control?

Morgan was famous for financing failing companies, gaining majority shareholdings, and then swooping in with his own managers and directors to aggressively focus on profitability. The king of consolidation, like Buffett, he knew that large firms with little competition were the best investments. Morgan built monopoly moats by combining businesses within industries and eliminating competition altogether. His technique of consolidating companies across industries became known as "Morganization."

In the late 1800s, local stores across America were owned and operated almost exclusively by families and entrepreneurs. Mom-and-pop shops dotted the main streets nationwide, and industry was based on small-scale production. But in a few short years, Morganization had caused the basic fabric of American capitalism to change. People bought their daily goods from trusts owned by bankers far away on Wall Street.

The world's first billion-dollar company, United States Steel, was created under Morgan's direction by consolidating the three major US steel producers of the early twentieth century. Formed in 1901, the company controlled almost 70% of US steel production in its first year. It attracted the attention of antitrust lawyers, who attempted to break it apart but were unsuccessful. US Steel still exists today, over 117 years later.

The same year, Morgan also formed the Northern Securities Company – a railroad trust that controlled most major American railroads. In a historic case, the Justice Department under President Roosevelt filed an antitrust case against NSC and, only three years after its formation, broke up the railroad monopoly in 1904. Although the owners claimed that NSC was simply a stock-holding company that did not engage in commercial activity, this case paved the way for dozens of other antitrust decisions in subsequent years. Roosevelt gained a reputation for taking on the big monopolists, but never again acted against Morgan.

The move to antitrust in the first half of the century was as a reaction against the concentration of economic and political power. If you controlled industries, you could control the government. It was a battle to determine who ultimately should control industries – the private or the public sector? Roosevelt is quoted as saying, "The great corporations which we have grown to speak of rather loosely as trusts are the creatures of the State, and the State not only has the right to control them, but it is duty bound to control them wherever the need of such control is shown."[2]

Despite the war on inequality today, the issue is not wealth but control. People have the sense that the system is rigged for the wealthy. The difficulty is that often wealth and control go hand in hand. As Robert Reich says in his book *Saving Capitalism*, "The invisible hand of the marketplace is connected to a wealthy and muscular arm." Titans with disproportionate influence over markets can use their power and wealth to dominate industries and rig the rules in their favor. Today, concentration of shareholders means that many Americans are deprived of the benefits of stock ownership altogether and have no say or control over how markets work.

Almost half of Americans do not own any stocks. According to Gallup, only 54% of Americans own stocks either in brokerage accounts or through retirement savings plans. This is a decline from 62% prior to the 2008 financial crisis.[3] And less than 14% of households directly own corporate stock.[4]

Despite record gains in the S&P in 2017, nearly half of Americans did not share in these historic profits. The wealthiest 1% own nearly 50% of stock and the top 10% own more than 81%. In contrast, the middle class owns only 8% of all stock.[5] Young Americans are particularly wary of investing in the stock market, according to a recent Gallup poll.[6] Many millennials graduated from college into the global financial crisis and saw first-hand that riding big waves in the market can also be followed by massive drops on the other side. In fact, there's only one demographic where stock market ownership is growing: rich, old people. They are the only ones who can afford to take risks.

Stock ownership is skewed by income. Most poor people are not stock owners because they don't have extra money to invest, and are rarely in jobs that offer 401(k)s or pension plans. Stock ownership is also divided by state – people in poorer states are less likely to be investing in the markets. Ultimately inequality is both a result of and is driven by stock ownership.

Today many investors are looking for opportunities to replicate the Gilded Age. As Morgan knew, those who own the stock control the companies. The most famous modern investor, Warren Buffett, is looking increasingly like the new JP Morgan. Buffett invests in monopolies. They are even more attractive if industries have the appearance of competition, but are in fact local monopolies. Airlines are the perfect example.

Buffett hated airlines, but when industries move from being competitive to tight oligopolies, he is willing to change his mind. For years, he hated airlines. In a 2002 interview with the British newspaper *The Telegraph*, he said, "If a capitalist had been present at Kitty Hawk back in the early 1900s, he should have shot Orville Wright. He would have saved his progeny money."[7] He thought airlines were a disaster for investors given high fixed costs, unions, and volatile fuel prices. It may seem curious that as late as 2013, Buffett called investing in airlines a "death trap."

Today, Buffett's firm Berkshire Hathaway owns stock in American, United, Delta, and Southwest airlines to the tune of nearly $9.5 billion. He is not betting on a company but exercising control over the industry. They all know he likes pricing power, and the message from his shareholding is clear. Berkshire owns between 7% and 10% of each company, a majority position. Buffett is now the first, second, or third largest shareholder in each of these four major airlines. He also recently said he "wouldn't rule out owning an entire airline." Why the dramatic change of heart?

Congress deregulated airlines in 1978. Many new entrants competed fiercely for market share. Deregulation increased profitability, but the industry went through cycles of boom and bust, primarily due to oil prices and high fixed costs. Then consolidation began. As the *New York Times* put it, "an industry that is not naturally competitive went from being a regulated cartel, to a brief period of ruinous competition, and then to an unregulated cartel — with predictable effects on the quality of service."[8] All US airlines consolidated into four majors: American, Delta, United, and Southwest.

Buffett waited until industry consolidation was complete with each major airline operating a regional monopoly. He then invested heavily . . . into all four of them. Little competition means there is little threat to your investment. Buffett is now a majority shareholder in every key competitor in the same industry.

New evidence is emerging that links common ownership of companies in the same industry, with anticompetitive behavior. The term is horizontal shareholding, and it refers to an investor holding significant shares in companies that are horizontal competitors. This type of stock ownership has increased dramatically in the past 40 years. In 1980, if you paired any random two US firms together, more than 75% of them would have no common owner. By 2012 only 8% of firm pairings had no common ownership.[9]

The big investors are no longer betting against the small. They now own the casino.

Concentration of ownership is problematic because it distills the control of entire industries into a few players' hands. But even more concerning is that recent studies are suggesting that common ownership incentivizes firms to avoid competing with one another altogether.

In a healthy economy, companies compete to offer better, cheaper products and services for their consumers. In a situation with horizontal share ownership, where competing firms are trying to please the same owner, firms can tacitly collude to maintain high corporate profits by swelling total *industry* performance. Investors make money when the industry (not individual companies) makes money. The easiest way to do this is to raise consumer prices.

Instead of stealing market share from one another by aggressively competing on price or quality, companies can simply raise prices on consumers and increase their profit margins. This isn't just theory – studies are now showing that increased common ownership correlates to higher consumer prices.[10]

Airlines illustrate this well – they nickel and dime us for things that used to be standard. Checking a bag or picking out a seat is now a luxury add-on. Won't be long before they'll charge a toll for using the bathroom. Extra charges will top $82 billion by the end 2017, according to a study of global carriers by IdeaWorks and CarTrawler. This is a 264% increase from the 2010 figure of $22.6 billion.[11]

In an important paper, economists José Azar, Marin Schmalz, and Isabel Tecu showed that horizontal shareholding increased airfare prices by anywhere from 3% to 12%.[12] The study controlled for lots of variables like the change in oil price. The price increases still held, and the only explanatory variable was horizontal shareholding.

In the banking sector, banks with horizontal shareholding have been known to raise fees and lower their deposit rates (the amount someone gets paid for keeping their money in the bank). Nearly 25% of all the major banks are owned by just a few large asset managers who have no vested interest in any one bank (Figure 9.1).

The ills of horizontal shareholding are a widespread problem, given that the Big 5 institutional investors – Blackrock, Vanguard, State Street, Fidelity, and JP Morgan – now own 80% of all stock in S&P 500 listed companies.

The phenomenon is global. In 2016, Blackrock was the largest shareholder of HSBC, Deutsche Bank, Banco Popolare di Milano, and Banco Bilbao Vizcaya Argentaria along with one-third of firms on both the FTSE 100 (London) and the DAX (Germany).[13] While Blackrock is mainly a passive shareholder and holds these stocks for its indices or

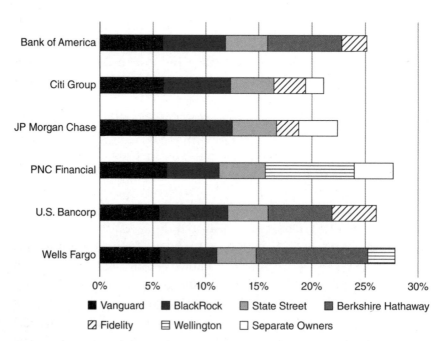

Figure 9.1   Largest Owners of US Banks (as of 2016 Q2)
Source: Competition Policy International.

exchange-traded funds, it is now one of the largest shareholders in the world with vast power.

Companies do not have to collude directly, but the nature of the incentive structure is enough to make this collusion attractive. The concept of horizontal shareholding helps explain the strange dynamics of CEOs being rewarded for industry performance, rather than company performance, and also why companies have not reinvested corporate profits into expanding their output in many industries in recent years. Without real competitors, the incentives to compete wither away.

Traditionally, when economists have worried about monopoly power, the focus has been on mergers that demonstrate antitrust risks. Horizontal shareholdings add another layer to the problem.

Today, you can own oligopolies, and those oligopolies are owned by other oligopolies. It's like an oligopoly layer cake. For Buffett, the oligopolies in the airline industry are like a dream come true. Just like Morgan before him, he hopes that his investments in entire industries will encourage less investment, higher prices (his beloved "pricing power") and no new competition.

Although almost half of Americans do not own any stocks, those who do own shares generally own them through an institution. Asset management firms can administer pension plans, 401(k)s, or direct investment products like exchange traded funds (ETFs) or mutual funds. Institutions now own about 80% percent of total US equity market by capitalization.

One of the major reasons for the enormous swelling of these institutional holdings is the history-making transition into "passive investing." In previous years, financial managers would actively direct investments. They felt that they could beat the market by researching, employing smart mathematicians and economists, and by spending a lot of time noodling about market trends. This is known as active investing – and in recent years it has come under fire for being ineffective and expensive.

Warren Buffett claims that investors have "wasted" upwards of $100 billion paying useless wealth managers high management fees.[14] He is a proponent of what's known as passive investing, or investing in index funds. These funds do not try to beat the market, but mimic a performance of a particular index like the S&P, Russell 500, and so forth. They do not have to be managed, so they are much less expensive than active funds, and they help investors lessen risk through diversification.

Passive investing has brought great benefits for average, middle-class investors. It has been somewhat of a Robin Hood story in finance. Small investors who had been paying absurdly high fees to Wall Street investment managers suddenly got access to a low-cost product that democratized investing. For the last decade, passive investing has outperformed active management, and it has involved a lot less effort or skill. The index does all the work. The highest paid investment managers in the world lost out to a simple index in which anyone could invest.

Jack Bogle is the godfather of index funds. He created the world's first retail index fund at Vanguard in 1974. Buffett has called him a hero for helping the average investor. Jack humbly responded, "I'm not a hero, I'm an ordinary guy . . . who gave a damn about the people investing and wanted to make sure they got a fair shake."

Bogle never could have anticipated the incredible inflows into this asset class. The appetite has been insatiable, and money has steadily flowed out of active funds and into passive over the last few years. Passive funds now own 40% of all US assets, and would own 100% by 2030 if this immense growth trajectory continued (Figure 9.2).

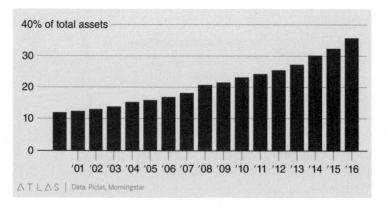

Figure 9.2   Share of Passively Managed Assets in US Markets
SOURCE: Atlas; Data: Pictet, Morningstar.[15]

Vanguard started with $11 million back in 1975 and has skyrocketed to over $5.1 trillion under management today. It is the second largest asset manager in the world, beat only by Blackrock at $6.2 trillion at the time of this writing. Between 2014-2017, Vanguard amassed over $800 billion in new funds, which is 8.5 times more than all its competitors. It is growing faster than every other mutual fund manager in the world combined.[16]

The popularity of passive funds has ballooned the assets of the top funds. The figure below shows that the "Big 3" index funds – Blackrock, Vanguard, and State Street – own nearly 19% of the S&P 500 between them (Figure 9.3).

Despite their popularity and outperformance, passive investments are starting to become more hotly contested. What began as a financial innovation to democratize access to investment products has morphed into a situation where a few huge players dominate access to these products. Exchange traded funds (ETFs) are super cheap for investors, but the Big 3 have more than 80% of the market between them. Not since the gilded age has so much power been highly concentrated.[17]

Asset management has, itself, become "Morganized." Control has, once again, concentrated in relatively few hands. Paul Singer, a billionaire hedge fund manager, has called passive investing "a blob which is

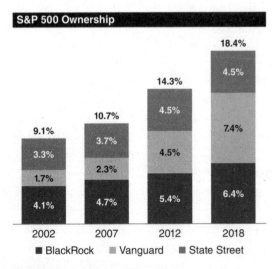

Figure 9.3   S&P 500 Ownership by "Big 3"
Source: Lazard, FactSet.

destructive to the growth–creating and consensus–building prospects of free market capitalism."

All of this begs the question – who do companies ultimately serve? And how much control and influence should shareholders have over company decisions? In the 1970s Milton Friedman threw his hat in the ring in an attempt to answer these questions. Following a now infamous essay by Friedman, who would later win the Nobel Prize in economics, a new intellectual dogma took hold.

Friedman argued that the only "social responsibility of business is to increase its profits" and that "a corporate executive is an employee of the owners of the business." By this, he meant that the CEO is "employed" by the shareholders and must serve them above all other parties, including workers, consumers, or society. It was a fine thought, within reason. Shareholders in fact do own the company.

The idea that a company's only purpose is to increase profits and maximize shareholder value is now so entrenched that few question it. *The Economist* claimed Friedman was "the most influential economist of the second half of the twentieth century . . . possibly of all of it."

Like all religions, once CEOs embraced this new gospel of maximizing shareholder value, a good idea often fell into the fervent hands of zealots. Anything that was a drag on cash for shareholders was cut – worker pay, health care and pensions, and R&D. CEOs were glad to do it if it made the stock price rise. They did not have to create innovative products, take market share from competitors, or provide value to society – all they had to do was pump up the stock price.

Companies are investing less for long–term returns or the development of their workers and instead myopically focus on quarterly earnings. They are under pressure from institutional shareholders and hedge funds that have their own need for continual high stock prices. Ironically, for all of the obsession with maximizing value, over the past 50 years, the real return on assets and invested capital has declined by three quarters since 1965. CEOs can reach their target of higher profits, but they are doing so with little regard to shareholder return. CEOs have created high prices for shareholders, without creating high returns for companies (Figure 9.4).

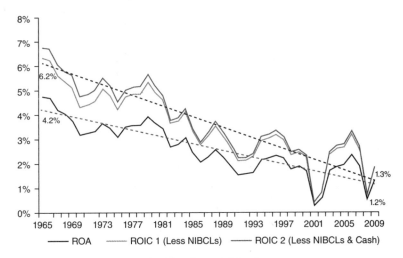

Figure 9.4   Net Investment by Nonfinancial Businesses
SOURCE: Deloitte Shift Index.

The stock market hit record highs in 2017 with record corporate profits. But where does all the cash flow go? Who decides this important question? There are five things companies can do with cash: reinvest in the business, acquire another company, pay down debt, pay dividends to shareholders, or buy back their own stock.

Businesses are investing less and less in their own people and factories and greater amounts in cannibalistic share buy-backs, which only benefit shareholders. Despite record profits, we have seen a sharp fall in reinvestment in the workforce, R&D, and capital projects. Investment averaged about 20% of corporate revenues between 1959 and 2001, but fell to only 10% between 2002 and 2015.

The culprit is not hard to find. Highly concentrated industries with common ownership invest less and spend a disproportionate amount of cash on share buy-backs.[18] They have little interest in increasing supply or capacity in their own industry. They would much prefer to have high pricing power.

If concentrated industries are investing less, what are they doing with their cash?

CEOs can be compensated in a variety of ways: salary, bonuses, and stock-based compensation. These forms, and various combinations of them, are meant to provide incentives to company leadership to make beneficial decisions for the company while minimizing disincentives. A large cash or base salary (that does not vary with company performance) is generally seen as an inadequate incentive structure.

In the 1970s, CEO to worker compensation was much more level with many other countries around the world today (about 30:1). That number has skyrocketed to 361:1 in the United States. Managers should certainly be compensated for the difficult work they do, but it is hard to believe CEOs, as a group, are now ten times more valuable relative to workers than they were in the 1970s.

Part of the issue is that, originally management pay was determined according to "internal equity." A manager's value to the firm was determined by his or her performance relative to other employees. In the 1970s, with the rise of executive compensation consulting, the focus shifted to "external equity" – or comparing CEOs to what others were being paid across the industry.

Boards and compensation committees agree to compensation packages based on benchmarking against other comparable companies, but they are all benchmarking against each other in a never-ending infinite loop of salary increases. Studies also show that the companies that serve as benchmarks are always chosen to maximize CEO pay.[19] Like in Garrison Keillor's Lake Wobegon, where all children are above average, in today's corporate boards all CEOs are exceptional.

CEOs are often rewarded with stock options as compensation. Bonuses are often tied to company performance in the form of stock options or stock ownership. The higher the stock price goes, the higher the value of management stock options. And when it comes to pumping the stock price, CEOs have a powerful tool to influence their stock price: share buybacks.

The all-star champions of financial market engineering are share buybacks. A share buyback is when companies use excess profits to buy back their own stocks. Buybacks reduce the shares available in the marketplace and drive up the share price. This process bumps the earnings per share, and these are numbers that Wall Street traders watch very closely.

The stock that the company has bought back can either be kept, can be used to pay out executives, or they can simply be made to disappear, Houdini style. The company can "retire" the stocks, which means fewer are available on the market, and those that are have now gone up in value as a result.

Stock buybacks used to be illegal following the 1929 crash. They were considered stock manipulation, because mechanically it does support the share price. But President Regan rescinded the law in 1982, giving companies the ability to send their cash back into their own pockets without shareholder approval.[20]

In 2018 the market is on track to set the all-time record for share buybacks (Figure 9.5). Companies have spent $5.1 trillion on them since the financial crisis. Again, this is cash that could be spent on wages, research and development, or capital expenditures. As Senator Elizabeth Warren of Massachusetts memorably put it, stock buybacks create a sugar high for already obese CEOs.

Buybacks continue to explode because of the 2018 Trump tax cuts. According to Bloomberg, about 60% of profits from the tax cuts are going to shareholders, while only 15% of those profits are going to workers.[21] Unfortunately for the economy, most people who own shares are generally rich and old and unlikely to spend any of the cash they get.

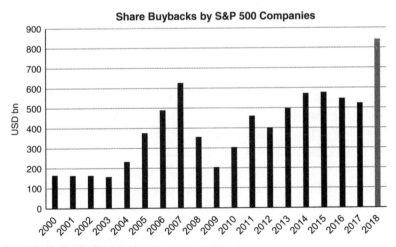

Figure 9.5 Buybacks Zoom to Record Highs
SOURCE: Variant Perception.

Many investors argue that buybacks happen only when there are no better alternative uses for excess cash. They argue buybacks don't limit growth or investment spending, but result from the lack of investment opportunities. It has become a vicious cycle, where low investing and low wages create low demand, which in turn dictates even less investing.

William Lazonick, Professor of Economics at the University of Massachusetts, claims that buybacks have created a short-term mentality for firms. He writes, "with its downsize-and-distribute resource-allocation regime, the 'buyback corporation' is in large part responsible for a national economy characterized by income inequity, employment instability, and diminished innovative capability – or the opposite of what I have called 'sustainable prosperity.'"[22]

Proponents argue that a rising stock market promotes consumer confidence, which increases spending and boosts the economy. Yet it is a cheap thrill when most workers do not own shares and do not see their wages rise.

Stock buybacks are not a disease. They are a symptom of little competition and abnormally high profits. They take the tolls everyone pays in their everyday lives and send them to modern-day robber barons.

When J.P. Morgan died in 1914, he left an inheritance of $80 million in financial assets. John D. Rockefeller is said to have announced, "And to think – he wasn't even a wealthy man."[23] Such was the wealth of Rockefeller.

Morgan, though, was fabulously wealthy, and his art collection was unparalleled. Morgan's biographer Jean Strouse calculated that, by 1912, Morgan had spent about $60 million on art.[24] Today, many of the pieces he bought are worth thousands of times more than what he paid for them. The total value of his estate was about 0.3% of the US GDP, which was $39 billion at the time. Adjusted to today's GDP, Morgan's net worth would have been almost $50 billion. It would make him one of the wealthiest Americans ever. But for Morgan, the chase was never about the money; it was always about control.

J.P Morgan inspired far more admiration and fear among the American public. Following the Panic of 1907, the public came to realize the vast power of JP Morgan when they saw that he could singlehandedly save the banking system. In 1912, Morgan was called to testify before Congress on charges that he exerted too much control over American commerce. His condescending manner did not go over well. In response, Congress created the Federal Reserve.

On December 23, 1913 President Woodrow Wilson signed the Federal Reserve Act. "There are only two choices," he said, "Either to give the central control to bankers or to give it to government."[25] No one man would ever again singlehandedly control the banking system.

A year later, Congress passed the Clayton Antitrust Act in 1914. This ushered in a new era of trust busting and monopoly disintegration. Contrary to perceptions today, antitrust was intended to dissipate control and power, not simply keep consumer prices low. The act singled out the practice of "Morganizing" or horizontal shareholding. It specifically stated that stock ownership should not be used as a means to limit competition. Section 7 of the Act states:

> No corporation shall acquire, directly or indirectly, the whole or any part of the stock or other share capital of two or more corporations engaged in commerce where the effect of such acquisition; or the use of such stock by the voting or granting of proxies or otherwise, may be to substantially lessen competition between such corporations, or any of them, whose stock or other share capital is so acquired, or to restrain such commerce in any section or community, or tend to create a monopoly of any line of commerce.

Morgan died in 1913 before witnessing the influence of the Clayton Act. His partners pleaded with Washington not to eliminate horizontal shareholdings. They even resigned as directors from over 30 companies, including banks, hoping they could still keep their shares. Congress banned horizontal shareholdings, anyway.

For years, the Clayton Act limited the emergence of a new J.P. Morgan. Yet the influence of the Act is waning. Today, horizontal shareholding has both increased ownership and concentrated power. In the words of Edward Rock, an antitrust expert at NYU School of Law, "The last time we had this degree of concentrated financial power was in the Morgan days."[26]

If Morgan were alive now, he would be happy to see that not much has really changed.

Key Thoughts from the Chapter

- Almost half of Americans don't own stock, and less than 14 percent of households own corporate stock directly.
- Oligopolies now exist not only within specific industries, but are funded and owned by oligopolistic shareholders. It's like an oligopoly layer cake.
- Stock buybacks were illegal following the 1929 financial markets crash. It was considered stock manipulation.
- Inequality is both a result of, and driven by, stock ownership.

Chapter Ten

The Missing Piece of the Puzzle

Something is rotten in the state of Denmark.
—Hamlet, Act 1, Scene 4, Marcellus to Horatio

In the months after the collapse of Lehman Brothers and the bailout of almost all global banks, politicians, businessmen, and pundits were convinced that we were in the midst of a crisis of capitalism that would bring about far reaching reforms.

Nothing would ever be the same again, we were told. "Another ideological god has failed," the dean of financial commentators, Martin Wolf, wrote in the *Financial Times*. Companies will "fundamentally reset" the way they work, said the CEO of General Electric, Jeffrey Immelt. "Capitalism will be different," said Treasury Secretary Timothy Geithner.

Months and years later, nothing has changed. Frustration boiled over, and people took to the streets and town halls. The Tea Party movement sprang up spontaneously on the right, and thousands of people marched on Washington and confronted their elected representatives across America. The Occupy Wall Street movement grew on the left and spread from the tip of Manhattan across the country. The populist movements were two sides of the same coin. Both resented the bailouts of large banks and bonus payments to executives who had brought down the financial system, while the middle class struggled with debt and unemployment. But the protests faded away like faint tremors. The big political earthquakes came later.

On the night of the US election in November 2016, the British went to bed expecting Hillary Clinton to win, but by the time they awoke, America had elected Donald Trump. A complete political outsider, a former reality-TV star, and a man who has had almost as many corporate bankruptcies as marriages would be the next president of the United States. The British should have seen it coming. A few months earlier, they had gone to bed expecting to stay in the European Union, only to wake up in shock and disbelief and find out that by a slim margin, a majority had voted for a divorce from their biggest trading partner.

The electoral earthquakes were a powerful statement of discontent. American and British voters had tired of playing chess against a bigger opponent. They decided that the best move was to toss the pieces in the air and see where they might land. The move might not win the game, but it might start a new one with different rules.

Americans and the British wanted change, even if it meant a leap into the unknown. If Trump had not won, it might well have been Bernie Sanders, an antiestablishment candidate who beat Hillary Clinton in dozens of states. He was a socialist most of his career. In America, according to Gallup polls, being a socialist is right beneath atheism and Islam as a disqualifying trait in a political candidate.

In Britain, the Labour Party had voted for a far-left-wing leader. They chose Jeremy Corbyn, a complete outsider and a throwback to a time when socialists called for nationalizing entire industries. He had once demanded the "complete rehabilitation" of Leon Trotsky, a Marxist revolutionary. Once Corbyn became Labor leader, he declared, "The people who run Britain have rigged the economy and business rules to line the pockets of their friends. The truth is the system simply doesn't work for most people."

Bernie Sanders and Donald Trump couldn't agree on anything, but they both told their followers that the US economy was rigged, and voters loved them for it.

On the campaign trail Trump said, "It's not just the political system that's rigged, it's the whole economy," President Trump told voters while campaigning. "It's rigged by big donors who want to keep down wages. It's rigged by big businesses who want to leave our country, fire our workers, and sell their products back into the United States with absolutely no consequences for them. It's rigged by bureaucrats who are trapping kids in failing schools."[1] Sanders argued during his campaign: "For the past 40 years, Wall Street and the billionaire class has rigged the rules to redistribute wealth and income to the wealthiest and most powerful people," adding, "We must send a message to the billionaire class: You can't have it all."[2]

Voters in the United States and the UK overwhelmingly perceive that capitalism is broken. In the United States, a poll by Marketplace and Edison Research found that an overwhelming majority of Americans, 71%, believe that the US economy is rigged. In the UK, a YouGov poll showed almost two thirds of Britons believe that capitalism makes inequality worse, while three quarters think that corporations have hurt the environment, dodged taxes, or bought favors from politicians.

The surge in populism spilled across borders. Italy saw the rise of the Cinque Stelle movement, Germany had the nationalist Alternative for Germany (AfD), France had to contend with the resurgence of the Front National, Spain saw the emergence of the far-left, quasi-Marxist party Podemos, France witnessed the collapse of the old political order and the rise of Macron, old nationalist grievances erupted in Scotland and Catalunya, and populists have reached power in Italy. Across all the democratic "capitalist" countries of the West, voters said "Enough!"

Voters know that something is rotten in capitalism, and the elite does as well. If voting for political outsiders is what the average person does, then pretending to read weighty books on capitalism is what the elite does.

Nothing highlights the search for a diagnosis of our ills more than the extraordinary, puzzling success of Thomas Piketty's *Capital in the Twenty-First Century*. A 700-page economics book that is full of data tables and charts is hardly anyone's idea of a bestseller. There were no murder cases like in a Grisham book or any magical spells like in a J.K. Rowling book, yet Piketty's book sold more than 1.5 million copies.

Everyone bought and pretended to read the book. We have yet to meet anyone who has read the entire book. We're not making that up. Professor Jordan Ellenberg, a mathematics professor, did a study of bookmarks on Kindle e-books and found that almost no one made it past 26 pages in Piketty's book.[3]

In retrospect, it is understandable that people would be interested in a book of this kind, given their intuitive sense of a problem. People bought the book in droves because his charts on inequality captured the imagination (Figure 10.1). They clearly showed what many had feared but could not prove: the United States was becoming more unequal. Who cared about hundreds of pages of text when he had such good charts?

The reviews of the book were ecstatic, even rapturous. *The Economist* said it was "the economics book that took the world by storm." According to the *Financial Times*, "Thomas Piketty's book, 'Capital in the Twenty-First Century', has been the publishing sensation of the year. Its thesis of rising inequality tapped into the zeitgeist

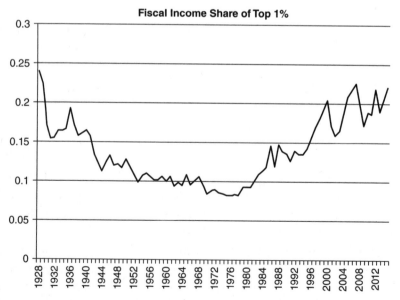

Figure 10.1 Income Inequality in the United States, 1910–2015

and electrified the post-financial crisis public policy debate." Lawrence Summers's said this research "has transformed political discourse and is a Nobel Prize–worthy contribution." Perhaps, most tellingly, Ed Miliband, the former Labour leader, said of Piketty at the time, "In a way, he is symptomatic of what people are actually feeling." Who cared if the arguments were right or wrong? He captured a *feeling*.

Piketty's reasoning and rhetoric often have strong echoes of Marx, which is not that odd for a French economist. He makes grand claims like Marx that there is a "central contradiction of capitalism." According to Piketty, capital "devours the future" as if high returns on capital inevitably cause economic ruin or revolution. These statements made him a hero to the left. Piketty's solution to high-income inequality is punitive tax rates on the rich to transfer the money to the poor. Piketty concluded that levying rates up to 80% on the top incomes and imposing a tax on wealth were the solutions. He was preaching to the choir.

Piketty argued that the origins of vast inequality comes from a lack of growth. Where structural growth is low, he thought capitalism would run up against a logical contradiction very close to what Marx described. Accumulated wealth from the past would take on great importance, while present-day labors would scarcely be rewarded. The greater the wedge between the growth in capital versus labor, the more socially destabilizing it would become. As he wrote, "The entrepreneur inevitably tends to become a rentier, more and more dominant over those who own nothing but their labor. Once constituted, capital reproduces itself faster than output increases. The past devours the future." The inner contradiction of capitalism is that it will inevitably be the victim of its own success if growth is low.

This insight into the origins of inequality was treated with great awe and reverence by a world searching for answers. Unfortunately, his data was flawed in important ways and his conclusion was incomplete.

Many journalists and economists uncovered serious flaws in his data. The *Financial Times* found that the Piketty's work contains a "series of errors that skew his findings." His book was riddled with "mistakes and unexplained entries in his spreadsheets." The economics professor Richard Sutch attempted to replicate his findings and could not do so. In a profoundly critical piece, he noted that "the procedures used to harmonize and average the data, the insufficient documentation, and the spreadsheet errors are more than annoying. Together they create a misleading picture of the dynamics of wealth inequality.[4] In short, Piketty's data was "unreliable." That is about as damning as you can get in an academic paper.

The International Monetary Fund could not prove his grand theory that low growth led to inequality. It shouldn't have been a surprise. Piketty himself showed inequality had risen, but his book hadn't even tried to prove his idea that capital takes more of the economic pie from labor when growth is low. When the IMF looked at 19 separate advanced economies over 30 years, they found there was "no empirical evidence that dynamics move in the way Piketty suggests." Some countries had high growth but falling inequality and returns on capital; others had low growth but falling inequality. There was no connection between growth and the returns on capital. In other words, his central conclusion about capitalism was wrong.

While the IMF was looking at developed countries in Europe and the United States, this is also true of developing countries. The Organisation for Economic Co-operation and Development (OECD) has shown that low growth and inequality don't go necessarily hand in hand with wide differences across emerging markets. At one extreme, strong economic growth over the past decade went hand in hand with declining income inequality in Brazil and Indonesia, while at the other extreme, China, India, Russia, and South Africa saw very big increases in inequality, even though their economies were also expanding strongly.[5] Again, Piketty's grand claims don't hold up to reality.

It would be easy to dismiss Piketty, given the complete lack of any supporting evidence for the "internal contradiction" theory. Unfortunately, because the book sold 1.5 million copies and became a media sensation, you cannot discuss capitalism without discussing Piketty. If we are going to fix what is rotten with capitalism, we need to correctly identify the disease.

Piketty's book may be flawed, but he identified a real issue that is gnawing away at our collective economic conscience. Readers instinctively knew that something was wrong. His data is not perfect, but he did an extraordinary job of documenting the growing gap between the very rich and the poor. Economic inequality within countries has been increasing around the world, and the rich have been getting richer, leaving the majority behind.

Piketty was correct that there has been a general trend higher in inequality within countries during the past 30 years, but he failed to figure out *why*. Rising inequality is a symptom. It is not the disease. He had a grand theory of capitalism but he failed to understand the mechanics of how capital was earning a lot more than labor. The problem of inequality is real, but it is not happening due to low growth.

Inequality is not so much a cause of economic and political changes as it is a consequence. Furthermore, inequality is not the same thing as unfairness. It is the feeling that ever growing inequality is unfair that has incited so much political unrest. The way that inequality has happened is the troubling part that Piketty failed to identify.

It is not low growth that is increasing inequality but the rise of market concentration and the death of competition. The evidence from recent economic studies is overwhelming: the economic and political power of monopolies and oligopolies has completely tilted the playing field in favor of dominant corporations against employees. Many industries are dominated by a very small number of firms. There are fewer new startups to compete with existing big companies. There are fewer companies competing to hire workers, and wages stagnate as the balance of power has shifted to large corporations. None of these outcomes is inevitable. Capitalism can be fixed.

You can measure inequality in a few different ways. The most common way is to look at income, which is what people earn as salaries in a given year. You can also look at wealth, which is the total of people's assets that have been built up over time, which would include stocks, bonds, real estate, art, and so forth. Both have shown a rising gap between the richest and the poorest. The rich are earning more money, and they own more of the world's assets.

If you look at wealth, rather than income, it is clear how skewed outcomes have become. This is extremely useful because some CEOs own lots of shares, which do not represent income, but do matter a great deal when comparing their wellbeing versus the average worker. The easiest way to look at wealth inequality is to see how much of the wealth is owned by the top 1% of a country and even the top 0.01%. It is for this reason that the "1%" has become part of our political vocabulary.

Every year Credit Suisse issues a report titled the *Global Wealth Report*, and it shows an unprecedented and increasing concentration of wealth among a handful of people.[6] As the bank noted, "Global wealth inequality has certainly been high and rising in the post-crisis period." The extremely wealthy have improved their position since 2000. According to Credit Suisse, the top 1% of global wealth holders started the millennium with 45.5% of all household wealth, but in 2017, "for the first time ever, the richest 1% now controls just over half, or 50.1%, of global wealth." The top of the wealth pyramid has done extremely well, but on the other end of the pyramid, 3.5 billion adults have a net worth of less than $10,000. You can see the number of households in each part of the global wealth pyramid in Figure 10.2.

As we write this book, stock markets are at all-time highs, and the wealthy have never had it so good. A key reason why wealth inequality has risen is that almost all central bank policies to respond to

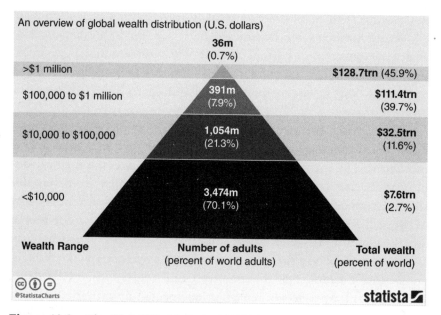

An overview of global wealth distribution (U.S. dollars)

Wealth Range	Number of adults (percent of world adults)	Total wealth (percent of world)
>$1 million	36m (0.7%)	$128.7trn (45.9%)
$100,000 to $1 million	391m (7.9%)	$111.4trn (39.7%)
$10,000 to $100,000	1,054m (21.3%)	$32.5trn (11.6%)
<$10,000	3,474m (70.1%)	$7.6trn (2.7%)

@StatistaCharts

statista

Figure 10.2   The Global Wealth Pyramid, 2017
SOURCE: Statista; Credit Suisse 2017 Global Wealth Report.

the financial crisis targeted asset prices. Central banks explicitly tried to lift stock markets and house prices, creating a "wealth effect" and hoping some of it would trickle down. The poor have almost no stocks or bonds, and the middle-class have far less than the wealthy. Unsurprisingly, extraordinary monetary policy by the Federal Reserve, the European Central Bank (ECB), the Bank of Japan (BOJ), and the Swiss National Bank (SNB) pumped up stock markets for those who already had large stockholdings and increased the wealth divide. While former Federal Reserve Chairman Benjamin Bernanke and others point out that unemployment would have been worse if they had not pursued extraordinary monetary policies, these measures have continued for over a decade after the financial crisis, and the net effect was that the wealthy got wealthier.

The trickle-down monetary policies were most extreme outside the United States. The ECB bought corporate debt, directly financing mergers and acquisitions for billionaire shareholders. They financed the merger that allowed the billionaire owners of AB Inbev to merge the company with SAB, which gave them control over 50% of the US beer market. The SNB bought over $85 billion of US stocks of large US corporations that were paying huge dividends to shareholders and buying back their own shares. They bought shares of local monopolies and oligopolies like Microsoft, Google, Facebook, Verizon, Visa, and so on. It would have been more efficient if central banks had simply wired money directly to the bank accounts of the very wealthy.

While wealth inequality is interesting, the standard way economists look at income disparities is by looking at something called a Gini coefficient. This measure shows the variation between the actual distribution of income in a country and what would apply if it were distributed perfectly evenly. It ranges from zero, indicating perfect equality, to a value of one, indicating perfect inequality with one household receiving all income. Globally, we have seen a steadily rising trend in inequality in emerging market countries, in the United States, the UK, and Australia. Europe has seen a smaller rise in income inequality, primarily due to high taxes and transfer payments to poorer households.[7] Higher taxes mitigate the symptoms but do not solve the problem (Figure 10.3).[8]

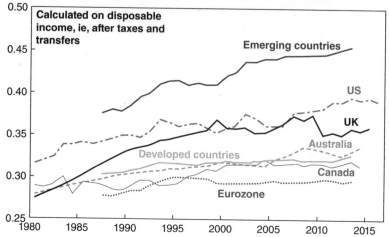

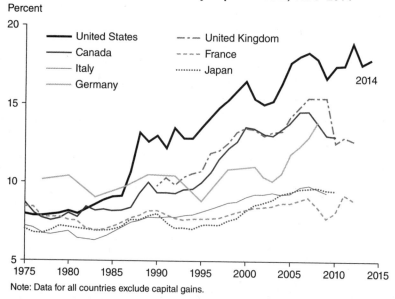

Note: Data for all countries exclude capital gains.

Figure 10.3 Rising Inequality. Selected Gini Coefficients
SOURCE: Dr. Shane Oliver and AMP Capital.[9]
SOURCE: http://www.presidency.ucsb.edu/economic_reports/2016.pdf.

It is not surprising that the United States has seen a big increase in inequality over the past 30 years. The extremes in income distribution are most clearly reflected in extraordinary CEO pay. In the US CEO pay has exploded. From 1978 to 2013, CEO compensation adjusted for inflation increased 937%. By contrast, the average worker's income grew by a pathetic 10% over the same period. To put the change in perspective, the CEO-to-worker pay ratio was 33-to-1 in 1978 and grew to 303-to-1 in 2014.[10] The United States is a big outlier in terms of how vastly overpaid the top corporate officers are versus the average worker. For CEOs in the UK, the ratio is 22; in France, it's 15; and in Germany it's 12.[11] US CEOs are vastly overpaid no matter how you look at it (Figure 10.4).

Given the gaping disparity in pay between the average worker and CEOs, you might imagine managers were superstars and the average worker was bad at his job. But that is hardly the case. While many executives go on the front cover of *Fortune* or *Forbes* and get all the credit for their company stock, worker productivity has been steadily rising for decades. Unfortunately, employee earnings have not kept up with productivity increases. Workers are producing more goods with

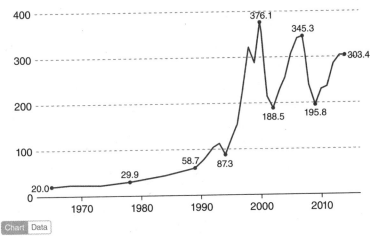

Note: CEO annual compensation is computed using the "options realized" compensation series, which includes salary, bonus, restricted stock grants, options exercised, and long-term incentive payouts for CEOs at the top 350 U.S. firms ranked by sales.

Figure 10.4   Rising CEO-to-Worker Compensation Ratio, 1965–2014
Source: Economic Policy Institute.

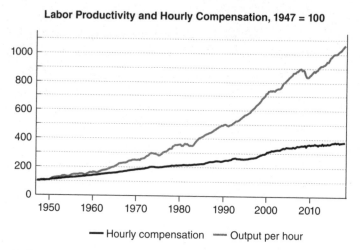

Figure 10.5   Worker Pay Is Not Keeping Up with Worker Productivity
SOURCE: Variant Perception.

less labor, and companies are making higher profits, but the benefits are not being shared with workers. Notice in Figure 10.5 that productivity growth has been rising in a straight line since the 1950s, but starting in 1980 hourly compensation has not risen much. The money from that gap doesn't vanish into thin air, and it has to show up somewhere.

Some economists have argued that the chasm between wages and productivity is an illusion. They argue that much of the gap can be explained by year-end bonuses, which are not included in hourly pay, by healthcare costs, which don't show up in a paycheck but which the worker benefits from, and by stock options, which also don't show up in a paycheck. However, we can discount these explanations. Healthcare, bonuses, and options are a real expense to companies, and if companies were getting hit with these costs instead of wages, it would show up in corporate profit margins. If that were true, corporate profit margins would not be at record highs, but they are. If the divergence between wages and productivity is real, the difference should clearly show up in corporate profits, and it does: profits have surged as wages have stagnated (Figure 10.6).

Companies have taken a record part of the economic pie. Corporate profits as a percentage of gross domestic product (GDP) are near record highs and labor's share of GDP is near record lows.

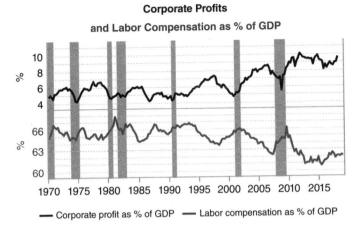

Figure 10.6 Corporate Profits versus Employee Compensation
SOURCE: Variant Perception.

You can see from Figure 10.6 that the chart looks like the jaws of a giant alligator. (You have to look at long-term trends, rather than the short-term ups and downs: corporate profits naturally rise and fall with recessions and expansions.) The divergence started in the early 1980s when the regular rise and fall of corporate profits and workers' compensation broke down. Only at the very peak of the internet bubble when labor markets were tight did workers' wages rise. The trend of higher corporate profits accelerated in 2001 after China opened up and joined the World Trade Organization. American workers found they had to compete with hundreds of millions of workers who joined the global labor pool, at the same time as European workers found they had to compete with the newly free Eastern European workers. Firms have gained market power, while workers now have to contend with a globalized world.

The trend in corporate profits is a mystery to economists and investment strategists. Jeremy Grantham, a well-known investor, has pointed out, "Profits are the most mean reverting series in finance. If margins don't revert something has gone wrong with capitalism."

Something has indeed gone very wrong. In a competitive market, if a company is making a lot of money, other companies will get excited by the prospects of high profits and will enter the industry and compete. Eventually margins decline as more competitors fight each other. Something is profoundly broken with capitalism if corporate profit margins do not revert to the historical mean.

Rising industrial concentration is a powerful reason why profits don't fall back toward their long-term average and a powerful explanation for the imbalance between corporations and workers. Workers in many industries have fewer choices of employers, and when industries are monopolists or oligopolists, they have significant market power versus their employees.

There is a strong and direct correlation between how few players there are in an industry and how high corporate profits are. Fewer competitors give companies significant market power to raise prices and to reduce wages. As Gustavo Grullon noted in his study of US industry, the trends are unmistakable, "The evidence quite clearly indicates that the relations between changes in industry concentration levels and changes in profit margins and shareholder wealth have become positive over the past two decades."[12]

Let's look again at Piketty's income chart, but this time paying attention to when the government cracked down on monopolies and oligopolies and when it didn't. There are two key dates in this chart. Up until the late 1930s, antitrust laws were on the books but not very well enforced. President Roosevelt began enforcing them vigorously in 1937–1938, and regulators frowned on most mergers that increased market share. That changed in the early 1980s when the government stopped enforcing antitrust laws and the US corporate sector started the first of a series of merger waves. Each economic boom has led to greater market power for corporations. It is unsurprising that income inequality then starts to rise again in the 1980s. When markets have become more concentrated after merger waves, income inequality has risen. When antitrust laws have been vigorously enforced, income inequality has been lower (Figure 10.7).

The increase in inequality started after the antitrust revolution under President Ronald Reagan. Sam Peltzman, an economist at the University of Chicago, found that that concentration, which had been unchanged over the previous decades, began rising at the same time that merger policy changed. Concentration has increased steadily over the entire period after antitrust policy changed. He noted

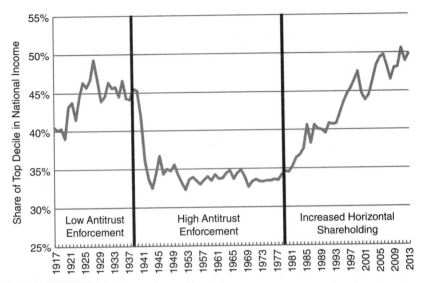

Figure 10.7   Income Inequality in the United States versus Antitrust Enforcement
Source: Einer Elhauge, "Horizontal Shareholding," *Harvard Law* Review 129, no. 5 (March 2016).

that the increase has been especially pronounced in consumer goods industries.[13]

The role of high industrial concentration on inequality is now becoming clear from dozens recent academic studies. In 2015, Jonathan Baker and Steven Salop found that "market power contributes to the development and perpetuation of inequality."[14]

Inequality comes not only from low wages, but from the everyday toll road of people's lives. Every time a consumer spends money, they are transferring a little of their paycheck to the seller and paying a small toll. Monopolies of goods and services turn the disposable income of the many into capital gains, dividends, and executive compensation of monopolies.

Evidence across a number of key industries in the United States shows that excessive market power allows companies to raise prices for consumers above competitive levels, while lower payouts to suppliers.

The transfer of wealth is vast. A study by Lina Khan and Sandeep Vaheesan outlined exactly how concentrated industries lead to inequality. They note that the aggregate wealth transfer effect from pervasive monopoly and oligopoly power is likely, at a minimum, hundreds of billions of dollars per year.[15]

If industries have a few dominant firms, then they should be able to charge a lot more for their goods than it costs to make them. That is exactly what we find. The economists Jan De Loecker of Princeton University and Jan Eeckhout of the University College London found that average markups, defined as the amount above cost at which a product is sold, have surged since the change in antitrust laws in the early 1980s. The average markup was 18% in 1980, but by 2014 it was nearly 70%. Higher markups suggest an increase in what economists refer to as "market power," which is the result of more highly concentrated industries.

A markup may sound like a very technical term, but you see it in everyday life. The best example is in luxury goods, where the right logo on a handbag will make the leather sell for a lot more than it costs to make. Part of what you're paying for is status and association. But true luxury goods are also often hand made, of exquisite high quality and rare. Paying markups on your cell phone service, glasses, or health-care should be unjustified by fundamentals.

High markups matter a great deal in the inequality debate because they are tightly correlated with lower wages for workers. De Loecker and Eechkhout noted that the rise in markups explains lower wages almost perfectly.[16] Their initial research was focused on the United States, but they extended their analysis, and *it applies to almost the entire developed world*. More of the economic pie goes to companies and less to workers when companies can squeeze workers (Figure 10.8). They noted, "Markups have risen most in North America and Europe, and least in emerging economies in Latin America and Asia."[17]

The role of markups is similar in other developed countries, and higher markups can lead to higher income inequality. Sean Ennis, Pedro Gonzaga, and Chris Pike examined the change in markups and the variation in incomes for the richest and the poorest. They showed that the presence of markups "reduces the income of the poorest 20% by between 14% and 19%."[18] They concluded that given how markups help the rich and hurt the poor, competition may help to reduce economic inequality. The IMF has confirmed this in

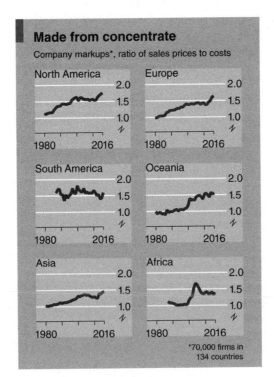

Figure 10.8 Higher Markups Lead to Lower Wages
SOURCE: *The Economist.*

recent research. They noted, "In advanced economies, markups have increased by an average of 39% since 1980. The increase is broad-based across industries and countries, and driven by the highest markup firms in each economic sector."

The trend toward fewer, larger companies is driving a wedge between the few at the top who are paid handsomely and the major-ity who have seen their wages go nowhere. Economists David Autor and his colleagues concluded in a recent paper that the rise of "super-star" firms with high profits and small workforces has contributed to income inequality.[19]

Rising economic inequality is not an inherent feature of capitalism. The growing gap between the rich and the poor is happening due to a decline in competition. This has been driven by industrial concentra-tion and extremely lax to nonexistent antitrust enforcement. This has

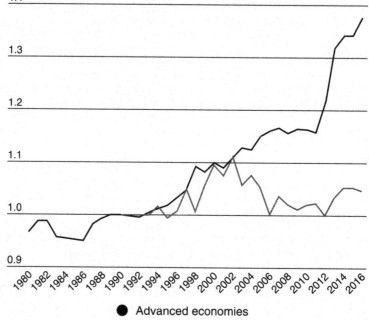

Figure 10.9   Markups in Advanced Economies Have Been Rising
since the 1980s
Source: International Monetary Fund.

enormous impacts on the ability of new companies to start and compete, the ability of workers to get higher wages, and the ability for consumers to access goods cheaply.

Given Piketty's diagnosis is incorrect, his solutions of very high income taxes and a wealth tax are also not the appropriate responses. It is like recommending opiates to a cancer patient. It may numb the pain, but it does not attack the cause of the distress.

The appropriate solutions are not higher taxes or the growth in government. The appropriate solution is more competition and more capitalism, not less.

Economic inequality is a bug that can be fixed with antitrust and with greater competition.

The correct answer is more vigorous antitrust enforcement. Government policy in antitrust enforcement should not have income inequality as an explicit goal. Inequality itself is not in itself a bad thing. Innovators who build companies will capture the benefit of their work. However, a growing part of inequality comes from entrenched monopolies that unfairly transfer wealth from consumers and suppliers to powerful monopoly owners. Unjust inequality is a side effect of lax antitrust enforcement. Fixing industrial concentration will have the side effect of reducing inequality. Reintroducing competition to markets will reduce the growing inequality in America.

The failure of wages to rise with economic growth and productivity is leading to a crisis in confidence, a fear that the American Dream is dead. The essence of American optimism is the belief in upward income mobility or the rags to riches story: the ideal that children have a higher standard of living than their parents. According to the Equality of Opportunity Project, a child's prospects of earning more than their parents have fallen from 90% to 50% over the past half century. Back in 1970, 92% of 30-year-olds were making more money than their parents did at that age. By 2010, only 50% of 30-year-olds could still say the same. And looking ahead, only a third of Americans now believe that the next generation will be better off.[20]

Progress has become elusive for the middle class, and despite economic growth, incomes for the middle class have in fact declined; in 2014, the median income of middle class households was 4% less than in 2000.[21]

The growing gap between CEOs and workers and between corporations and laborers has created two economies in the United States. Ray Dalio, the billionaire founder of Bridgewater Associates, one of the largest hedge funds in the world, wrote a piece titled "The Two Economies: The Top 40% and the Bottom 60%." He convincingly argues that it is a serious mistake to think you can analyze or understand "the" economy because we now have two of them. The wealth and income levels are so skewed between very top and bottom that "average" indicators are no longer meaningful. As you can see in Figure 10.10, the top 0.1% now own as much of the US wealth as the

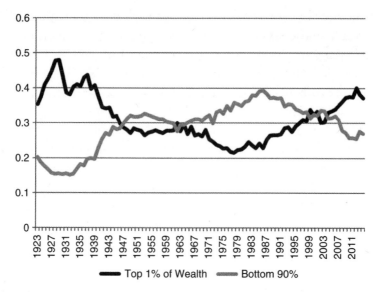

Figure 10.10   US Net Wealth Shares: Top 0.1% versus Bottom 90%

bottom 90%. The last time that happened was in the 1930s, when populism surged around the world and helped lead to World War II. Today we are seeing similar results.

In 1951 Eric Hoffer wrote *True Believer: Thoughts on the Nature of Mass Movements.* He analyzed the mass movements of the 1930s and offered an explanation for how populist movements start. This book is now more relevant than ever. No two populist movements are alike, but they promote the power of the people against a privileged elite. According to Bridgewater, if you look at the total of third-party votes, populism has surged and is currently at its highest level since the late 1930s.

Hoffer noted that revolutions do not tend to arise from abject poverty, but rather from deteriorating economic conditions. Those on the verge of starvation make unlikely "true believers" and followers of populist movements, as their daily struggle for existence is more important than any broader political concerns. The "New Poor" are the most likely converts for mass movements. They bitterly recall their former wealth and blame others for their current misfortune. This was true of British farmers who had suffered during the enclosure movement and gravitated toward Cromwell before the British Civil War

(1641–1652). This was certainly the case with the Germans, who lost their wealth due to war and hyperinflation, before the rise of Hitler and the Nazi Party in the 1930s. Today, votes for Sanders, Trump, and Brexit are the expression of discontent by the "Newly Poor." They feel the system is rigged against them and the future is not as bright as the past.

Historian Will Durant warned that societies fall apart when inequality is too severe. "Civilization begins with order, grows with liberty, and dies with chaos." He wrote that a society might find itself divided between a cultured minority and an unfortunate majority. As the majority grows and is left behind, "the internal barbarization by the majority is part of the price that the minority pays for its control of educational and economic opportunity."

In many ways, San Francisco is a microcosm for the US economy and the increasing gap between a wealthy minority and a majority that is left behind. The city is extraordinarily prosperous, but the middle class is starting to feel like the new poor. San Francisco ranks first in California for economic inequality. The average income of the top 1% of households in the city averages $3.6 million, 44 times the average income of the bottom 99%, which stands at $81,094.[22]

While Silicon Valley is recording record profits from monopolies on social networks and search advertising, and overall, the Bay Area has been shedding jobs for the past few months. This paints an unsettling picture of dramatically slowing job growth for the majority of workers.[23] The lack of housing also makes it tough for employees to live near their workplaces, forcing many into lengthy commutes.

Locals have been protesting the inequality for the past few years. The corporate buses that Google and other tech companies offer to ferry their workers from the city to Silicon Valley, 30 miles to the south, are being targeted by an increasingly assertive guerrilla campaign of disruption.[24] Protestors burned effigies of the private buses and held parties to smash them as piñatas. Protesters have rallied at the San Francisco International Airport and outside Twitter's offices to protest gentrification and inequality.

These foreshocks are easy to ignore, but the elite is starting to feel them. Last year Nick Hanauer, one of the early investors in Amazon and part of the 0.01%, wrote an open memo to "My Fellow

Zillionaires." The piece was appropriately titled, "The Pitchforks Are Coming . . . for Us Plutocrats":

> If we don't do something to fix the glaring inequities in this economy, the pitchforks are going to come for us. No society can sustain this kind of rising inequality. In fact, there is no example in human history where wealth accumulated like this and the pitchforks didn't eventually come out. You show me a highly unequal society, and I will show you a police state. Or an uprising. There are no counterexamples. None. It's not if, it's when.[25]

Hanauer did not think that a revolution was inevitable, but he argued that changing course would require action to look after the 99% who were not at the top.

There are much bigger earthquakes ahead if we do not recognize the reasons and create the solutions for the problems of rising income inequality.

Key Thoughts from the Chapter

- Rising inequality is a symptom. It is not the disease.
- Companies have taken a record part of the economic pie.
- Fewer competitors give companies significant market power to raise prices and to reduce wages.
- The economic and political power of monopolies and oligopolies has completely tilted the playing field in favor of dominant corporations against employees.

Conclusion

Economic and Political Freedom

Economic freedom is an essential requisite for political freedom.
—*Milton Friedman*

We must make our choice. We may have democracy, or we may have wealth concentrated in the hands of a few, but we can't have both.
—*Justice Louis Brandeis*

During World War I, as hundreds of thousands of men were dying in the trenches, the French Prime Minister George Clemenceau said, "War is too important to be left to the generals." Today, capitalism is too important to be left to the economists.

As we have shown throughout this book, in many industries monopolies are squeezing workers, choking suppliers, raising prices, stifling the economy, and capturing lawmakers and regulators. Left to their own devices, these companies will not reform themselves. They greet more regulation as a chance to erect further barriers around their industry. They welcome watchdogs and regulators as powerful, government-appointed allies. They shrug at the threat of antitrust laws, which they have hijacked through economists and lawyers for hire.

233

Because companies will not reform themselves, we must change the laws and regulations. We must remember that antitrust laws are enacted by Congress and interpreted by the courts. Antitrust decisions and policy cannot be outsourced to economists or corporate shills. The role of the courts is not to determine economic policy, but rather to implement antitrust policies enacted by the legislature.

A century ago, when Theodore Roosevelt argued for a square deal and reining in corporate trusts, he said, "I mean not merely that I stand for fair play under the present rules of the game, but that I stand for having those rules changed so as to work for a more substantial equality of opportunity and of reward for equally good service."

Once again, we must reform the rules of the game. We need a legislative change to institute new antitrust laws that serve the people. We need to empower local communities and workers rather than distant CEOs or shareholders. We need to change the way we go about our daily lives to restore a balance of power to markets. We need specific remedies to change the rules of the game.

In this conclusion we will show the basis for fixing the problem.

Reforming markets cannot be left to business alone. Markets do not exist in a vacuum untouched by society and the rule of law. While commerce concerns itself with prices, the law concerns itself with values. These values go beyond "efficiency" and "consumer welfare." The citizen is more than a one-dimensional consumer; he is a worker, a producer, a consumer, and a voter.

Friedrich Hayek wrote, "Personally, I should much prefer to have to put up with some such inefficiency than have organized monopoly control my ways of life."[1]

Even if consumer welfare were the only acceptable standard, it has failed on its own terms. Monopolists promise efficiency and lower prices, yet have delivered neither. It is worth remembering the words of Benjamin Franklin who said, "Those who would give up essential liberty, to purchase a little temporary safety, deserve neither liberty nor safety." We have given up economic freedom for the promise of consumer welfare, and we gained neither.

We have lost our way, but the past offers a path back. The challenges of monopoly go back centuries, and we are not the first generation to fight them. There is a long and powerful Anglo-American political tradition that attacks vested rights, special interests and monopolies.

In 1637 John Lilburne was arrested for printing books that had not been licensed by The Stationers Company. As punishment, he was whipped, pilloried, and dragged by an oxcart to Westminster. During the trial, he demanded to see his indictment, asked to face his accusers, and refused to incriminate himself. He claimed these were natural rights of a freeborn Englishman. He spent the rest of his life fighting for his ideas. He inspired the first mass political movement in history, one that became known as the Levellers.

Lilburne wrote the first written constitution titled *An Agreement of the People of England* in 1649. His Agreement not only listed the powers of government, but also contained a bill of rights limiting the power of the legislature as well as the executive. The values and ideals of Lilburne's *Agreement* became the basis for the US Constitution and the Bill of Rights, including freedom of speech and religion, the separation of church and state, the right against self-incrimination, and more. The Supreme Court frequently cites Lilburne as precedent for the rights we now take for granted.

Most important, the Levellers advocated not only for personal rights, but for free trade and an end to monopolies. A clause in Lilburne's constitution declares of Parliament, "That it shall not be in their power to continue or make any Laws to abridge or hinder any person or persons, from trading or merchandizing into any place beyond the seas, where any of this Nation are free to trade."[2]

A key Leveller legacy is their concern for protection of individuals from coercion from concentrations of power. For them, society was divided not between workers and owners of property, but rather between those who profited from monopolies and government favors and the rest of the people. Lilburne and his fellow Levellers attributed low wages to monopolies and restrictions on trade and urged their abolition.[3]

When after the English Civil war, the monopoly on printing remained. Lilburne was again placed in Newgate prison, where he wrote an eloquent piece in which he called for the dissolution of the "insufferable, unjust, and tyrannical Monopoly of Printing." Lilburne attacked the state-granted monopolies of printing, preaching, and foreign trade as infringing on "the Common right of all the free-men of England." He argued that monopolies put the people "in a condition of vassalage," and reduced them to "servility."[4]

Toward the end of his life, when faced with defeat, Lilbume encouraged his followers. "And posterity," he wrote, "we doubt not shall reap the benefit of our endeavours, what ever shall become of us."[5]

Lilburne did not live to see the effect of his ideas, but we owe him a debt of gratitude. His ideas became the bedrock of American civic life and have been exported around the world.

As the Levellers were suppressed, their ideas spread to the American colonies. Many Levellers became Quakers, and William Penn and his followers took the Leveller ideals to Pennsylvania. The Pennsylvania Constitution of 1776 with its declaration of rights, opposed concentrations of economic and political power, "That government is, or ought to be, instituted for the common benefit, protection and security of the people, nation or community; and not for the particular emolument or advantage of any single man, family, or sett of men, who are a part only of that community."[6]

Americans inherited Lilburne's hatred of monopolies. The thread opposing monopolies and concentrations of power runs from Lilburne to Jefferson, Jackson, and to Sherman and beyond. The Maryland State Constitution in 1776 declared, "Monopolies are odious, contrary to the spirit of free government . . . and ought not to be suffered."[7] When the Continental Congress issued its Declaration of Independence from Britain, like Lilburne, they resented the monopoly of the East India Company. The Boston Tea Party was in response to the Company's monopoly on tea. Among their reasons for rebellion against Britain were, "For cutting off our Trade with all parts of the world: For imposing Taxes on us without our Consent." James Madison believed in economic rights; and in an essay, he warned against "arbitrary restrictions, exemptions, and monopolies."[8]

The monopolies Englishman and Americans opposed were based on government grants of monopolies. While many monopolies today are not explicitly based on government grants, the helping hand of government can be found everywhere – approving mergers that grant effective monopolies, endlessly extending patents and copyright for large companies, and enacting friendly regulatory barriers that keep competitors away.

When we see the arc of history, the Sherman Act and Clayton Act are but stepping-stones in the opposition to concentrated economic power. In the landmark judgment in *United States v. Topco Associates*, Justice Thurgood Marshall eloquently wrote:

> Antitrust laws in general, and the Sherman Act in particular, are the Magna Carta of free enterprise. They are as important to the preservation of economic freedom and our free-enterprise system as the Bill of Rights is to the protection of our fundamental personal freedoms. And the freedom guaranteed each and every business, no matter how small, is the freedom to compete – to assert with vigor, imagination, devotion, and ingenuity whatever economic muscle it can muster.

Antitrust does not exist in isolation from the long reach of the past.

Opposing monopolies is not merely a matter of economics and the dislike of higher prices that monopolists might charge. Figures from the left and right have warned about the problems that come from economic concentrations of power and lack of economic freedom. They have warned that you cannot have political without economic freedom, and the concentration of power corrupts both.

From the left, Louis Brandeis, a social reformer who became Supreme Court Justice, championed the battle for economic freedom. "What does democracy involve?" Louis Brandeis said in 1912. "Not merely political and religious liberty, but industrial liberty also."

Brandeis wrote a book titled *The Curse of Bigness*, and renewed interest in antitrust has been called the New Brandeis movement. But the roots of opposition to monopolies run much deeper. The struggle against monopoly did not start or end with Brandeis. Arguments against monopolies have little to do with bigness, and everything to do with dispersing economic and political power.[9]

Milton Friedman, the arch free marketer, echoed Brandeis and saw economic and political freedom as inextricably linked. He wrote, "Economic freedom is an essential requisite for political freedom. By enabling people to cooperate with one another without coercion or central direction, it reduces the area over which political power is exercised." The principal reason for supporting free markets was not lower prices or consumer welfare, but strengthening of democracy and freedom. "In addition, by dispersing power, the free market provides an offset to whatever concentration of political power may arise. The combination of economic and political power in the same hands is a sure recipe for tyranny." It is the great irony of history that Friedman's disciples have done so much to concentrate power. They have achieved a private tyranny.

Brandeis and Friedman were fortunate to live and work in the United States, but European economists viewed the dangers of concentration even more acutely. The Ordoliberals saw how large trusts aided the rise of Hitler. As Friedrich Hayek wrote, "It is only because the control of the means of production is divided among many people acting independently that nobody has complete power over us, that we as individuals can decide what to do with ourselves." He went on to warn, "If all the means of production were vested in a single hand, whether it be nominally that of "society" as a whole or that of a dictator, whoever exercises this control has complete power over us."[10]

After World War II, the United States exported its tradition to Europe, and the Ordoliberals helped extend it further. As the US report on the German economy on year after Potsdam so powerfully stated:

> The German people must be taught that a democratic economy is the most favorable medium for the full development of an individual. . . Just as we must convince the Germans on the political side of the unsoundness of making an irrevocable grant of power to a dictator or an official authoritarian group, we must also convince them on the economic side of the unsoundness of allowing a private enterprise to acquire dictatorial power over any part of the economy.

The reconstruction of Germany was not concerned with efficiency or consumer welfare, but in the full economic and political rebuilding of the German people. The Germans were not seen as mere consumers, but as whole people that had an economic and civic life.

Before Bork's antitrust revolution, the Supreme Court recognized that "efficiency" was not the only object of antitrust law. Chief Justice

Earl Warren wrote, "Congress appreciated that occasional higher costs and prices might result from maintenance of fragmented industries and markets. It resolved these competing considerations in favor of decentralization."[11]

In practice, for most people economic freedoms are of much greater importance than political freedoms. Elections allow the public to vote at the ballots every few years, but in an economic democracy people can vote every single day with their spending choices, often many times a day. While such freedom is appealing in theory, in practice, most people don't have a choice in many of the essential economic decisions in their lives. Monopolies, effectively, represent an economic tyranny.

If we are to reform capitalism and avoid the concentration of economic power, we must return to the roots of capitalism and antitrust. We must restore competition where it is missing. We must safeguard markets for new entrants, and we must end regulatory capture that corrupts politics.

Those who do not like change will oppose any sensible reform of antitrust laws. Monopolists and their allies will decry the creeping fascism of state interference. They will squeal that governments are distorting free markets. Conservatives and true capitalists must remember that entrenched monopolies and oligopolies do not represent the triumph of free-market capitalism but rather its corruption. Open competition is the essence of free markets, and competition requires reasonable regulation. Every government action is not an invasion of individual freedom, while burdensome regulation stifles economic freedom; the key is finding the right balance.

If we do not choose reform, we will get a revolution that we have not chosen. There is nothing more conservative than reformation. In *Reflections on the Revolution in France*, one of the founding texts of conservatism, Edmund Burke recognized that the failure of the French monarchy to reform sowed the seeds for revolution. The French monarchy failed to recognize the need to adapt in order to preserve itself. Without reform, conservation is not possible.

When Theodore Roosevelt was fighting trusts 100 years ago, he said, "constructive change offers the best method of avoiding destructive change, reform is the antidote to revolution . . . social reform is not the precursor but the preventive of socialism." Roosevelt always stressed he was not opposed to corporations, only to monopolies and the abuse of power. Roosevelt reminded his listeners, as Burke did, that revolution would come from failure to reform, "Those who oppose reform will do well to remember that ruin in its worst form is inevitable if our national life brings us nothing better than swollen fortunes for the few and the triumph in both politics and business of a sordid and selfish materialism."[12]

If idealism is not enough for reform and political self-interest is the stumbling block, it is worth looking at the example of Disraeli.

In the 1870s, Conservative Prime Minister Benjamin Disraeli faced high income inequality, rapid industrialization, and the growth of the modern corporation. He could have resisted reforms, but he chose to embrace them. As prime minister, Disraeli passed progressive legislation that caused Alexander Macdonald, one of the first Labor MPs, to conclude that "the Conservative party have done more for the working classes in five years than the Liberals have in fifty."

Disraeli and the Conservatives passed landmark laws improving the lives of workers. They passed the Artisans Dwellings Act, which cleared slums and built public housing works. They passed the Employers and Workmen Act, which made it legal for trade unions to strike and the Factory Act, which limited the work hours of women and children.

The electorate loved Disreali for it. He served twice as Prime Minister. Disraeli's government was a landmark in Conservative fortunes and its domestic measures widened its appeal to the urban lower and middle classes. It should be no surprise that the Conservatives dominated British politics from 1886 to 1906.

The fight for antitrust reform may be difficult, but it is the right thing to do to reform the economy.

True capitalism works because it provides freedom. It makes everyone better by expanding limits of what is possible. It rewards hard work, innovation and ingenuity. It rewards risk-taking and invention.

The history of capitalism is not without dark blots, but it is the best system we have. Today, the average person enjoys far more comforts and freedom than J.P. Morgan or John D. Rockefeller ever had. At their time, they lived like kings because they were the first to have electricity.

Now, we take electricity, telephones, radio, television, film, digital music, and air travel for granted. All are the fruits of inventors and the capitalists who funded them and delivered them to the masses.

Capitalism and invention stagnate without competition. When monopolists have controlled markets – trade at sea, airwaves, phone lines, cable systems, banks, ratings agencies, or computer operating systems – they have stifled innovation and creativity. When capitalism with healthy competition has thrived, it has represented nothing less than the triumph of the human spirit.

What are the guiding principles for reform? What are the values that should underpin the economy? What are the solutions to the problems we face?

We do not have all the answers, but we humbly set out some key principles and suggest reforms based on them. We hope these are principles that should appeal to left and right alike. We hope this list of recommendations will provide a specific roadmap for Congress to reform.

Principles for Reform

Capitalism without competition is not capitalism. Capitalism is not merely a high return on capital. Investors have created monopolies to extract higher returns on capital, and markets and society have suffered the consequences.

The essential role of capitalism is not maximizing efficiency. The genius of capitalism is the creation of value for firms, consumers, and workers. Our lives are immeasurably better today than they were a century ago not because we have been allocating more efficiently the resources of the twentieth-century economy. Innovation and solving human problems is the driver of progress, and that comes from competition.

Monopolies – not big businesses – are the enemy of competition. Big is neither beautiful nor ugly. Many businesses do benefit from economies of scale, but monopolies, in almost all cases, are bad for markets, workers, competitors, consumers and society. There are a limited number of industries that only work as natural monopolies, and these should be regulated to serve the public interest.

Competition is a critical element of capitalism because it promotes the diffusion of economic power and political freedom. Economic freedom is a requisite for political freedom. Monopolies may be benign dictatorships today, but even so a form of dictatorship. Historically, we have preferred the danger of inefficiency with democracy, rather than the comfort of efficiency with economic and political tyranny.

Markets must remain competitive and open to new entrants. The only way to preserve competition is by eliminating unnecessary barriers to entry. Government has a role to play by actively enforcing antitrust and ensuring regulations do not serve monopolists. Vigorous antitrust enforcement is only one part of the solution.

Capitalism must be in favor of equal opportunity, but not equal outcomes. Antimonopoly efforts are not intended to weaken competition or promote firms that would fail in a competitive environment. The only goal is to ensure a level playing field to promote competition, innovation, and growth.

Capitalism does not exist independently of government and society. Markets operate within rules set by society and by government. Whether it is through common law contracts or through legislative acts, markets work because of clear rules. There has never been an unfettered free market without the rule of law.

Solutions and Remedies

Antimonopoly and Mergers

Mergers that materially reduce the number of competitors should be prevented. Today merger enforcement is dead. Over 90% of mergers close, and antitrust decisions are almost never challenged. Companies should be able to grow organically, and any merger that artificially increases the market share of a dominant firm should be prohibited.

The standard for rejecting mergers must be based on simple, clear rules. The easiest rule of thumb is that industries of fewer than six players should not be allowed to merge. You could even put this on the back of a postcard for legislators. This principle can also be stated simply in one sentence for economists: no company in an industry with a CR4 ratio above 66% or with a HHI score above 1,666 should be allowed to merge.

Today, the Department of Justice and FTC consider markets in which the HHI is between 1,500 and 2,500 points to be moderately concentrated, and consider markets in which the HHI is in excess of 2,500 points to be highly concentrated. It is important to prevent industries from becoming concentrated and limit mergers *before* they're already highly concentrated.

A six-player industry rule is a clear standard that is easily enforced. Without clear standards, companies with vast resources will employ economists for hire who will use theoretical models to justify even outright monopolies on the grounds of efficiency and consumer welfare. This biased pretense of justification is contrary to the public interest.

Previous mergers that have reduced competition should be reversed. Unless we right previous wrongs, we cannot fix markets. Many mergers have been approved over the past few decades that have created monopolies and lessened competition. When the courts broke up trusts in the twentieth century, the world did not end, and society benefited. Even shareholders generally benefited, as Standard Oil discovered. Today, any highly concentrated industries that have come through mergers should be broken up and reversed.

Antitrust is not a field that can be handed over exclusively to economists. The field of antitrust has been taken far from its original aims and handed over entirely to economists. Economics is not a science, and it is not equipped to answer what values we want to promote or how we want to organize our society. Not every theory or fad in economics has been correct, and we cannot entrust our economy to professors for hire who bear no consequences for their decisions.

Antimonopoly is more than antitrust. While competition policy and antitrust laws are the main way to fight monopolies, they are not the only ways. Law and regulation must be geared toward preventing dominant companies from preventing new entrants.

Vertical integration should face significant hurdles. Vertical integration by dominant firms should be prevented in any moderately to highly concentrated industry.

Local monopolies should be broken up. Large companies should not be allowed to carve markets up like the mob, dividing the turf. For example, the McCarran Ferguson Act exempted insurance companies from antitrust and subjected them to state regulation where they enjoy local monopolies. Similarly, the hub and spoke model of airports has created local monopolies and duopolies. Airlines should be forced to divest routes to restore competition

Industries should not be exempt from antitrust supervision. Unions have specifically been exempted from antitrust, as collective bargaining does not represent a restraint of trade. However, many industries have gained exemption over the years, for example, the insurance industry. Unwarranted exceptions limit competition and are contrary to the spirit of antitrust.

Antitrust authorities should face greater transparency. They should be forced to report about their work and show why they decided not to bring cases against any mergers that happened during the quarter. They should also be forced to report on an annual basis and show when their analysis was wrong and reverse previous mergers.

New laws should be instituted punish predatory pricing by firms in highly concentrated industries. The United States needs new laws that allow the government to punish firms that engage in predatory pricing. This practice often takes the form of a monopolist raising prices for consumers, but can also happen when monopolists price goods below cost for a period of time in order to forestall new entrants. Much like antitrust in general, existing laws are not enforced or even used.

Antitrust trials should be speeded up rapidly. Laws are not enforced in part because individual cases, such as the Justice Department's Microsoft investigations, can last for a decade and consume an outsize share of an agency's resources. Before 1974, the rules allowed trials to skip appellate review and automatic appeals of district courts' antitrust decisions to the Supreme Court. We must eliminate frequent appeals.

Regulation

Regulations must serve society, not erect barriers to entry for monopolists. Not all government regulations are intrusions on freedom. Regulation plays a critical role in preventing pollution, keeping us safe and healthy and promoting the common good. Rules should be calibrated to avoid killing small companies.

Regulation should be based on principles, not complex rules. Simple principles encourage following the spirit of the law, while complex regulations encourage following the letter of the law but violating its spirit. Complex rules impose substantial costs on new entrants, and prevent competition. For example, Glass Steagal was 35 pages long and served the United States well for over 70 years. Dodd-Frank is over 2,200 pages long, and it has killed new bank startups.

Regulatory capture and the revolving door are evils that should be avoided at all costs. Monopolists influence regulation through a revolving door by which industry workers join government and return to industry in never ending circle. Rules should ban moves between industry and government, as well as restrict the ability of legislators and members of the executive from lobbying on behalf of companies.

Create common carriage rules for internet platforms that sell third-party services. Common carriage rules require the carrier to treat all customers equally and transparently. Where tech companies have a monopoly, they must provide access to their services on fair, reasonable nondiscriminatory terms to all competitors. Without common carriage, dominant transportation or logistics companies can decide what packages get delivered at what cost and what speed, discriminating against clients. Common carriage rules preserve equal opportunity for competitors.[13]

Create rules that reduce switching costs and customer lock-in. Rules reducing or eliminating switching costs promote competition by eliminating a barrier to entry. For example, "number portability" rules allowed users to take their phone to another carrier, which promoted lower prices and competition.

Patents and Copyright

To promote competition, patents and copyrights must only be granted for a limited time without extension. Innovation and creativity must be rewarded, but only for a limited time. Extending the life of patents, even through bureaucracy and regulation, is the granting of a private monopoly and the death of competition.

Competition must be encouraged once patents expire. Regulation, bureaucracy, and legal prohibitions have made it difficult if not impossible for many patients in the United States to get access to cheap, competitive generic drugs even after patents expire. Faster approval of generics, and the importation of generics from Canada and Europe must be allowed to promote competition.

Congress should remove patent protection for areas that are rife with abuse. Almost half of all patents are for things like software and business methods that have been abused by "patent trolls" who drive up costs for producers and consumers.

Shareholders

Workers must be granted shares so that labor can become owners of capital. The gap between labor and capital comes in large part because the vast majority of Americans do not own any meaningful shares in companies. Until the fruits of the economy are shared with workers, the benefits of markets will only go to CEOs, managers, and the very wealthy. Employee share programs should be encouraged via legislation and regulation.

Horizontal shareholdings should be disallowed. No shareholder should be able to buy more than 5% of competitors in the same industry. The only possible reason for an investor to buy most of the major companies in an industry is to induce them to collude or to merge. (This rule would have an exemption for passive investments for index funds.)

Share buybacks should be severely limited. Companies should not be able to buy their shares in the open market and drive prices up while CEO compensation is tied to the share price. Share buybacks should only be done via an organized tender. Insiders should not be able to sell shares within 90 days of a share buyback. Companies should not be able to buy back their own shares if they have underfunded pension plans. Companies have used share buybacks to prop up share prices while insiders sell.

Managers should be forced to own shares they purchase via stock options for at least a year. Stock options have inflated pay at firms, and incentivized a short-term obsession with stock prices rather than longer-term investments in companies.

And Finally, What You Can Do . . .

The fact that you've read to the end means that you care deeply about the economy and politics. You want to know more about the problem and the solutions. Fixing capitalism does not depend entirely on Congressmen and judges; it also depends on you and millions of others.

Whenever possible, choose to spend your money away from dominant firms and monopolies. Sometimes you have no choice when it comes to local high-speed internet, insurance, or even airlines. But where you do, support Davids, not Goliaths. You can even buy local if there are good businesses you like. Every day in capitalism is an election, and you get to cast your vote with your wallet.

Avoid the internet giants; remember, if their services are free, you and your privacy are the product. Studies show that spending time on Facebook and social networks makes you miserable. Enjoy life instead. You'll be much happier. And Google does lots of wonderful things, but there are other email programs besides Gmail, and there are search engines like Bing and DuckDuckGo.

You might even want to subscribe to a newspaper and support journalism.

Become politically active and encourage your Representatives and Senators to restore competition. Reforming markets is not a left or right issue. It is a human issue to get more freedom and promote a healthier economy. If you're left leaning, competitive markets will help reduce unjust inequality. If you're right leaning, restoring competition will promote entrepreneurial activity.

If you liked this book, give a copy to a friend. Unless more people are aware of how capitalism has been weakened and competition is dying, things will never be reformed.

Notes

Introduction

1. http://www.bbc.co.uk/news/world-us-canada-39586391.
2. https://www.wired.com/2017/04/uniteds-greed-turned-friendly-skies-flying-hellscape/.
3. https://splinternews.com/airlines-can-treat-you-like-garbage-because-they-are-an-1794192270.
4. http://www.denverpost.com/2015/07/17/airline-consolidation-has-created-airport-monopolies-increased-fares/.
5. http://www.denverpost.com/2017/04/11/united-boycott/;https://skift.com/2017/07/14/delta-holds-an-edge-over-competitors-by-dominating-less-competitive-markets/.
6. https://www.dallasnews.com/business/business/2015/07/14/airlines-carve-us-into-markets-dominated-by-1-or-2-carriers.
7. https://www.nytimes.com/2015/11/01/opinion/sunday/how-mergers-damage-the-economy.html.
8. https://www.economist.com/graphic-detail/2016/03/24/corporate-concentration.

9. Milton Friedman and Rose D. Friedman, *Capitalism and Freedom: Fortieth Anniversary Edition* (University of Chicago Press, 2002).

10. https://www.npr.org/2016/09/06/492849471/an-economic-mystery-why-are-men-leaving-the-workforce.

Chapter 1: Where Buffett and Silicon Valley Billionaires Agree

1. Warren Buffett, *Berkshire Hathaway Letters to Shareholders, 2016* (Kindle Location 14589). Explorist Productions, Kindle Edition.

2. Ibid.

3. http://www.thebuffett.com/quotes/How-to-Think-About-Businesses.html.

4. Roger Lowenstein, *Buffett: The Making of an American Capitalist* (Random House, 2008).

5. https://businessmanagement.news/2017/05/05/warren-buffet-would-rather-invest-in-your-idiot-nephew-than-with-mark-zuckerberg-or-jeff-bezos/.

6. https://www.ft.com/content/fd27245a-9790-11e7-a652-cde3f882dd7b.

7. https://www.wsj.com/articles/elon-musks-uncontested-3-pointers-1519595032.

8. http://gawker.com/322852/is-peter-thiel-silicon-valleys-godfather.

9. https://www.wsj.com/articles/peter-thiel-competition-is-for-losers-1410535536.

10. Joseph A. Schumpeter, *Capitalism, Socialism, and Democracy*, 2nd ed. (Dancing Unicorn Books, 2016).

11. http://consumerfed.org/wp-content/uploads/2016/12/Overcharged-and-Underserved.pdf.

12. https://www.freepress.net/blog/2017/04/25/net-neutrality-violations-brief-history.

13. https://www.cnet.com/news/fcc-formally-rules-comcasts-throttling-of-bittorrent-was-illegal/.

14. Barry C. Lynn, *Cornered: The New Monopoly Capitalism and the Economics of Destruction* (Hoboken, NJ: Wiley, 2010).

15. https://www.salon.com/2013/07/08/how_%E2%80%9Cecon_101%E2%80%9D_is_killing_america/.

16. Michał Kalecki, *Capitalism: Business Cycles and Full Employment*, vol. 1 of *Collected Works* (Oxford, UK: Oxford University Press, 1990), 252.

17. http://investigativereportingworkshop.org/connected/story/comcast-lures-former-fcc-aides-lobby-nbc-merger/.

18. https://www.newyorker.com/tech/elements/the-oligopoly-problem.

19. *Capital Returns: Investing Through the Capital Cycle: A Money Manager's Reports 2002–15* (Palgrave Macmillan), p. 27. Kindle Edition.

20. https://www.economist.com/news/finance-and-economics/21731441-new-measure-growing-problem-what-annual-reports-say-or-do-not-about.

21. Simon Clarke, *Marx's Theory of Crisis* (Springer, July 2016), p. 255.

22. Credit Suisse, The Incredible Shrinking Universe of Stocks: The Causes and Consequences of Fewer U.S. Equities http://www.cmgwealth.com/wp-content/uploads/2017/03/document_1072753661.pdf.

23. Gustavo Grullon, Yelena Larkin, and Roni Michaely, " Are U.S. Industries Becoming More Concentrated?" (August 31, 2017). Available at SSRN: https://ssrn.com/abstract=2612047.

24. https://www.barrons.com/articles/unicorns-what-are-they-really-worth-1510974129?mod=hp_MTS&

25. Grullon, Larkin, and Michaely, "Are U.S. Industries."

26. https://qz.com/1040046/30-firms-earn-half-the-total-profit-made-by-all-us-public-companies/.

27. Grullon, Larkin, and Michaely, "Are U.S. Industries."

28. http://equitablegrowth.org/report/u-s-merger-policy-amid-the-new-merger-wave/.

29. http://fortune.com/2015/10/22/mba-ethics-volkswagen/.

30. http://www.nbcnews.com/id/18472476/ns/business-us_business/t/duke-cheating-scandal-shows-need-law/.

31. https://www.marketwatch.com/story/wal-mart-ceo-consumers-feeling-greater-pressure-2011-04-27.

32. http://www.saturdayeveningpost.com/2014/01/03/history/post-perspective/ford-doubles-minimum-wage.html.

33. https://www.ucg.org/world-news-and-prophecy/the-eurozone-debt-crisis-calamity-still-looms.

34. http://www.economist.com/node/9832838.

35. https://ecology.iww.org/texts/JohnBellamyFoster/CapitalismandtheCurseofEnergyEfficiency.

36. http://www.newyorker.com/magazine/2010/12/20/the-efficiency-dilemma.

37. https://www.wired.com/2011/09/att-conquered-20th-century/.

38. Tim Wu, *The Master Switch* (Alfred Knopf, 2010).

Chapter 2: Dividing Up the Turf

1. David Critchley, *The Origin of Organized Crime in America* (New York: Taylor & Francis Group, 2009), p. 144.

2. http://americanmafiahistory.com/five-families/.

3. https://www.americanmafia.org/families/the-commission-and-the-mafia-families/.

4. Nicholas deRoos, "Examining Models of Collusion: The Market for Lysine," *International Journal of Industrial Organization* 24, no. 6 (2006): 1083–1107.

5. http://articles.chicagotribune.com/2004-06-19/business/0406190182_1_lysine-and-citric-acid-mark-whitacre-corn-syrup.

6. OECD, Report on the Nature and Impact of Hard Core Cartels and Sanctions under National Competition Laws, DAFFE/COMP (2002) (Paris: Organisation of Economic Co-operation and Development, 2003), p. 7.

7. John M. Connor, *Price-Fixing Overcharges*, rev. ed. (February 24, 2014). Available at SSRN: https://ssrn.com/abstract=2400780.

8. John Connor and Douglas Miller, "The Predictability of DOJ Cartel Fines," *Antitrust Bulletin* 56, no. 3 (September 1, 2011): 525–541.

9. Sean F. Ennis Pedro Gonzaga, and Chris Pike, "Inequality: A Hidden Cost of Market Power (March 6, 2017). Available at SSRN: https://ssrn.com/abstract=2942791.

10. https://www.economist.com/news/business/21599799-trustbusters-have-got-better-detecting-cartels-and-bolder-punishing-them-incentives.

11. https://www.economist.com/news/business/21599799-trustbusters-have-got-better-detecting-cartels-and-bolder-punishing-them-incentives.

12. https://www.theatlantic.com/magazine/archive/1982/02/have-you-ever-tried-to-sell-a-diamond/304575/.

13. http://www.bbc.co.uk/news/business-30003693.

14. http://www.telegraph.co.uk/finance/newsbysector/banksandfinance/9568087/RBS-traders-boasted-of-Libor-cartel.html.

15. Margaret C. Levenstein and Valerie Y. Suslow, "Price-Fixing Hits Home: An Empirical Study of U.S. Price Fixing Conspiracies," Ross School of Business Working Paper No. 1290, November 2015.

16. Stephen Martin, "Competition Policy, Collusion, and Tacit Collusion," *International Journal of Industrial Organization* 24, no. 6 (November 2006): 1299–1332.

17. Miguel Alexandre Fonseca and Hans-Theo Normann, "Explicit vs. Tacit Collusion: The Impact of Communication in Oligopoly Experiments" (July 3, 2011). Available at SSRN: https://ssrn.com/abstract=1937803.

18. Federico Ciliberto, Eddie Watkins, and Jonathan W. Williams, "Two Screening Tests for Tacit Collusion: Evidence from the Airline Industry" (July 29, 2017). Available at SSRN: https://ssrn.com/abstract=3012580.

19. Gary Noesser, *Stalling for Time* (Random House, 2010).

20. https://www.nytimes.com/2013/03/03/magazine/beer-mergers.html.

21. William E. Kovacic, Robert C. Marshall, Leslie M. Marx, and Halbert L. White, "Plus Factors and Agreement in Antitrust Law." *Michigan Law Review* 110, no. 3 (2011): 393–436.

22. Simon, Hermann. *Confessions of the Pricing Man: How Price Affects Everything* (Springer International Publishing, 2015). Kindle Edition.

23. Ibid.

24. http://antitrustconnect.com/2017/08/07/rejection-of-containerboard-conspiracy-claims-shows-difficulty-of-getting-an-antitrust-case-to-a-jury/.

25. https://www.healthaffairs.org/do/10.1377/hblog20170905.061802/full/.

26. Steven G. Calabresi, "The Right to Buy Health Insurance across State Lines: Crony Capitalism and the Supreme Court," 81 *U. Cin. L. Rev.* (2013)." Available at: https://scholarship.law.uc.edu/uclr/vol81/iss4/5; "Focus on Health Reform: How Competitive are State Insurance Markets?" The Henry J. Kaiser Family Foundation (October 2011), http://www.kff.org/healthreform/upload/8242.pdf; and Bob Cook, "AMA: Health Plan Market Dominance Causes 'Competitive Harm,' " *American Medical News* (December 10, 2012), http://www.ama-assn.org/amednews/2012/12/10/bisb1210.htm.

27. Luis Suarez-Villa, *Corporate Power, Oligopolies, and the Crisis of the State* (State University of New York Press, 2015), p. 63. Kindle Edition.

28. http://rafiusa.org/programs/contract-agriculture-reform/understanding-contract-agriculture/.

29. Barry C. Lynn, *Cornered: The New Monopoly Capitalism and the Economics of Destruction* (Hoboken, NJ: Wiley, 2010).

30. James M. MacDonald, "Technology, Organization, and Financial Performance in U.S. Broiler Production," Economic Information Bulletin 126, USDA Economic Research Service.

31. http://www.justice.gov/atr/public/workshops/ag2010/comments/255196.pdf.

32. http://www.chicagotribune.com/business/ct-biz-winn-dixie-tyson-chicken-prices-20180115-story.html

33. https://www.newsweek.com/2014/04/18/death-farm-248127.html   and   https://www.theguardian.com/us-news/2017/dec/06/why-are-americas-farmers-killing-themselves-in-record-numbers.

34. Suarez-Villa, *Corporate Power, Oligopolies, and the Crisis of the State*, p. 63.

35. http://www.kunc.org/post/poultry-plant-workers-face-abuse-job-report-says.

36. https://www.nytimes.com/2014/03/13/opinion/kristof-the-unhealthy-meat-market.html.

37. http://www.businessinsider.com/maps-showing-regional-supermarkets-2013-6.

38. Gustavo Grullon, Yelena Larkin, and Roni Michaely, " Are U.S. Industries Becoming More Concentrated?" (August 31, 2017). Available at SSRN: https://ssrn.com/abstract=2612047.

39. https://www.marketwatch.com/story/americas-most-successful-companies-are-killing-the-economy-2017-05-24 and https://www.census.gov/econ/concentration.html.

40. http://www.nationalhogfarmer.com/ar/numbers-fall

41. https://www.forbes.com/sites/csr/2012/08/06/choice-at-the-supermarket-is-our-food-system-the-perfect-oligopoly/#594a687f334e.

Chapter 3: What Monopolies and King Kong Have in Common

1. http://abcnews.go.com/Health/PainManagement/story?id=6309464&page=1.

2. http://www.digitaljournal.com/article/262552.

3. http://abcnews.go.com/Health/PainManagement/story?id=6309464&page=1.

4. http://senseaboutscience.blogspot.co.uk/2011/07/tapeworm.html.

5. http://rooseveltinstitute.org/how-widespread-labor-monopsony-some-new-results-suggest-its-pervasive/; José Azar, Ioana Elena Marinescu, and Marshall Steinbaum, "Labor Market Concentration" (December 15, 2017). Available at SSRN: https://ssrn.com/abstract=3088767.

6. http://rooseveltinstitute.org/how-widespread-labor-monopsony-some-new-results-suggest-its-pervasive/ .

7. Lina Khan and Sandeep Vaheesan, "Market Power and Inequality: The Antitrust Counterrevolution and Its Discontents," *Harvard Law & Policy Review* 235 (2017). Available at SSRN: https://ssrn.com/abstract=2769132.

8. Holger M. Mueller, Paige Ouimet, and Elena Simintzi, "Wage Inequality and Firm Growth" (February 1, 2015). Available at SSRN: https://ssrn.com/abstract=2540321.

9. https://gizmodo.com/5797022/googles-secret-class-system and https://www.bloomberg.com/news/articles/2018-07-25/inside-google-s-shadow-workforce.

10. Gustave Grullon, Yelena Larkin, and Roni Michaely, "Are U.S. Industries Becoming More Concentrated?" (August 31, 2017). Available at SSRN: https://ssrn.com/abstract=2612047.

11. Bruce A. Blonigen and Justin R. Pierce, "Evidence for the Effects of Mergers on Market Power and Efficiency," Finance and Economics Discussion Series 2016-082. (Washington, DC: Board of Governors of the Federal Reserve System, 2016), https://doi.org/10.17016/FEDS.2016.082.

12. Jan De Loecker and Jan Eeckhout, "The Rise of Market Power and the Macroeconomic Implications" (August 2017). NBER Working Paper No. 23687. http://www.nber.org/papers/w23687.

13. Sarah Gordon, "Record Year for M&A with Big Deals and Big Promises." *Financial Times,* December 16, 2015, https://www.ft.com/content/0fd15156-9e5b-11e5-b45d-4812f209f861.

14. Craig Peters, "Evaluating the Performance of Merger Simulations: Evidence from the U.S. Airline Industry." *Journal of Law and Economics 49* (2006), pp. 627–649; Matthew Weinberg, "An Evaluation of Mergers Simulations," working paper, University of Georgia, 2006.

15. Matthew Weinberg, "The Price Effects of Horizontal Mergers," *Journal of Competition Law & Economics 4,* no. 2 (June 1, 2008), pp. 433–447, https://doi.org/10.1093/joclec/nhm029.

16. Orley Ashenfelter, Daniel Hosken, and Matthew Weinberg, "Did Robert Bork Understate the Competitive Impact of Mergers? Evidence from Consummated Mergers," *The Journal of Law and Economics 57,* no. S3 (August 2014): S67–S100, https://doi.org/10.1086/675862.

17. John Kwoka, *Mergers, Merger Control, and Remedies: A Retrospective Analysis of U.S. Policy* (MIT Press, 2014).

18. Joseph Kowka, "U.S. Antitrust and Competition Policy Amid the New Merger Wave," July 27, 2017, http://equitablegrowth.org/report/u-s-merger-policy-amid-the-new-merger-wave/.

19. https://news.yale.edu/2015/12/15/hospital-prices-show-mind-boggling-variation-across-us-driving-health-care-costs and http://www.healthcarepricingproject.org/papers/paper-1.

20. http://thehealthcareblog.com/blog/2017/02/28/drexit-costs-of-a-hospital-monopoly-in-one-underserved-county/.

21. http://www.modernhealthcare.com/article/20170413/NEWS/170419935.

22. https://www.economist.com/news/finance-and-economics/21725552-new-research-suggests-too-little-competition-deters-investment-americas.

23. Paul S. Dempsey and Andrew R. Goetz, "Airline Deregulation and Laissez-Faire Mythology," ABC-CLIO (September 8, 1992): 252.

24. "Why It Costs So Much to Fly From These Airports," *Wall Street Journal*, August 25, 2011; https://centreforaviation.com/insights/analysis/houston-intercontinental-airport-enjoys-solid-traffic-growth-and-wins-new-key-long-haul-service-245295; https://skift.com/2017/07/14/delta-holds-an-edge-over-competitors-by-dominating-less-competitive-markets/; http://houston.culturemap.com/news/travel/11-27-12-the-most-expensive-airport-in-america-thats-houstons-iah-again/. Houston has consistently been the most expensive airport in the country, providing a cash cow for United.

25. Robert Kulick, *Ready-to-Mix: Horizontal Mergers, Prices, and Productivity*, U.S. Census Bureau, CES 17–38 (April 2017), https://ideas.repec.org/p/cen/wpaper/17-38.html.

26. Philip Howard, *Concentration and Power in the Food System: Who Controls What We Eat?* (Bloomsbury Publishing, February 25, 2016): 61.

27. https://www.justice.gov/file/486606/download.

28. https://www.nytimes.com/2017/04/07/opinion/is-it-last-call-for-craft-beer.html.

29. https://www.fool.com/investing/2017/12/24/this-analyst-thinks-a-b-inbev-stock-has-nothing-le.aspx; http://uk.businessinsider.com/r-ab-inbev-increases-profit-despite-selling-less-beer-2017-10.

30. John B. Kirkwood, "Powerful Buyers and Merger Enforcement." *Boston University Law Review 1485* (October 1, 2012); Seattle University School of Law Research Paper No. 13-04. Available at SSRN: https://ssrn.com/abstract=1809985.

31. Barry Lynn, "Breaking the Chain." *Harpers*, http://www.barryclynn.com/wp-content/Harpers_Breaking.pdf.

32. http://grist.org/food/2011-12-30-eaters-beware-Walmart-is-taking-over-our-food-system/.

33. https://www.brookings.edu/research/declining-business-dynamism-in-the-united-states-a-look-at-states-and-metros/.

34. https://aeon.co/essays/what-does-small-business-really-contribute-to-economic-growth.

35. Gustavo Grullon, Yelena Larkin, and Roni Michaely, "Are U.S. Industries Becoming More Concentrated?" August 31, 2017. Available at SSRN: https://ssrn.com/abstract=2612047.

36. Ian Hathaway, Mark Schweitzer, and Scott Shane, *The Shifting Source of New Business Establishments and New Jobs*, Economic Commentary, August 2014. http://www.clevelandfed.org/research/commentary/2014/2014-15.pdf.

37. http://money.cnn.com/2013/01/18/news/companies/boeing-dreamliner-parts/index.html.

38. https://www.pcworld.com/article/3272468/components-processors/intels-loihi-roadmap-calls-for-its-brain-chips-to-be-as-smart-as-a-mouse-by-2019.html.

39. http://fathom.lib.uchicago.edu/2/21701757/.

40. William Poundstone, *Are You Smart Enough to Work at Google?* (Oneworld Publications), pp. 15–16; Kindle Edition.

41. John C. Haltiwanger, Steven Davis, and Scott Schuh, *Job Creation and Destruction* (MIT Press, 1998).

42. R.I.M. Dunbar, "Cognitive Constraints on the Structure and Dynamics of Social Networks." *Group Dynamics: Theory, Research, and Practice* 12, no. 1 (2008): 7–16. http://dx.doi.org/10.1037/1089-2699.12.1.7.

43. Robin Dunbar, *How Many Friends Does One Person Need?: Dunbar's Number and Other Evolutionary Quirks* (Faber and Faber, 2014).

44. http://www.pewresearch.org/fact-tank/2014/02/03/6-new-facts-about-facebook/.

45. http://www.statista.com/statistics/264097/number-of-1st-level-connections-of-linkedin-users/.

46. https://www.npr.org/2011/06/04/136723316/dont-believe-facebook-you-only-have-150-friends.

47. Geoffrey West, *Scale* (Penguin Books, 2018).

48. http://voxeu.org/article/decline-high-growth-entrepreneurship; Ryan Decker, John Haltiwanger, Ron S. Jarmin, and Javier Miranda, "Where Has All the Skewness Gone? The Decline in High-Growth (Young) Firms in the U.S." (December 2015), NBER Working Paper No. w21776. Available at SSRN: https://ssrn.com/abstract=2700005.

49. Zoltan J. Acs and David B. Audretsch, "Innovation in Large and Small Firms: An Empirical." *The American Economic Review* 78, no. 4 (September 1988): 678–690. American Economic Association, http://www.jstor.org/stable/1811167.

50. Zoltan J. Acs and David B. Audretsch, "Testing the Schumpeterian Hypothesis," *Eastern Economic Journal* XIV, no. 2 (1988).

51. https://www.marketwatch.com/story/americas-most-successful-companies-are-killing-the-economy-2017-05-24.

52. https://www.bloomberg.com/news/articles/2017-10-12/google-has-made-a-mess-of-robotics.

53. http://blog.luxresearchinc.com/blog/2016/03/the-downfall-of-google-robotics/.

54. Michael A. Hiltzik, *Dealers of Lightning: Xerox PARC and the Dawn of the Computer Age* (HarperBusiness, 1999).

55. Barry C. Lynn, *Cornered: The New Monopoly Capitalism and the Economics of Destruction* (Hoboken, NJ: Wiley, 2010).

56. https://qz.com/801706/innovation-guru-clayton-christensens-new-theory-will-help-protect-you-from-disruption/.

57. Frederic M. Scherer, "Technological Innovation and Monopolization" (October 2007). KSG Working Paper No. RWP07-043. Available at SSRN: https://ssrn.com/abstract=1019023.

58. John J. McConnell, John J. Sibley, E. Steven, and Wei Xu, "The Stock Price Performance of Spin-Off Subsidiaries, Their Parents, and the Spin-Off ETF, 2001–2013," *Journal of Portfolio Management; New York* 42, no. 1 (Fall 2015): 143–152.

59. http://larrysummers.com/2016/02/17/the-age-of-secular-stagnation/.

60. Robin Döttling, German Gutierrez Gallardo, and Thomas Philippon, "Is There an Investment Gap in Advanced Economies? If So, Why?" (July 2017). Available at SSRN: https://ssrn.com/abstract=3002796.

61. Christopher Lasch, *The Revolt of the Elites and the Betrayal of Democracy* (W.W. Norton & Co., 1995).

62. https://evolution.berkeley.edu/evolibrary/article/agriculture_02.

63. http://www.pbs.org/thebotanyofdesire/potato-control.php.

64. https://www.bloomberg.com/view/articles/2017-12-21/the-banana-pocalypse-is-nigh.

65. https://www.csmonitor.com/1991/1002/02191.html.

66. https://www.theguardian.com/us-news/2018/jan/10/hurricane-maria-puerto-rico-iv-bag-shortage-hospitals.

67. https://www.theatlantic.com/business/archive/2015/11/cities-economic-fates-diverge/417372/.

68. Richard Brunell, "The Social Costs of Mergers: Restoring Local Control as a Factor in Merger Policy," *North Carolina Law Review* 85, no. 1 (2006). Available at SSRN: https://ssrn.com/abstract=992272.

69. http://abcnews.go.com/Business/Walmart-closures-leaving-small-towns-broken-residents/story?id=36559225.

Chapter 4: Squeezing the Worker

1. "Silicon Valley," *American Experience* PBS Series, Season 25, Episode 3. http://www.pbs.org/video/american-experience-silicon-valley/.

2. Alex Tabarrok, "Non Compete Clauses Reduce Innovation," June 9, 2014, http://marginalrevolution.com/marginalrevolution/2014/06/non–compete–clauses.html.

3. Mike McPhate, "California Today: Silicon Valley's Secret Sauce," May 19, 2017, https://www.nytimes.com/2017/05/19/us/california-today-silicon-valley.html.

4. https://www.csmonitor.com/Technology/2011/1212/Robert-Noyce-Why-Steve-Jobs-idolized-Noyce.

5. Jim Edwards, "Emails from Google's Eric Schmidt and Sergey Brin Show a Shady Agreement Not to Hire Apple Workers," March 23, 2014, http://www.businessinsider.com/emails-eric-schmidt-sergey-brin-hiring-apple-2014-3.

6. Barry Levine, "4 Tech Companies Are Paying a $325M Fine for Their Illegal Non-compete Pact," May 23, 2014, https://venturebeat.com/2014/05/23/4-tech-companies-are-paying-a-325m-fine-for-their-illegal-non-compete-pact/.

7. Rachel Abrams, "Why Aren't Paychecks Growing? A Burger-Joint Clause Offers a Clue," September 27, 2017, https://www.nytimes.com/2017/09/27/business/pay-growth-fast-food-hiring.html.

8. Evan P. Starr, Norman Bishara, and J.J. Prescott, "Non-competes in the U.S. Labor Force," December 8, 2017, https://papers.ssrn.com/sol3/papers.cfm?abstract_id=2625714.

9. Ryan Nunn, "Leveling the Playing Field for Workers by Reforming Non-competes," May 6, 2016, https://www.brookings.edu/opinions/leveling-the-playing-field-for-workers-by-reforming-non-competes/.

10. Office of Economic Policy, US Department of the Treasury, *Non-compete Contracts: Economic Effects and Policy Implications.* March 2016. https://www.treasury.gov/resource-center/economic-policy/Documents/UST%20Non-competes%20Report.pdf.

11. Ibid.

12. Matt Marx and Lee Fleming, "Non-compete Agreements: Barriers to Entry . . . and Exit?" *Innovation Policy and the Economy* 12 (April 2012), p. 49, eds. Josh Lerner and Scott Stern. National Bureau of Economic Research, http://www.nber.org/chapters/c12452.pdf.

13. Phil Longman, "Why the Economic Fates of America's Cities Diverged," November 28, 2015, https://www.theatlantic.com/business/archive/2015/11/cities-economic-fates-diverge/417372/.

14. Marshall Steinbaum, "How Widespread Is Labor Monopsony? Some New Results Suggest It's Pervasive," December 18, 2017, http://rooseveltinstitute.org/how-widespread-labor-monopsony-some-new-results-suggest-its-pervasive/.

15. Nathan Wilmers, "Wage Stagnation and Buyer Power: How Buyer-Supplier Relations Affect U.S. Workers' Wages, 1978 to 2014," *American Sociological Review* 83, no. 2 (2018): 213–242, https://doi.org/10.1177/0003122418762441.

16. Jade Scipioni, "10% of Amazon's Workforce in Ohio Is on Food Stamps, Report Says,"

    January 8, 2018, https://finance.yahoo.com/news/10-amazon-apos-workforce-ohio-162700977.html.

17. Policy Matters Ohio, "SNAP feeds Ohio," September 6, 2017,

    https://www.policymattersohio.org/research-policy/pathways-out-of-poverty/basic-needs-unemployment-compensation/snap-feeds-ohio.

18. "Contingent Workforce: Size, Characteristics, Earnings, and Benefits, April 20, 2015." The Honorable Patty Murray, Ranking Member Committee on Health, Education, Labor, and Pensions, United States Senate, The Honorable Kirsten Gillibrand, United States Senate. https://www.gao.gov/assets/670/669899.pdf.

19. https://www.theatlas.com/charts/4yUS6B7fe.

20. https://www.theatlas.com/charts/4yUS6B7fe.

21. Dan Kopf, "Almost All the US Jobs Created since 2005 Are Temporary," December 5, 2016, https://qz.com/851066/almost-all-the-10-million-jobs-created-since-2005-are-temporary/.

22. Bloomberg, "Shift: The Commission on Work, Workers, and Technology," May 16, 2017.

23. Hanna Wheatley, "More Than Half of Self-employed Not Earning a Decent Living," August 15, 2017, http://neweconomics.org/2017/08/self_employed_not_earning/,

24. Brad Stone, "Costco CEO Craig Jelinek Leads the Cheapest, Happiest Company in the World," June 7, 2013, https://www.bloomberg.com/news/articles/2013-06-06/costco-ceo-craig-jelinek-leads-the-cheapest-happiest-company-in-the-world.

25. Connor Dougherty and Andrew Burton, "A 2:15 Alarm, 2 Trains and a Bus Get Her to Work by 7 a.m.," *New York Times*, August 17, 2017, https://www.nytimes.com/2017/08/17/business/economy/san-francisco-commute.html.

26. Nicole Wredberg, "Subverting Workers' Rights: Class Action Waivers and the Arbitral Threat to the NLRA," *Hastings Law Journal* 67, no. 3 (2016), 881–912.

27. Anna Boiko-Weyrauch, "Seattle Workers Accuse Airline Caterer of Backtracking on Fines and Wages," October 20, 2017, http://kuow.org/post/seattle-workers-accuse-airline-caterer-backtracking-fines-and-wages.

28. Bureau of Labor Statistics, "Union Members Summary," January 26, 2017, https://www.bls.gov/news.release/union2.nr0.htm.

29. Phil Ebersole, June 12, 2012, https://philebersole.wordpress.com/2012/06/12/the-decline-of-american-labor-unions/.

30. Drew Harwell, "Hundreds Allege Sex Harassment, Discrimination at Kay and Jared Jewelry Company," February 27, 2017, https://www.washingtonpost.com/business/economy/hundreds-allege-sex-harassment-discrimination-at-kay-and-jared-jewelry-company/2017/02/27/8dcc9574-f6b7-11e6-bf01-d47f8cf9b643_story.html?utm_term=.e92c302f0d99.

31. Theodore Eisenberg and Elizabeth Hill, "A 2003 Study by Professors Eisenberg and Hill Reported Employee Win Rates in Employment Discrimination Trials of 36.4%," *Arbitration and Litigation of Employment Claims: An Empirical Comparison* 58, DIsP. RESOL. J. 44 (2003). 2014 79 80 *Berkeley Journal of Employment & Labor Law.* The same study reported a higher employee win rate of 57% in a sample of state court, noncivil rights–based employment cases. This latter win rate is similar to the 50% employee win rate in California state court trials involving common law discharge-based claims found in research by Professor David Oppenheimer. By contrast, my own research on outcomes of mandatory arbitration hearings found a 21.4% employee win rate amongst cases administered by the AAA. Around half of all mandatory arbitration cases administered by the AAA involve employment discrimination claims, with the majority of the remainder involving noncivil rights, common law-based claims.

32. Ceilidh Gao, "Can Companies Force Workers to Go to Arbitration?" September 19, 2017, http://www.newsweek.com/can-companies-force-workers-go-arbitration-667623.

33. Liz Moyer, "Were You Affected by the Equifax Data Breach? One Click Could Cost You Your Rights in Court," September 8, 2017, https://www.cnbc.com/2017/09/08/were-you-affected-by-the-equifax-data-breach-one-click-could-cost-you-your-rights-in-court.html.

34. Alexander J. S. Colvin, "The Growing Use of Mandatory Arbitration," September 27, 2017, http://www.epi.org/publication/the-growing-use-of-mandatory-arbitration/.

35. Megan Leonhart, "Getting Screwed at Work? The Sneaky Way You May Have Given Up Your Right to Sue," September 27, 2017, http://time.com/money/4958168/big-companies-mandatory-arbitration-cant-sue/.

36. https://www.washingtonpost.com/news/the-watch/wp/2014/09/19/federal-appeals-court-stop-using-swat-style-raids-for-regulatory-inspections/.

37. Radley Balko, *Rise of the Warrior Cop: The Militarization of America's Police Forces* (New Yorks: PublicAffairs, 2013).

38. Dick M. Carpenter II, Ph.D., Lisa Knepper, Kyle Sweetland, and Jennifer McDonald, "License to Work: A National Study of Burdens from Occupational Licensing," Institute for Justice, https://ij.org/report/license-work-2/.

Chapter 5: Silicon Valley Throws Some Shade

1. https://www.theregister.co.uk/2010/12/01/google_eu_investigation_comment/.

2. http://europa.eu/rapid/press-release_IP-17-1784_en.htm.

3. https://www.wired.com/story/yelp-claims-google-broke-promise-to-antitrust-regulators/.

4. https://www.nytimes.com/2018/02/20/magazine/the-case-against-google.html.

5. http://theweek.com/articles/693488/google-monopoly--crushing-internet.

6. https://theoutline.com/post/1399/how-google-ate-celebritynetworth-com.

7. https://www.idc.com/promo/smartphone-market-share/os.

8. https://www.netmarketshare.com/browser-market-share.aspx.

9. https://www.wsj.com/articles/how-google-swayed-efforts-to-block-annoying-online-ads-1518623663.

10. https://www.rollingstone.com/politics/features/taibbi-facebook-can-we-be-saved-social-media-giant-w518655.

11. https://www.forbes.com/sites/stevendennis/2017/06/19/should-we-care-whether-amazon-is-systematically-destroying-retail/#62085ff66b1f.

12. https://www.axios.com/regulators-ftc-facebook-google-doj-advertising-5ea0f001-eca8-4f07-b7d0-6ed22782800f.html.

13. https://lpeblog.org/2017/12/06/from-territorial-to-functional-sovereignty-the-case-of-amazon/.

14. http://www.nationalreview.com/article/450476/silicon-valleys-anti-conservative-bias-solution-treat-major-tech-companies-utilities.

15. https://www.wired.com/story/heres-what-facebook-wont-let-you-post/.

16. https://www.nytimes.com/2016/11/22/technology/facebook-censorship-tool-china.html.

17. https://www.washingtonpost.com/news/volokh-conspiracy/wp/2014/12/21/facebook-should-stop-cooperating-with-russian-government-censorship/.

18. http://iasc-culture.org/THR/THR_article_2017_Fall_Pasquale.php.

19. https://www.bloomberg.com/news/articles/2018-01-02/google-s-dutch-sandwich-shielded-16-billion-euros-from-tax.

20. https://moderndiplomacy.eu/2018/05/17/the-google-tax/.

21. https://www.theatlantic.com/business/archive/2016/04/corporate-tax-avoidance/478293/.

22. https://www.theguardian.com/commentisfree/2017/nov/08/tax-havens-dodging-theft-multinationals-avoiding-tax.

23. https://cyber.harvard.edu/interactive/events/conferences/2008/09/msvdoj/smith.

24. https://www.nytimes.com/2018/02/20/magazine/the-case-against-google.html.

25. https://www.theringer.com/tech/2018/5/18/17362452/microsoft-antitrust-lawsuit-netscape-internet-explorer-20-years.

26. https://www.wsj.com/articles/inside-the-u-s-antitrust-probe-of-google-1426793274.

27. https://theintercept.com/2016/04/22/googles-remarkably-close-relationship-with-the-obama-white-house-in-two-charts/.

28. https://www.recode.net/2018/1/23/16919424/apple-amazon-facebook-google-uber-trump-white-house-lobbying-immigration-russia.

29. http://www.stateofdigital.com/eric-schmidt-at-google-hearings-close-to-monopoly-but-weve-not-cooked-anything/.

30. https://laweconcenter.org/wp-content/uploads/2018/05/manne-the_real_reaon_foundem_foundered_2018-05-02-1.pdf.

31. https://www.salon.com/2015/11/24/googles_insidious_shadow_lobbying_how_the_internet_giant_is_bankrolling_friendly_academics_and_skirting_federal_investigations/.

32. https://www.nytimes.com/2017/08/30/us/politics/eric-schmidt-google-new-america.html.

33. https://qz.com/1206184/bill-gates-warns-silicon-valley-not-to-be-the-new-microsoft/.

34. https://www.npr.org/sections/thetwo-way/2017/06/27/534524024/google-hit-with-2-7-billion-fine-by-european-antitrust-monitor.

35. http://ec.europa.eu/competition/antitrust/cases/dec_docs/39740/39740_14996_3.pdf.

36. https://www.newyorker.com/magazine/2017/08/28/who-owns-the-internet.

37. https://www.cjr.org/special_report/facebook-media-buzzfeed.php.

38. https://www.theguardian.com/technology/2017/oct/23/facebook-non-promoted-posts-news-feed-new-trial-publishers.

39. https://www.socialmediatoday.com/social-networks/complete-list-facebooks-misreported-metrics-and-what-they-mean.

40. https://www.socialmediatoday.com/social-networks/complete-list-facebooks-misreported-metrics-and-what-they-mean.

41. https://nypost.com/2016/11/03/facebook-sued-over-its-fraudulent-ad-metrics/.

42. https://www.broadcastingcable.com/news/facebook-s-video-move-may-aid-nielsen-comscore-168497.

43. http://adcontrarian.blogspot.com/2013/06/the-75-billion-ad-swindle.html.

44. https://www.theguardian.com/technology/2017/sep/07/facebook-claims-it-can-reach-more-people-than-actually-exist-in-uk-us-and-other-countries.

45. https://www.theguardian.com/technology/2017/mar/11/tim-berners-lee-web-inventor-save-internet.

46. https://staltz.com/the-web-began-dying-in-2014-heres-how.html.

47. http://www.vulture.com/2018/02/how-facebook-is-killing-comedy.html.

48. https://medium.com/humane-tech/tech-and-the-fake-market-tactic-8bd386e3d382.

49. https://staltz.com/the-web-began-dying-in-2014-heres-how.html.

50. https://www.rollingstone.com/politics/features/taibbi-facebook-can-we-be-saved-social-media-giant-w518655.

51. https://www.theatlantic.com/technology/archive/2018/04/amazon-may-have-a-counterfeit-problem/558482/.

52. https://www.theatlantic.com/technology/archive/2018/04/amazon-may-have-a-counterfeit-problem/558482/.

53. https://www.forbes.com/sites/stevendennis/2017/06/19/should-we-care-whether-amazon-is-systematically-destroying-retail/#62085ff66b1f.

54. https://www.yalelawjournal.org/note/amazons-antitrust-paradox.

55. https://www.theguardian.com/technology/2015/jun/23/amazon-marketplace-third-party-seller-faustian-pact.

56. https://www.forbes.com/sites/retailwire/2014/10/30/is-amazon-undercutting-third-party-sellers-using-their-own-data/#700a08a953d8.

57. https://www.propublica.org/article/amazon-says-it-puts-customers-first-but-its-pricing-algorithm-doesnt

58. https://rainforests.mongabay.com/0202.htm.

59. https://www.rand.org/pubs/research_briefs/RB77/index1.html.

60. https://www.ncbi.nlm.nih.gov/books/NBK236347/.

61. https://www.vox.com/new-money/2017/7/11/15929014/end-of-the-internet-startup.

62. David S. Evans and Richard Schmalensee, *Matchmakers: The New Economics of Multisided Platforms* (Harvard Business Review Press, 2016). Kindle Edition, locations 322–323.

63. https://www.seattletimes.com/business/tech-giants-put-the-squeeze-on-startups-squelching-their-chances-of-success/.

64. https://www.theguardian.com/technology/2017/oct/20/tech-startups-facebook-amazon-google-apple.

65. https://www.recode.net/2017/5/10/15602814/amazon-invested-startup-nucleus-cloned-alexa-echo-show-voice-control-touchscreen-video.

66. https://en.wikipedia.org/wiki/Google_data_centers.

67. https://peering.google.com/#/infrastructure.

68. http://www.dailymail.co.uk/sciencetech/article-5275893/Google-reveals-plan-build-THREE-new-undersea-cables.html.

69. http://www.wired.co.uk/article/google-facebook-plcn-internet-cable/.

70. https://www.ben-evans.com/benedictevans/2017/10/12/scale-wetxp.

71. https://www.theringer.com/tech/2018/5/18/17362452/microsoft-antitrust-lawsuit-netscape-internet-explorer-20-years.

72. https://www.sfgate.com/politics/article/Microsoft-Asked-Apple-to-Knife-the-Baby-Court-2980345.php.

73. https://promarket.org/google-facebooks-kill-zone-weve-taken-focus-off-rewarding-genius-innovation-rewarding-capital-scale/.

Chapter 6: Toll Roads and Robber Barons

1. http://www.wired.co.uk/article/chinese-government-social-credit-score-privacy-invasion.

2. https://www.ft.com/content/6250e4ec-8e68-11e7-9084-d0c17942ba93.

3. https://www.npr.org/sections/alltechconsidered/2016/05/18/477819617/facebooks-facial-recognition-software-is-different-from-the-fbis-heres-why.

4. https://washingtonmonthly.com/magazine/january-february-march-2018/how-to-fix-facebook-before-it-fixes-us/.

5. https://www.buzzfeed.com/bensmith/george-soros-just-launched-a-scathing-attack-on-google-

6. http://www.telegraph.co.uk/news/worldnews/northamerica/usa/11155959/The-sleepy-American-suburb-turned-super-rich-playground.html.

7. https://www.thedailybeast.com/californias-new-feudalism-benefits-a-few-at-the-expense-of-the-multitude.

8. https://www.mercurynews.com/2017/03/24/san-jose-and-oakland-area-job-markets-tumble/.

9. http://www.reuters.com/article/2011/05/19/us-usa-economy-california-idUSTRE74I88V20110519.

10. https://www.ocregister.com/2016/01/31/serfs-up-with-californias-new-feudalism/.

11. https://www.paloaltoonline.com/news/2017/02/17/report-more-people-leaving-valley-than-coming-in.

12. https://www.businesswire.com/news/home/20110506005600/en/Research-Markets-Soft-Drinks-Market-Analysis.

13. https://www.nytimes.com/2017/04/07/opinion/is-it-last-call-for-craft-beer.html.

14. Debra M. Desrochers, Gregory T. Gundlach, and Albert A. Foer, "Analysis of Antitrust Challenges to Category Captain Arrangements." *Journal of Public Policy & Marketing* 22, no. 2 (Fall 2003): 201–215, https://doi.org/10.1509/jppm.22.2.201.17635.

15. http://www.zocalopublicsquare.org/2010/09/06/how-much-do-monopolies-control/books/readings/.

16. http://newbrunswicktoday.com/article/walgreens-rite-aid-merger-agreement-terminated-after-ftc-feedback.

17. http://www.gao.gov/assets/670/667245.pdf.

18. http://www.commonwealthfund.org/publications/in-the-literature/2017/sep/health-care-market-concentration and https://www.healthaffairs.org/doi/abs/10.1377/hlthaff.2017.0556.

19. http://www.cnn.com/2010/POLITICS/04/23/sec.porn/index.html.

20. See fiber-optic penetration by state https://broadbandnow.com/Fiber.

21. http://lowendmac.com/2008/rise-of-microsoft-monopoly/. Bill Gates, in a 1994 email, wrote, "We should wait until we have a way to do a high level of integration that will be harder for likes of Notes, WordPerfect to achieve, and which will give Office a real advantage . . . . We can't compete with Lotus and WordPerfect/Novell without this."

22. http://gs.statcounter.com/social-media-stats.

23. https://marketingland.com/emarketer-facebook-dominate-15-9-pct-digital-ad-spend-growth-2017-209045.

24. https://www.lrb.co.uk/v39/n16/john-lanchester/you-are-the-product.

25. http://gawker.com/5636765/facebook-ceo-admits-to-calling-users-dumb-fucks.

26. http://ec.europa.eu/competition/antitrust/cases/dec_docs/39740/39740_14996_3.pdf.

27. http://www.antitrustinstitute.org/files/Google_DoubleClick_memo_110620071437.pdf.

28. http://fortune.com/2017/04/26/google-facebook-digital-ads/.

29. https://www.reuters.com/article/fitch-affirms-dean-foods-idr-at-bb-withd/fitch-affirms-dean-foods-idr-at-bb-withdraws-all-ratings-idUSFit8kPvMh.

30. https://www.agweb.com/article/dfa_agrees_to_pay_140_million_in_milk-price_fixing_lawsuit/ and https://hoards.com/blog-1936-dean-foods-will-pay-$30-million-after-northeast-price-fixing-lawsuit.html.

31. https://www.foodengineeringmag.com/articles/91700-dean-foods-dairy-farmers-of-america-and-national-dairy-holdings-antitrust-lawsuit-reinstated.

32. http://thehill.com/blogs/congress-blog/economy-budget/241697-the-catalyst-that-transformed-freight-rail-transport.

33. https://www.economist.com/news/briefing/21695385-profits-are-too-high-america-needs-giant-dose-competition-too-much-good-thing.

34. http://consumerfed.org/wp-content/uploads/2015/10/Bulk-Commodities-and-the-Rails.pdf.

35. https://ageconsearch.umn.edu/bitstream/164478/2/Concentration.pdf.

36. http://fortune.com/2014/06/26/monsanto-gmo-crops/.

37. https://www.reuters.com/article/us-monsanto-m-a-bayer-antitrust/bayers-monsanto-acquisition-to-face-politically-charged-scrutiny-idUSKCN11K2LG.

38. https://www.eteknix.com/amd-gain-intelpassmarkq3/.

39. https://www.nytimes.com/2017/09/06/business/intel-eu-antitrust-fine.html.

40. Michael Singer and Dawn Kawamoto ."AMD Files Antitrust Suit against Intel," CNET.com.

41. https://www.attn.com/stories/173/fear-reaper-cost-death-soaring and http://www.nfda.org/news/trends-in-funeral-service.

42. https://www.bloomberg.com/news/articles/2013-10-24/is-funeral-home-chain-scis-growth-coming-at-the-expense-of-mourners.

43. https://www.theatlantic.com/national/archive/2011/07/how-38-monks-took-on-the-funeral-cartel-and-won/242336/ and http://www.al.com/opinion/index.ssf/2016/04/why_does_alabama_allow_a_monop.html.

44. https://www.nbcnews.com/business/visa-mastercard-7-3-billion-settlement-over-credit-card-fees-881386.

45. https://www.nytimes.com/2017/04/07/opinion/is-it-last-call-for-craft-beer.html.

46. https://lpeblog.org/2017/12/06/from-territorial-to-functional-sovereignty-the-case-of-amazon/.

47. https://www.recode.net/2017/3/14/14890122/google-search-ad-market-share-growth.

48. Matthew Garrahan, "Google and Facebook Dominance Forecast to Rise," *Financial Times* (December 4, 2017), https://www.ft.com/content/cf362186-d840-11e7-a039-c64b1c09b482.

49. https://www.statista.com/statistics/241805/market-share-of-facebooks-us-social-network-ad-revenue/.

50. https://www.justice.gov/opa/pr/davita-pay-350-million-resolve-allegations-illegal-kickbacks and http://www.corpwatch.org/article.php?id=16027.

51. https://www.denverpost.com/2017/02/22/davita-dialysis-patients-lawsuit/.

52. https://www.forbes.com/sites/anaswanson/2014/09/10/meet-the-four-eyed-eight-tentacled-monopoly-that-is-making-your-glasses-so-expensive/#ce421a06b66b.

53. https://www.reuters.com/article/us-luxottica-group-m-a-essilor-usa/eyewear-mega-deal-could-hurt-u-s-consumers-but-still-be-approved-idUSKBN1D72KL.

54. https://newrepublic.com/article/144780/break-credit-reporting-racket.

55. https://qz.com/1079490/the-equifax-breach-is-proof-its-time-to-overhaul-the-credit-bureau-industry/.

56. https://www.washingtonpost.com/news/the-switch/wp/2017/09/08/what-to-know-before-you-check-equifaxs-data-breach-website/.

57. http://www.sfchronicle.com/business/article/Quest-for-easier-cheaper-online-tax-tools-11053412.php

58. https://www.justice.gov/atr/case-document/file/498231/download.

59. https://www.warren.senate.gov/files/documents/Tax_Maze_Report.pdf.

60. https://www.nytimes.com/2017/04/17/opinion/how-the-airlines-became-abusive-cartels.html?_r=0.

61. Ron Chernow, *Titan: The Life of John D. Rockefeller, Sr.* (Vintage, 1998), p. 208.

62. https://www.forbes.com/sites/christinenegroni/2017/11/28/airlines-on-track-to-nickel-and-dime-travelers-for-record-82b-in-extra-fees-in-2017-study-says/#3e03d00b4792.

63. https://www.salon.com/2014/04/03/your_cellphone_company_is_robbing_you_blind_partner/.

64. https://www.wired.com/2010/06/wireless-oligopoly-is-smother-of-invention/.

65. https://www.economist.com/news/united-states/21603078-why-thieves-love-americas-health-care-system-272-billion-swindle.

66. http://www.gao.gov/assets/670/667245.pdf.

67. https://www.forbes.com/sites/realspin/2017/06/28/health-cares-crushing-lack-of-competition/#405e998f14ff.

68. https://www.healthcaredive.com/news/hospital-competition-consolidation-macra/441679/.

69. Lina Khan and Sandeep Vaheesan, "Market Power and Inequality: The Antitrust Counterrevolution and Its Discontents" (April 22, 2016), *Harvard Law & Policy Review 235* (2017). Available at SSRN: https://ssrn.com/abstract=2769132.

70. http://www.latimes.com/business/hiltzik/la-fi-hiltzik-healthcare-mergers-20160527-snap-story.html.

71. https://www.statnews.com/2017/09/06/hospital-mergers-monopolies/.

72. http://www.hallrender.com/2016/01/20/common-themes-emerge-as-ftc-challenges-three-hospital-mergers-in-two-month-period/.

73. http://www.bendbulletin.com/opinion/5118579-151/letter-congress-should-repeal-safe-harbor-provision.

74. http://www.motherjones.com/kevin-drum/2010/07/problem-gpos/.

75. Pharmaceutical Care Management Association, "That's What PBMs Do" (Washington, DC: PCMA, March 14, 2016).

76. http://prospect.org/article/hidden-monopolies-raise-drug-prices.

77. https://www.fiercepharma.com/special-report/big-3-distributors.

78. https://www.marketwatch.com/story/growing-share-of-big-three-drug-wholesalers-gets-attention.

79. https://www.forbes.com/sites/nathanvardi/2017/11/06/states-focus-on-incentives-of-wholesalers-and-pharmacies-in-drug-price-fixing-probe/#3dd205ba402b.

80. https://www.drugabuse.gov/related-topics/trends-statistics/overdose-death-rates.

81. https://www.dailykos.com/stories/2017/12/18/1725603/-The-Corporations-That-Created-The-Opioid-Epidemic-Continue-To-Evade-Responsibility.

82. https://www.theguardian.com/global-development/poverty-matters/2011/jun/02/abcd-food-giants-dominate-trade.

83. https://www.avclub.com/the-writers-guild-is-not-happy-about-the-disney-fox-dea-1821301494.

84. htt/medium.com/@PeterGonzalezNY/how-technology-is-transforming-the-title-insurance-market-739e23b0503.

85. https://www.forbes.com/forbes/2006/1113/148.html#10b59ec45266.

86. http://www.gao.gov/new.items/d07401.pdf.

87. https://www.nytimes.com/2015/05/12/opinion/the-title-insurance-scam.html.

88. Edward N. Wolff, "Household Wealth Trends in the United States, 1962 to 2016: Has Middle Class Wealth Recovered?," NBER Working Paper No. 24085, November 2017,http://www.nber.org/papers/w24085.

Chapter 7: What Trusts and Nazis Had in Common

1. https://www.theatlantic.com/magazine/archive/1881/03/the-story-of-a-great-monopoly/306019/.

2. Edward J. Renehan Jr., *Commodore: The Life of Cornelius Vanderbilt* (Basic Books, 2019). Kindle Edition.

3. T. J. Stiles, *The First Tycoon: The Epic Life of Cornelius Vanderbilt* (Alfred A. Knopf, 2009).

4. https://www.theatlantic.com/magazine/archive/1881/03/the-story-of-a-great-monopoly/306019/.

5. Ron Chernow, *Titan* (Vintage Books, 1998).

6. Matthew Josephson, *The Robber Barons* (Harcourt, 1934).

7. *Theodore Roosevelt: Ultimate Collection* (Madison & Adams Press, 2017).

8. Patrick Gaughan, *Mergers and Acquisitions: An Overview* (Harper Collins, 1991).

9. http://law.jrank.org/pages/4362/Antitrust-Law-Sherman-Act-Early-Enforcement.html.

10. Theodore J. St. Antoine, "Connell: Antitrust Law at the Expense of Labor Law," *Virginia Law Review* 62 (1976): 603–631.

11. Chernow, *Titan*.

12. http://archive.org/stream/crossroadsoffree007728mbp/crossroadsof-free007728mbp_djvu.txt.

13. Klaus Peter Gugler, Dennis C. Mueller, and B. Yurtoglu, Burcin, "The Determinants of Merger Waves" (January 2006). WZB: Markets and Politics Working Paper No. SP II 2006-01. Available at SSRN: https://ssrn.com/abstract=507282.

14. George J. Stigler, "Monopoly and Oligopoly by Merger," *American Economic Review* 40 (May 1950): 23–34.

15. Lina Khan and Sandeep Vaheesan, "Market Power and Inequality: The Antitrust Counterrevolution and Its Discontents" (April 22, 2016), *Harvard*

Law & Policy Review 235 (2017). Available at SSRN: https://ssrn.com/abstract=2769132.

16. https://www.theatlantic.com/business/archive/2017/06/word-monopoly-antitrust/530169/.

17. Diarmuid Jeffreys, *Hell's Cartel: IG Farben and the Making of Hitler's War Machine* (Metropolitan Books, 2008).

18. https://www.bayer.com/en/carl-duisberg.aspx

19. https://www.bayer.com/en/carl-duisberg.aspx

20. Jeffreys, *Hell's Cartel*.

21. https://archive.is/20120415021424/http://www.mazal.org/archive/nmt/07/NMT07-C001.htm.

22. https://www.ushmm.org/wlc/en/article.php?ModuleId=10007077.

23. https://www.jewishvirtuallibrary.org/i-g-farben-trial-1947-1948.

24. Jeffreys, *Hell's Cartel*.

25. Summation for the Prosecution by Justice Robert Jackson, Nuremberg Trials, July 26, 1946, available at http://www.law.umkc.edu/faculty/projects/ftrials/nuremberg/Jacksonclose.htm.

26. Franz Leopold Neumann, *Behemoth: The Structure and Practice of National Socialism 1933–1944* (Oxford University Press, 1944; reprint, Octagon, 1983).

27. Wyatt Wells, *Antitrust and the Formation of the Postwar World* (Columbia University Press, 2003).

28. Arthur Schweizer, *Big Business in the Third Reich* (Indiana University Press), 1964.

29. Herbert Block, "Industrial Concentration versus Small Business: The Trend of Nazi Policy," *Social Research* 10, no. 2 (May 1943): 175–199.

30. Franz Neumann, Herbert Marcuse, and Otto Kirchheimer, *Secret Reports on Nazi Germany: The Frankfurt School Contribution to the War Effort*, edited by Raffaele Laudani (Princeton University Press, 2013).

31. Philip C. Newman, "Key German Cartels under the Nazi Regime," *The Quarterly Journal of Economics* 62, no. 4 (1948): 576–595. JSTOR, www.jstor.org/stable/1881766.

32. Neumann, Marcuse, and Kirchheimer, *Secret Reports*.

33. https://newrepublic.com/article/104346/standard-oil-axis-ally.

34. Wells, *Antitrust*.

35. Jeffreys, *Hell's Cartel*.

36. Ibid.

37. Wells, *Antitrust*.

38. Ibid.

39. Wendell Berge, *Cartels: Challenge to a Free World* (Beard Books – Business Classic, 2000 reprint). Originally published 1944.

40. The Potsdam Declarations, Tripartite Agreement by the United States, the United Kingdom, and Soviet Russia concerning Conquered Countries, August 2, 1945. At http://www.ibiblio.org/pha/policy/1945/450802a.html.

41. Wells, *Antitrust*.

42. John M. Kleeberg, *German Cartels: Myths and Realities*, http://www.econ.barnard.columbia.edu/~econhist/papers/Kleeberg_German_Cartels.pdf.

43. Wells, *Antitrust*.

44. *A Year of Potsdam: German Economy Since Surrender*, prepared by the Economics Division, Office of Military Government for Germany (US). United States War Department, 1946.

45. **A.** Pelle, *The German Roots of the European Community's Cartel Regulation: From a Historical and Theoretical Perspective* (LAP Lambert Academic Publishing, 2011).

46. F.A. Hayek, *The Road to Serfdom* (University of Chicago Press, 2007), pp. 93–94.

47. Simon Tilford, "Is EU Competition Policy an Obstacle to Innovation and Growth?," http://www.cer.eu/sites/default/files/publications/attachments/pdf/2011/essay_competition_st_20nov08-1359.pdf.

48. https://www.economist.com/europe/2015/05/09/of-rules-and-order .

49. Ignacio Herrera Anchustegui, Competition Law Through an Ordo-liberal Lens (March 1, 2015). Available at SSRN: https://ssrn.com/abstract=2579308 or http://dx.doi.org/10.2139/ssrn.2579308.

50. Robert H. Bork and Ward S. Bowman Jr, "The Crisis in Antitrust," *Columbia Law Review* 65, no. 3 (1965).

51. Steven C. Salop, Symposium on Mergers and Antitrust. *Economic Perspectives* 1, no. 2 (Fall 1987): 3–12.

52. Milton Friedman, "The Business Community's Suicidal Impulse," *Cato Policy Report* 21, no. 2 (March/April 1999).

53. Richard A. Posner, "The Chicago School of Antitrust Analysis," *University of Pennsylvania Law Review* 127, no. 4 (April 1979): 925–948.

54. http://keever.us/greenspanantitrust.html.

55. Robert H. Bork, "The Goals of Antitrust Policy," *American Economic Review* 57 (1967): 242.

56. B.Y. Orbach, "The Antitrust Consumer Welfare Paradox," *Journal of Competition Law and Economics* 7, no. 1 (2001): 133–164. [nhq019]. doi: 10.1093/joclec/nhq019.

57. Alan A. Fisher, Frederick I. Johnson, and Robert H. Lande, "Price Effects of Horizontal Mergers," https://papers.ssrn.com/sol3/papers.cfm?abstract_id=1134826.

58. Barry C. Lynn, *Cornered: The New Monopoly Capitalism and the Economics of Destruction* (Hoboken, NJ: Wiley, 2010).

59. Lynn E. Browne and Eric Rosengren, "The Merger Boom: An Overview," Conference Series [Proceedings] 31 (1987): 1–16.

60. https://www.alternet.org/story/83668/in_the_last_gilded_age%2C_people_stood_up_to_greed_--_why_aren%C3%A2%E2%82%AC%E2%84%A2t_we.

61. Lynn, *Cornered*.

62. http://www.ibtimes.com/obamas-latest-executive-order-designed-break-monopolies-boost-market-competition-2354605.

63. Gustavo Grullon, Yelena Larkin, and Roni Michaely, "Are U.S. Industries Becoming More Concentrated?" (August 31, 2017). Available at SSRN: https://ssrn.com/abstract=2612047.

64. https://www.propublica.org/article/these-professors-make-more-than-thousand-bucks-hour-peddling-mega-mergers.

65. Grullon, Larkin, and Michaely, "Are U.S. Industries Becoming More Concentrated?"

66. https://promarket.org/economists-totality-evidence-underscores-concentration-problem-u-s/.

67. https://promarket.org/study-politically-connected-firms-likely-receive-favorable-merger-reviews-antitrust-regulators/; Mihir N. Mehta, Suraj Srinivasan, and Wanli Zhao, "Political Influence and Merger Antitrust Reviews" (September 13, 2017). Available at SSRN: https://ssrn.com/abstract=2945020.

68. Orley Ashenfelter, Daniel Hosken, and Matthew Weinberg, "Did Robert Bork Understate the Competitive Impact of Mergers? Evidence from Consummated Mergers," *The Journal of Law and Economics 57,* no. S3 (August 2014): S67–S100. https://doi.org/10.1086/675862.

Chapter 8: Regulation and Chemotherapy

1. http://www.jeffslegacy.com/book.html and http://www.wilsonsdisease.org/for-patients-families/stories.

2. https://www.vanityfair.com/news/2016/06/the-valeant-meltdown-and-wall-streets-major-drug-problem.

3. https://en.wikipedia.org/wiki/Valeant_Pharmaceuticals.

4. https://www.nytimes.com/2016/07/31/business/how-valeant-cashed-in-twice-on-higher-drug-prices.html.

5. http://fortune.com/2016/10/17/valeant-new-drug-price-hikes/.

6. https://www.consumeraffairs.com/news/valeant-increases-price-on-lead-poisoning-drug-by-2700-but-american-kids-dont-need-it-anyway-110416.html.

7. https://www.streetinsider.com/Corporate+News/Imprimis+Pharma+(IMMY)+Announces+Lower-Cost+Option+to+Valeants+(VRX)+Lead+Poisoning+Treatment/12136830.html.

8. https://www.forbes.com/sites/emilywillingham/2016/10/16/cost-for-valeants-lead-poisoning-treatment-increased-7250-in-six-years/#22903eef26a8.

9. https://www.prnewswire.com/news-releases/imprimis-pharmaceuticals-announces-availability-of-lower-cost-option-for-the-treatment-of-lead-poisoning-300345605.html.

10. Naren P. Tallapragada, "Off-Patent Drugs at Brand-Name Prices: A Puzzle for Policymakers," *Journal of Law and the Biosciences* 3, no. 1 (April 2016): 238–247, https://doi.org/10.1093/jlb/lsw008.

11. http://uk.businessinsider.com/valeant-2700-price-increase-on-lead-poisoning-drug-2016-10?r=US&IR=T.

12. http://uk.businessinsider.com/pearson-salary-2015-2016-4.

13. http://www.bloomberg.com/news/articles/2016-02-02/shkreli-not-alone-in-drug-price-spikes-as-skin-gel-soars-1-860.

14. https://qz.com/514553/massive-unexpected-drug-price-increases-are-happening-all-the-time/.

15. https://www.scientificamerican.com/article/analysis-drugmakers-take-big-price-increases-on-popular-meds-in-u-s/.

16. http://www.modernhealthcare.com/article/20171228/NEWS/171229930.

17. http://www.bbc.co.uk/newsbeat/article/31664223/the-curse-of-blade-runners-adverts.

18. https://www.wsj.com/articles/science-affliction-are-companies-cursed-by-cameos-in-blade-runner-1506356096.

19. https://www.nationalreview.com/2013/03/hey-wheres-my-corporate-dystopia-kevin-d-williamson/.

20. https://www.nationalreview.com/2017/09/science-fiction-corporations-not-omnipotent-capitalism-ensures-competition/.

21. F.A. Hayek, *The Road to Serfdom* (University of Chicago Press, 2007).

22. https://www.wired.com/2012/03/march-19-1474-venice-enacts-a-patently-original-idea/.

23. http://altlawforum.org/publications/a-history-of-patent-law/.

24. https://www.mercatus.org/publication/number-patents-has-exploded-1982-and-one-court-blame.

25. https://promarket.org/intellectual-property-laws-wolves-sheeps-clothing/.

26. http://www.gao.gov/assets/660/657103.pdf.

27. https://priceonomics.com/how-mickey-mouse-evades-the-public-domain/.

28. https://hbr.org/2016/07/price-gouging-and-the-dangerous-new-breed-of-pharma-companies.

29. Aaron S. Kesselheim, Jerry Avorn, and Ameet Sarpatwari, "The High Cost of Prescription Drugs in the United States: Origins and Prospects for Reform," *JAMA* 316, no. 8 (2016): 858–871, https://jamanetwork.com/journals/jama/article-abstract/2545691.

30. https://io9.gizmodo.com/5865283/three-sleazy-moves-pharmaceutical-companies-use-to-extend-drug-patents.

31. https://www.biosimilardevelopment.com/doc/the-impact-of-reformulation-strategies-on-pharmaceuticals-biologics-0001.

32. https://hbr.org/2016/07/price-gouging-and-the-dangerous-new-breed-of-pharma-companies.

33. https://americansforprosperity.org/fda-hesitant-approve-generic-drugs/.

34. https://www.healthline.com/health-news/drug-price-gouging-laws-becoming-new-trend#3.

35. http://sourceonhealthcare.org/drug-money-part-4-the-return-of-the-creates-act-fourth-times-a-charm/.

36. https://theintercept.com/2018/02/08/spending-bill-creates-act-drug-prices/.

37. https://www.forbes.com/sites/matthewherper/2017/02/10/a-6000-price-hike-should-give-drug-companies-a-disgusting-sense-of-deja-vu/#5ebf70af71f5.

38. http://www.newser.com/story/255796/sufferers-of-rare-disease-get-lesson-in-us-drug-economics.html.

39. https://www.mdanderson.org/publications/annual-report/annual-report-2015/the-man-who-helped-cure-childhood-leukemia.html.

40. http://www.davisliumd.com/why-doctors-should-read-malcolm-gladwells-david-and-goliath/.

41. https://www.theatlantic.com/business/archive/2011/06/will-the-cure-for-systemic-risk-kill-the-economy/240600/.

42. https://www.chron.com/local/history/innovators-inventions/article/Dr-Emil-Freireich-attacked-cancer-on-multiple-9135603.php.

43. Bruce C. Greenwald and Judd Kahn, *Competition Demystified: A Radically Simplified Approach to Business Strategy* (Penguin Publishing Group, 2007), p. 26.

44. Milton Friedman and Rose D. Friedman, *Capitalism and Freedom: Fortieth Anniversary Edition* (University of Chicago Press, 2002).

45. http://www.nfib.com/assets/NFIB-Problems-and-Priorities-2016.pdf.

46. https://www.mercatus.org/publications/regulation-entrepreneurship-and-firm-size.

47. https://www.uschamberfoundation.org/smallbizregs/.

48. https://www.uschamberfoundation.org/sites/default/files/CityReg%20Report_0.pdf.

49. https://townhall.com/columnists/monacharen/2017/12/29/the-new-york-times-covers-overregulation-n2427916.

50. J.B. Bailey and D.W. Thomas, *Journal of Regulatory Economics* 52 (2017): 237, https://doi.org/10.1007/s11149-017-9343-9.

51. Fabio Schiantarelli, "Product Market Regulation and Macroeconomic Performance: A Review of Cross Country Evidence," World Bank Policy Research Working Paper No. 3770; IZA Discussion Paper No. 1791. November 2005. Available at SSRN: https://ssrn.com/abstract=826453

52. https://www.federalreserve.gov/econresdata/feds/2014/files/2014113pap.pdf.

53. https://www.manhattan-institute.org/sites/default/files/R-NG-0417.pdf.

54. https://ilsr.org/vanishing-community-banks-national-crisis/.

55. http://mjperry.blogspot.com/2011/09/dodd-frank-2010-full-employment-act-for.html.

56. http://www.washingtonexaminer.com/goldman-and-jpmorgan-sit-safely-behind-the-walls-of-dodd-frank/article/2560179.

57. https://www.wsj.com/articles/regulation-is-good-for-goldman-1423700859.

58. https://www.nytimes.com/2018/06/22/business/dealbook/banks-stress-test.html.

59. https://www.washingtonexaminer.com/goldman-sachs-wants-regulation-not-laissez-faire.

60. http://business.financialpost.com/news/economy/sp-moodys-boosting-rating-fees-faster-than-inflation.

61. https://www.reuters.com/article/businesspro-us-usa-ratings-competition-a-idUSTRE55N4VU20090624

62. https://www.fdic.gov/regulations/reform/altman1.pdf.

63. https://www.washingtonpost.com/blogs/wonkblog/post/the-pentagons-435-hammer/2011/05/19/AGoGKHMH_blog.html?noredirect=on&utm_term=.f17af71dda37.

64. "Onward and Upward: Transdigm Non-Deal Roadshow," May 2017, https://www.transdigm.com/investor-relations/presentations/.

65. https://www.glassdoor.co.uk/Reviews/TransDigm-Reviews-E22279.htm.

66. http://www.hassoninvestments.com/investment-journal-blog/2016/9/30/transdigm-compounding-value.

67. http://www.citronresearch.com/wp-content/uploads/2017/03/TDG-Citron-part-2-final-d.pdf.

68. https://www.investorvillage.com/smbd.asp?mb=4143&mn=386614&pt=msg&mid=17064056.

69. http://www.crainscleveland.com/article/20170201/NEWS01/170209988/transdigm-groups-stock-is-up-1500-the-ceos-flush-and-short-seller.

70. http://www.crainscleveland.com/article/20170404/BLOGS03/170409936/transdigm-group-ceo-is-no-stranger-to-politics.

71. Matthew D. Hill, G. Wayne Kelly, G. Brandon Lockhart, and Robert A. Van Ness, "Determinants and Effects of Corporate Lobbying," *Financial Management* 931 (2013): 944–955, https://doi.org/10.1111/fima.12032.

72. Raquel Meyer Alexander Stephen W. Mazza, and Susan Scholz, "Measuring Rates of Return for Lobbying Expenditures: An Empirical Case Study of Tax Breaks for Multinational Corporations," *Journal of Law and Politics* 25, no. 401(April 8, 2009). Available at SSRN: https://ssrn.com/abstract=1375082 or http://dx.doi.org/10.2139/ssrn.1375082

73. https://www.nytimes.com/2018/06/20/opinion/prescription-drug-costs-naloxone-opioids.html

74. https://www.thestreet.com/politics/creates-act-clears-committee-vote-could-ease-way-for-generic-drug-makers-14623054

75. https://www.barrons.com/articles/lobbying-index-beats-the-market-1524863200

76. http://www.politifact.com/wisconsin/statements/2015/mar/02/scott-walker/scott-walker-says-most-10-richest-counties-are-aro/

77. https://hbr.org/2016/05/lobbyists-are-behind-the-rise-in-corporate-profits

78. https://hbr.org/2016/05/lobbyists-are-behind-the-rise-in-corporate-profits

79. Brink Lindsey and Steven Teles, *The Captured Economy: How the Powerful Enrich Themselves, Slow Down Growth, and Increase Inequality* (New York: Oxford University Press, 2017).

80. http://cms.marketplace.org/sites/default/files/EMR23033%20Marketplace%20Wave%20Three%20Web%20Only%20Banner.pdf.

81. http://www.ibtimes.com/political-capital/donald-trump-said-goldman-sachs-had-total-control-over-hillary-clinton-then.

82. http://thehill.com/blogs/pundits-blog/the-administration/309966-trump-continues-white-houses-goldman-sachs-revolving.

83. https://www.cbsnews.com/news/goldman-sachs-revolving-door/.

84. http://thinkreadact.com/goldman-sachs-revolving-door/.

85. https://www.huffingtonpost.com/2010/09/14/geithner-blankfein-pelosi_n_715334.html.

86. Daniel Carpenter and David A. Moss, eds., *Preventing Regulatory Capture: Special Interest Influence and How to Limit It* (New York: Cambridge University Press 2014).

87. http://www.citizen.org/documents/financial-services-conflict-of-interest-act-report.pdf.

88. https://www.thedailybeast.com/donald-trump-pledged-to-drain-the-swamp-instead-he-filled-it-with-industry-sharks.

89. http://thehill.com/blogs/pundits-blog/finance/247962-reforming-the-financial-services-revolving-door.

90. https://steemit.com/corporatism/@geke/gekevenn-monsanto-updated.

91. http://review.chicagobooth.edu/public-policy/2017/article/should-we-stop-revolving-door.

92. https://obamawhitehouse.archives.gov/blog/2011/12/06/archives-president-teddy-roosevelts-new-nationalism-speech.

Chapter 9: Morganizing America

1. http://s3.amazonaws.com/armstrongeconomics-wp/2013/07/NYSE-Closings.pdf.

2. http://www.theodore-roosevelt.com/images/research/txtspeeches/16.txt.

3. Gallup, "U.S. Stock Ownership Down Among all but Older, Higher-income," May 24, 2017, http://news.gallup.com/poll/211052/stock-ownership-down-among-older-higher-income.aspx?g_source=link_newsv9&g_medium=topic&g_campaign=item_&g_content=U.S.%2520stock%2520ownership%2520down%2520among%2520all%2520but%2520older%2c%2520higher-income.

4. http://rooseveltinstitute.org/wp-content/uploads/2018/06/The-Shareholder-Myth.pdf.

5. Edward Wolff, "Household Wealth in the United States, 1962 to 2016: Has Middle Class Wealth Recovered?" National Bureau of Economic Research. Working Paper Series, no. 24085, 2017, http://www.nber.org/papers/w24085.

6. Jim Norman, "Young Americans Still Wary of Investing in Stocks," Gallup, May 4, 2018, http://news.gallup.com/poll/233699/young-americans-wary-investing-stocks.aspx?g_source=link_NEWSV9&g_medium=TOPIC&g_campaign=item_&g_content=Young%2520Americans%2520Still%2520Wary%2520of%2520Investing%2520in%2520Stocks.

7. https://www.forbes.com/sites/tedreed/2013/05/13/buffett-decries-airline-investing-even-though-at-worst-he-broke-even.

8. https://www.nytimes.com/2017/04/17/opinion/how-the-airlines-became-abusive-cartels.html?_r=0.

9. Erik Gilje, Todd A. Gormley, and Doron Levit, "The Rise of Common Ownership," April 19, 2018, https://ssrn.com/abstract=3165574.

10. Einer Elhauge, "Horizontal Shareholding," *Harvard Law Review* 129 (March 10, 2016), http://www.antitrustinstitute.org/sites/default/files/Elhauge.pdf.

11. https://www.forbes.com/sites/christinenegroni/2017/11/28/airlines-on-track-to-nickel-and-dime-travelers-for-record-82b-in-extra-fees-in-2017-study-says/#3e03d00b4792.

12. José Azar, Martin Schmalz, and Isabel Tecu, "Why Common Ownership Creates Antitrust Risks," *CPI Antitrust Chronicle* (June 2017).

13. Ibid.

14. https://www.forbes.com/sites/laurengensler/2017/02/25/warren-buffett-annual-letter-2016-passive-active-investing/#1bae82286bbd.

15. https://www.theatlas.com/charts/S1lPjxkM-.

16. https://www.nytimes.com/2017/04/14/business/mutfund/vanguard-mutual-index-funds-growth.html.

17. https://www.theatlantic.com/magazine/archive/2017/09/are-index-funds-evil/534183/?utm_source=twb.

18. National Bureau of Economic Research, "Explaining Low Investment Spending," http://www.nber.org/digest/feb17/w22897.html.

19. https://www.theatlantic.com/business/archive/2017/06/how-companies-decide-ceo-pay/530127/.

20. https://www.mercurynews.com/2018/05/07/butler-who-do-stock-buy-backs-leave-behind/.

21. https://www.bloomberg.com/gadfly/articles/2018-03-05/five-charts-that-show-where-those-corporate-tax-savings-are-going.

22. https://www.brookings.edu/wp-content/uploads/2016/06/lazonick.pdf.

23. Youssef Cassis, *Capitals of Capital: The Rise and Fall of International Financial Centres* (Cambridge University Press, 2006), p.137.

24. https://www.apollo-magazine.com/j-p-morgan-the-man-who-bought-the-world/.

25. Ron Chernow, *The House of Morgan: An American Banking Dynasty and the Rise of Modern Finance* (Gove Press, 1990).

26. https://www.theatlantic.com/magazine/archive/2017/09/are-index-funds-evil/534183/.

Chapter 10: The Missing Piece of the Puzzle

1. https://www.politico.com/story/2016/06/transcript-trump-speech-on-the-stakes-of-the-election-224654.

2. https://berniesanders.com/issues/income-and-wealth-inequality/.

3. http://www.huffingtonpost.co.uk/entry/piketty-book-no-one-read_n_5563629.

4. Richard Sutch, "The One Percent across Two Centuries: A Replication of Thomas Piketty's Data on the Concentration of Wealth in the United States," *Social Science History* 41, no. 4 (Winter 2017): 587–613, https://doi.org/10.1017/ssh.2017.27.

5. "Divided We Stand: Why Inequality Keeps Rising," OECD, 2011, https://www.oecd.org/els/soc/49170475.pdf.

6. https://www.credit-suisse.com/corporate/en/research/research-institute/global-wealth-report.html.

7. http://www.ampcapital.com.au/article-detail?alias=/olivers-insights/august-2017/inequality-is-it-increasing.

8. Economists normally calculate the Gini coefficient looking at people's incomes after taxes and transfers payments from the government. In many countries, particularly Europe, the poor do receive large payments from the government, which is why their measures appear lower.

9. www.ampcapital.com.au/article-detail?alias=/olivers-insights/august-2017/inequality-is-it-increasing.

10. http://www.epi.org/publication/ceo-pay-continues-to-rise/.

11. http://work.chron.com/ceo-compensation-vs-world-15509.html.

12. Gustavo Grullon, Yelena Larkin, and Roni Michaely, "Are U.S. Industries Becoming More Concentrated?" (August 31, 2017). Available at SSRN: https://ssrn.com/abstract=2612047.

13. Sam Peltzman, "Industrial Concentration under the Rule of Reason," *The Journal of Law and Economics* 57, no. S3 (August 2014): S101–S120, https://doi.org/10.1086/675719.

14. Jonathan Baker and Steven Salop, "Antitrust, Competition Policy, and Inequality," American University Washington School of Law Working Papers, February 25, 2015, http://digitalcommons.wcl.american.edu/fac_works_papers/41/.

15. Lina Khan and Sandeep Vaheesan, "Market Power and Inequality: The Antitrust Counterrevolution and Its Discontents" (April 22, 2016), *Harvard Law & Policy Review* 235 (2017). Available at SSRN: https://ssrn.com/abstract=2769132.

16. Jan De Loecker and Jan Eeckhout, "The Rise of Market Power and the Macroeconomic Implications" (August 2017). NBER Working Paper No. 23687 http://www.nber.org/papers/w23687.

17. Jan De Loecker and Jan Eeckhout, "Global Market Power," CEPR Discussion Paper No. DP13009, 18, Posted June 26, 2018.

18. Sean F. Ennis, Pedro Gonzaga, and Chris Pike, "Inequality: A Hidden Cost of Market Power" (March 6, 2017). Available at SSRN: https://ssrn.com/abstract=2942791.

19. David H. Autor, David Dorn, Lawrence F. Katz Christina Patterson, and John Van Reenen, "The Fall of the Labor Share and the Rise of Superstar Firms" (May 2017). NBER Working Paper No. w23396. Available at SSRN: https://ssrn.com/abstract=2968214.

20. Raj Chetty, David Grusky, Maximilian Hell, Nathaniel Hendren, Robert Manduca, and Jimmy Narang, "The Fading American Dream: Trends in Absolute Mobility since 1940," National Bureau of Economic Research Working Paper no. 22910, December 2016, http://www.nber.org/papers/w22910; Alex Johnson, "Exit Polls: NBC News' Analysis of 2016 Votes and Voters," November 9, 2016, http://www.nbcnews.com/storyline/2016-election-day/election-%20polls-nbc-news-analysis-2016-votes-voters-n680466. Equality of Opportunity Project, http://www.equality-of-opportunity.org/.

21. http://www.pewsocialtrends.org/2015/12/09/the-american-middle-class-is-losing-ground/.

22. https://qz.com/711854/the-inequality-happening-now-in-san-francisco-will-impact-america-for-generations-to-come/.

23. http://www.mercurynews.com/2017/10/20/san-jose-san-francisco-oakland-job-losses-hammer-bay-area-employers-slash-thousands-of-jobs/.

24. https://www.theguardian.com/world/2014/jan/25/google-bus-protest-swells-to-revolt-san-francisco.

25. https://www.politico.com/magazine/story/2014/06/the-pitchforks-are-coming-for-us-plutocrats-108014.

Conclusion: Economic and Political Freedom

1. Friedrich Hayek, *The Road to Serfdom* (New York: George Routledge & Sons, 1944), p. 204.

2. http://bcw-project.org/church-and-state/second-civil-war/agreement-of-the-people.

3. Geoffrey M. Hodgson, *Wrong Turnings: How the Left Got Lost* (University of Chicago Press, January 3, 2018).

4. Elizabeth Anderson's first Tanner 2015 lecture, "When the Market Was 'Left.'" Published as Elizabeth Anderson, *Private Government* (Princeton, 2017). http://tannerlectures.utah.edu/Anderson%20manuscript.pdf.

5. Michael Kent Curtis, "In Pursuit of Liberty: The Levellers and the American Bill of Rights," *Constitutional Commentary* 737 (1991), https://scholarship.law. umn.edu/concomm/737

6. http://www.phmc.state.pa.us/portal/communities/documents/1776-1865/pennsylvania-constitution-1776.html.

7. Charles R. Geisst, *Monopolies in America: Empire Builders and Their Enemies from Jay Gould to Bill Gates* (Oxford University Press, 2000).

8. David J. Bodenhamer, *The Revolutionary Constitution* (New York: Oxford University Press, 2012).

9. Jonathan Sallet, "Louis Brandeis: A Man for This Season," *Colorado Technology Law Journal* (March 1, 2018), https://ssrn.com/abstract=3132482 or http://dx.doi.org/10.2139/ssrn.3132482.

10. Carl T. Bogus, "The New Road to Serfdom: The Curse of Bigness and the Failure of Antitrust," 49 *U. Mich. J. L. Reform 1* (June 15, 2015); Roger Williams Univ. Legal Studies Paper No. 161. Available at SSRN: https://ssrn.com/abstract=2618522.

11. *Brown Shoe Co., Inc, v. United States,* 370 U.S. 294 (1962).

12. http://www.theodorerooseveltcenter.org/Blog/Item/New%20Nationalism.

13. https://openmarketsinstitute.org/wp-content/uploads/2018/05/05.30.18-DOJ-Comments-Costs-of-Regs.pdf.

Acknowledgments

JONATHAN TEPPER would like to thank friends for ideas and reading recommendations. Ziv Gil, Turi Munthe, Roy Bahat, James Mumford, Patrick Gray, Alex Burghart, Warwick Sabin, Adeel Qalbani, Keir McGuinness, and Cullen Taniguchi provided many ideas and helped spur the writing of the book. My father, Elliott Tepper, was unfailingly patient while reading drafts and sending me research pieces and articles. Ziv Gil, Danny Tocatly, and Zvi Limon kindly encouraged me and provided an office where I could write in Tel Aviv. Countless scholars have done extensive research on competition, industrial concentration, and antitrust. Without them, this book would not be possible. They are all in the footnotes, and I hope readers will read more from Gustavo Grullon, Barry Lynn, Lina Khan, Marshall Steinbaum, John Kwoka, Tim Wu, and others. Sam Hiyate always believed in this project and is a wonderful agent and friend.

Denise Hearn would like to acknowledge husband, Ryan Glasgo, whose unwavering support encouraged me to take on this project. Thanks to my parents, Tim and Susan Hearn, who were models of hard work and social consciousness, and the many friends who contributed their edits and thoughts to my work, including: Karen Campbell, Katie Leninger, Mary Casas Knapp, Andy Kass, and Gabriela Hernández, to name a few. And thank you to my colleague and friend, Jonathan Tepper, for the opportunity to be involved in this project.

About the Authors

JONATHAN TEPPER is the coauthor of *Endgame*, a book on the sovereign debt crisis, and *Code Red*, a book on unconventional monetary policy after the global financial crisis. Jonathan is founder of Variant Perception, a macroeconomic research group that caters to hedge funds, banks, and family offices. Jonathan has worked as an equity analyst at SAC Capital and as a vice president in proprietary trading at Bank of America. Jonathan is a founder of Demotix, a citizen-journalism photo agency. In 2012 he and his partner Turi Munthe sold Demotix to Corbis, which was owned by Bill Gates. He received a BA with highest honors in history and honors in economics from the University of North Carolina at Chapel Hill. Jonathan is a Rhodes Scholar and earned an MLitt in Modern History from Oxford University.

Denise Hearn is Head of Business Development at Variant Perception, a global macroeconomic research and investment strategy firm. She has an MBA from the Oxford Saïd Business School, where she cochaired the Social Impact Oxford Business Network, and a BA in International Studies from Baylor University. Denise has always been interested in human flourishing. Denise resides in Seattle with her husband.

Index